Managing Lives

Managing Lives

❑ ❑ ❑

Corporate Women
and Social Change

Sue Joan Mendelson Freeman

The University of Massachusetts Press

Amherst

Copyright © 1990 by
The University of Massachusetts Press
All rights reserved
Printed in the United States of America
LC 89–20539
ISBN 0–87023–716–0 (cloth); 717–9 (pbk.)
Designed by Jack Harrison
Set in Baskerville by Keystone Typesetting, Inc.
Printed and bound by Thomson Shore

Library of Congress Cataloging-in-Publication Data
Freeman, Sue Joan Mendelson, 1944–
Managing lives : corporate women and social change /
Sue Joan Mendelson Freeman.
p.   cm.
Includes bibliographical references.
ISBN 0–87023–716–0 (alk. paper). — ISBN 0–87023–717–9
(pbk. : alk. paper)
1. Women executives—Psychology.
2. Women executives—United States—Interviews.
3. Social change. 4. Interpersonal relations.
I. Title.
HD6054.3.F74   1990
658.4'09'082—dc20   89–20539
CIP

British Library Cataloguing in Publication data are available.

To my lifelong loves, my family, Evan, Owen, and Emily

*For my father, the late M. Monte Mendelson,
and my adoptive father, the late David Freeman*

*And for my mother, Sally E. Freeman, whose exceptional
beauty, gentle grace, wit, wisdom, and unconditional love
have given me so much*

Contents

III   Connections and Context

Acknowledgments

This project has been in process for most of my children's lives. Stretching over the last decade, it has become an integral part of our family as well as my professional work. Consequently, I am at once reluctant and joyous about its culmination.

The inspiration for this research came from Jill Ker Conway, whose steadfast dedication to fostering women's development continues beyond her tenure as president of Smith College. I count myself a fortunate part of two programs begun under her auspices: the Project on Women and Social Change and the Smith Management Program.

The Project stimulated multidisciplinary exchange among colleagues engaged in individual and collective research endeavors. My involvement with the Project gave me a new way of thinking about psychology and the questions it might profitably address. I liken my years with the Project to a unique postdoctoral experience wherein enormous learning and intellectual exploration took place in the company of a collaborative community of scholars. This study was generously supported by the Andrew W. Mellon Foundation.

I began the interviews of women managers with another Project principal investigator, Kay B. Warren, professor of anthropology at Princeton University. Kay's expertise in ethnographic research contributed to the early stages of the study, particularly in constructing and conducting the interviews. Shortly after completion of the interviews, Kay turned her attention to other projects. Thus, I bear full responsibility for the analyses and writing found here.

The Smith Management Program has been a continuous source of support and assistance to me. The interviews were begun with the help of its first director, Brenda Lerner. Susan C. Lowance, the current director, has been remarkable as a scholarly colleague and perceptive consultant.

Many women have contributed to this study. Foremost, of course, are those whose words appear throughout the book. The compelling interviews with these women confirmed my commitment to write about their experience. Their willingness to reveal thoughts and feelings as well as the trajectories of their lives both inspired and facilitated my writing. I remain indebted and attached to them.

The enthusiasm of Sara Ackerman, Pam Kelly, and Ann Driscoll, who served as research assistants, further fueled my own passion about the work. My admiration could not be greater for Carol Smith whose tireless transcribing strikes me as an incomparable feat. Finally, I am grateful for the indefatigable help of two peerless administrative assistants: Christine Barbuto, of the Department of Education and Child Study, and Kathleen Thayer, of the Project on Women and Social Change.

Smith College has facilitated this research through its support of the Project on Women and Social Change and through grants provided by the Committee on Faculty Compensation and Development. The Department of Education and Child Study has functioned as a second home, and I thank my family of colleagues there for their sustenance. Outside of my department, I have benefited enormously from the thoughts and friendship of Susan C. Bourque, Donna R. Divine, and Martha A. Ackelsberg.

I consider myself most fortunate to have worked with the University of Massachusetts Press. From my first inquiries, Dick Martin guided me with sound suggestions and heartening encouragement. I am grateful to Bruce Wilcox, who has been unfailingly responsive to all questions and concerns, and to Barbara Palmer and Pam Wilkinson for their editorial acumen.

Finally, so much of my professional life has been made possible by my entirely wonderful children addressing their question, "What's for dinner?" to my extraordinary husband, rather than to me.

To all the many other friends, colleagues, and family who have supported me in countless ways, thank you.

Managing Lives

Introduction

Are women who have assumed what had been men's roles in our society playacting? Do their daily pursuits contradict their true natures as females? Or has women's psychological nature been misapprehended? Is it possible that, psychologically, women resemble men as much as they do one another? Could it be that social change has produced a blending of gender roles that cannot be adequately accommodated within existing social structures?

The experience of corporate women can instruct us about gender and about the interaction between individual development and social change. The psychology of corporate women seems particularly pertinent to questions of male–female difference, since these women operate primarily in what has been and continues to be "a man's world." That women can and, moreover, want to occupy this formerly male preserve has dramatically altered conventional understandings of what women are about.

The traditional view of females as emotional caretakers was clear-cut and allowed a simple understanding of female identity and life path. More recent notions of females as both caretakers and executives are more complicated and difficult for some to accept. Examination of the literature on psychological development reveals a struggle between these conflicting ideas. Findings that males and females might be more alike than different, particularly when they function in the same profession, have been countered by a theory of basic gender difference that has been widely embraced. Carol Gilligan's description of a path of care and connection for females and one of interpersonal separateness for males harks back to traditional precepts of gender difference.[1] Acceptance of this idea comes more readily, perhaps because it is familiar and linear, or perhaps because we are still resistant to countervailing premises of androgyny that require more complex understanding and behavior from us.

When Gilligan's theory is applied to corporate women, as it has been by Sarah Hardesty and Nehamah Jacobs in *Success and Betrayal*, women are portrayed as having unconscious motives that sabotage appropriate professional behavior.[2] Thus, women act one way but feel another. Their ambivalence serves to undermine their success, and that ambivalence stems from suppressed needs for attachment and connection. Hardesty and Jacobs describe women as transferring, albeit unwittingly, their relationship needs from the domestic sphere to the corporation. We might conclude, then, that underneath their business suits women still fit the traditional psychological model; they have just learned to act differently. *Success and Betrayal* keeps the premise of a basic gender difference intact by postulating an unconscious, conventionally female nature underlying the behavior of women who are ostensibly succeeding in a man's world.

Like Gilligan, Hardesty and Jacobs listened to women's own voices in order to arrive at their interpretations. In this book we will also listen to corporate women, this time in an effort to understand women's psychological development in light of recent social change. By examining firsthand accounts of women's personal and professional development, we have access to their thoughts and feelings, motivations and satisfactions, in both public and private, business and domestic spheres.

What emerges is not a path or pattern of development peculiar to females but rather a diversity of experience that reflects the interaction between psychological development and social context. The women in this study experienced changing views of themselves and their life directions, as well as collective shifts in our social belief system about female identity and place. Women in corporations are in a prime position to demonstrate the interaction between individual and social change, since their careers are affected by both. But institutional change lags behind individual change. That women, and not men, continue to be faced with a choice between career and family attests to the uneven nature of social change. For the most part, our corporate organizations are still structured as though there were a full-time wife at home tending to the domestic needs of the male employee. Now that women are in corporations to stay, our institutions must face up to the need for fundamental reforms. A recent suggestion that a separate corporate track be established for women who plan to have families could perpetuate the notion that females are the family's caretaking mainstay and further mitigate against structural change that would assume more equality between men and women—at home and at work.[3]

This book examines the interaction of psychological change with that of our institutional structures. Moreover, the women in this book are particularly interesting because they have reckoned with conventional and countervailing ideologies. Their experiences demonstrate the process of change, how it occurs, under what conditions, and with what consequences for the individual and the organization. From testimony about women's development at work and at home, we learn firsthand how individual change and social change affect and are affected by each other.

This study presents evidence of women's ability to meet the challenges of top executive positions. It argues that their absence in those positions is not a function of contrary psychological needs or personal shortcoming; rather, it is a function of the limits of structural social change. Examining both individual change and corporate adaptation, this volume reveals that difficulties persist not because of females' unmet, unconscious needs for connection but because of structural obstacles and persistent, albeit subtle, discrimination. The need is not for more individual adaptation by women but for more change on the part of corporations to adapt to human needs, male and female, for both work and family.

This Study

The testimony presented here comes from forty women who were or were about to become middle managers. The women ranged in age from their early twenties to their late fifties, and they were diverse in class and ethnic backgrounds, although most were white Americans; included were three black and three foreign-born women.

Their organizations ranged from large to *Fortune* 500 companies. The women worked in financial services; retail industries; large, diversified conglomerates; media and publishing; high-technology industries; transportation; manufacturing; natural resources; and consumer products. They could be found in production on the shop floor, in regional offices in the field, and in corporate headquarters. Their positions ranged from sales representative to vice-president, with project leaders, instructors, accountants and auditors, writers and overseers of company publications represented. About half of the women already held the title of manager, and their areas included marketing, personnel and human resources, equal employment opportunity, product manufacturing and distribution, in-house education and training, sales, legislative affairs. The range of their responsibilities is depicted by the woman who scouted real estate for new company locations, the administrator in a private medical facility for the critically injured, and the representative of her employer on legislative floors.

These women were a special group because they had been chosen by their companies for further training at a college-affiliated management program. That these women were singled out for such support by their companies is subject to various interpretations, including the implication of professional promise, perhaps in the form of advancement within the organization. Thus, we are listening not just to female middle managers but to a select subset of that population, those to whom some kind of company commitment has been implied.

Interviews were conducted over a four-year period during the early 1980s. Each woman was interviewed at the beginning and end of her participation in the management program, which stretched over a year's time. Interviews were held when the women were on campus for two summers a year apart. The interview format could be called semi-structured or open-ended, as each participant received the same questions, but responses were allowed to dictate the direction of follow-up queries. Questions were focused not on the management program itself but on the professional and personal experiences that each woman brought to campus (see Appendix).

In the first interview respondents were asked about their career paths (Who and what had been important in their career development?); their personal development (How had their family influenced them, and what dilemmas had they faced?); their own and others' management styles (How had their styles developed, and how might they be perceived by others?).

In the second interview respondents were asked about personal and professional changes over the year's time (How might their perspectives on the future be affected?); the relationship between their work lives and their home lives; the evolution of their management responsibilities and experiences; structural elements of their organizations that affect their working lives.

Interviewees were generous with their time, their thoughts, and their experiences. Participation in the study was purely voluntary, but almost everyone agreed to talk to us. Not all participants are represented here, however, as some were not available at the end of their program year (for example, a job change or relocation). Included here are only those forty women for whom two interviews were completed.

Each interview, lasting usually sixty to ninety minutes, was taped and later transcribed. Since the women's testimony constitutes the data, illustrative quotations are found throughout the text, but the names of all people, places, and organizations have been changed to protect privacy and insure confidentiality. The intention is not to reveal information about specific people or organizations but rather to learn from firsthand accounts about the psychosocial development of women who hold positions of responsibility in our corporations. This study reveals the process of change as it occurs between individuals and social structures.

This is not a study of numbers. We hear the voices of forty women here. Their words are not subjected to a coding system or to statistical analyses in order to make general or generalizable statements about them. We approach them qualitatively, listening to what they say and finding the meanings they express. We neither expect nor seek sameness. Though their commonalities are not neglected, the aim is to document their diversity and individuality. Both their commonalities and their differences are instructive for us. The fact that their numbers are small is balanced by our being able to listen attentively to their recounting of experiences both personal and professional.

The use of a phenomenological approach to data collection and interdisciplinary analyses allowed careful examination of the processes of human development and structural change. Because this study looks at human development from the inside out, from the point of view of women's internal processing of change, it begins to examine the meanings of change on various levels. That is, women describe revised thoughts and feelings as well as behavior, and the synergism among them. These aspects of self are ultimately reconciled with each other, although not necessarily all at once. Further, there must be some degree of fit between individual change and what is offered by society's institutions of work and family.

Psychological Study of Individual Development

Social change has affected not only individual lives but also the shape of research in developmental psychology over the past two decades. Prior to the recent wave of feminist scholarship, researchers generally studied men and assumed that theories thereby derived applied to females as well. Attention to the fallacy of that assumption paired with a purposeful study of women has yielded a different view of development by gender.

The idea that female development could not be accounted for by male-derived theories gave rise to extensive study of male–female difference, while maintaining that difference did not imply deficit. Similarities and crossover between males and females effected a generic conclusion that individual differences among members of each sex superseded male–female distinctions. Females could be as different from each other as they might be from men. Though this discovery bespeaks an equality that could well serve agendas of the current women's movement, it leaves the popular experience of gender difference largely unexplained.

The idea that females could be as psychically different from each other as they were from men contradicted long-standing cultural ideology and socialization practice and flew in the face of popular belief and experience. Social scientists' findings of insignificant differences between male and female did not provide the encompassing concept that distinguished the sexes, as we knew them to be. Carol Gilligan's book, *In a Different Voice,* supplied what was missing.

That Gilligan gave us what we sought is evident in the overwhelming response to her work. She eloquently elucidated what we intuitively believed: that there was a split in psychological development along gender lines, that females followed a path of interpersonal relatedness and caring and males one of personal separateness and independent achievement. Gilligan's descriptive theory has been hailed as a breakthrough in the study of psychological development and as particularly enlightening for the understanding of gender difference.

It seems that our need for validation of gender difference has pressed us into yet another set of biases that could categorize women along conventional lines. Neither Gilligan nor feminists who cheered her findings intended them to be interpreted to anyone's detriment, male or female. Nonetheless, the paths of development for males and females bear strong resemblance to our traditional ideas of what boys and girls are made of. To declare an orientation toward connection and care as characteristic of females and one toward separation and individuation as a male propensity represents a throwback to the association of instrumentality with male and affectivity with female. Although, as Gilligan observes, these paths may cross in midlife when men become more concerned with attachment and women with individuation, her descriptions relegate men and women to their customary places for at least the first forty years of life.

Gender-distinct paths of development are related to the idea of separate male and female personality traits. Personality trait theory had a substantial and credible history in psychology until the work of Walter Mischel and the rise of behavioral theory displaced it.[4] Whereas personality traits were assumed to be predictable and consistent, Mischel found that the same person could manifest strikingly different characteristics in varying circumstances, individual behavior being a function less of internal and unchanging traits and more of social context. An individual's personality was no longer defined as a stable disposition but was considered a dynamic interaction with a particular environment.

Behavioral theory readily follows from this dramatically revised notion of personality. If personality is not an immovable cornerstone but changes in relation to situation, then people's behavior can be modified through learning and environmental contingencies.[5]

Evidence of behavior's modifiability abounds in the literature of clinical and educational psychology.[6] Living testimony to change also comes in the form of female identities and endeavors of the past two decades. Women's activities have overturned traditional ideas about their predispositions and abilities. They have demonstrated the fallacy of personality trait theory and the adaptability of human behavior by assuming positions heretofore occupied by and presumed fit for men only. In contrast to a personality explanation of females' traditionally subordinate corporate positions, a structural view asserts that traits ordinarily cited as causes are better understood as results of subordinate positions in organizations.[7] For example, a recent study found that women in high management positions demonstrate less dependency and need for approval than women at lower management levels and than high ranking men.[8]

Ostensibly, women holding professional positions in corporate organizations exemplify a gender-free concept of behavior. To succeed in an environment that requires characteristics ordinarily associated with

Alice Sargeant
Marilyn Loden
not cited

maleness, women must eschew a relationship orientation and adopt an independent achievement stance that has been assumed to be typical of men. Management and psychological literature attests to women's capabilities, even so far as finding that managerial behavior cannot be distinguished by gender.[9] Now that similarity has been established between men and women, we are, curiously, looking for difference by maintaining a distinction in underlying traits and behavior.

In *Success and Betrayal,* Hardesty and Jacobs, who are themselves successful executives, portray women's managerial accomplishments in relationship terms. Drawing upon psychodynamic analyses of women's corporate experiences, the authors describe female projection of a desire for connection, attachment, and the kind of individual recognition ordinarily associated with family onto the corporation. Whereas men's goals and expectations coincide with what the corporation offers, women's are extrapolated from the promise and reward system of their youth. Naive about politics, power, and money, women are working for learning and individual recognition. Though behaviorally correct, they are in for a psychological fall because their "innately female" needs cannot be met by the corporation. Women's salvation lies in heeding their "authentic voice," which is tied to a self grounded in feminine, intuitive insight. Their mistake was the unconscious denial of their true selves in the process of corporate assimilation. Their continued success depends upon an ability to reconcile individual needs with what is available. Corporations also must change to accommodate and recognize the strengths and needs of their individual employees.

Thus, the portrayal of women's psychological development has gone from pillar to post and back again. When trait theory became unreliable in predicting and explaining personality, the modifiability of human behavior promised change and enhanced potential. But when this idea is fully applied to females, and behavior is shown to be gender-free, some turn back to trait theory by postulating innate, albeit unconscious, motives unique to females. Because traits are defined as permanent parts of personality, they are granted a validity that discredits surface behavior.

Perhaps there are unconscious motives at work here in the form of societal resistance to relinquishing entrenched ideology and accepting the complexity of a world without gender stereotypes. Postulating traits that gainsay behavior is preferable to dealing with anomalies of personal interaction and institutional structure that result from the absence of gender guideposts.

Similarly, our understanding of gender has gone back and forth.

Research findings served to overturn notions of mutually exclusive male and female characteristics, and differences were viewed as greater within than between genders. Apparently this conclusion confused rather than clarified. A large conceptual missing piece was then provided by Gilligan's theory, which recognized and affirmed what many had believed all along: that the female identity was formed primarily through attachment, the male through separation.[10] Accounting for much of the difference that people of both sexes have experienced, this notion allows for continued belief in traditional ideology about the nature of men and women.

Theories of Gender Development and Corporate Women

Gilligan's theory is descriptive of general gender differences; its application specifically to corporate women can be found in the work of Hardesty and Jacobs. A more detailed explanation of the position derived from Gilligan's work is necessary before we can consider other explanations of womens' psychosocial development.

According to Hardesty and Jacobs, ostensibly successful corporate women subscribe to certain myths that are grounded in their childhood experiences. These myths shape expectations that are not held by men and cannot be met by corporations as they currently function. For example, the myths of Individual Recognition, Meritocracy, and Reward operate such that women believe that their own individual excellence, talent, and effort will culminate in recognition and reward. Presumably, women have transferred their early school experience, where performance alone sufficed to bring recognition. Thus, women have been described as passive in their simple reliance on task recognition to promote them without further effort on their part.

Moreover, the rewards that hold sway for women are the psychic ones of mastery and excellent performance, whereas men thrive on gamesmanship and seek the traditional, tangible corporate rewards, which are frequently awarded on the basis of politics, power, and position rather than individual performance. In sum, for men it is a matter of "I'm going to win this game," whereas for women it is "I want to be wonderful at what I do."

Finally, women are captivated by the Myth of Growth, "an inherently female yearning for self-improvement." Whereas men think about salary and title in relation to a position, women focus on its challenge and potential for new learning. This "uniquely female level of satisfaction" ultimately falls victim to the repetition and tedium common to corporate enterprise. In contrast, men measure their success not by new learning but by increased control, title, and position.

This female belief structure is reflected in certain corporate behavior patterns. Women are seen as accepting positions for the wrong reasons—as a challenge rather than a career path opportunity. They may stay in a position too long or cling to a company because of female needs for affiliative bonding, what Hardesty and Jacobs call the Myth of the Corporation as Family. And when they do move, it is again for misguided reasons of individual fulfillment rather than as part of a career game plan. Since behavior motivated by misplaced individual achievement needs is ultimately out of place in the corporate setting, women are destined for disappointment and disillusionment. Their choice, then, is either to adapt to the organization's reward system or to leave.

In this study, the apparently successful adaptation to the corporate environment by most of the women could be interpreted as evidence of a chameleonlike conformity, which maintains the corporate status quo. In contrast, we will see that these women are not focused on gender in the workplace but on business. The fact that they are not explicitly challenging gender stereotypes does not imply that they are upholding them. Women who have successfully negotiated male professions psychologically resemble their male counterparts. They bear little psychological semblance to women who conform to customary female social roles.[11]

The women interviewed provide ample evidence that they cannot be categorized along gender lines and that their behavior is ultimately measured against an internal criterion of integrity. We see them gauging their work according to their own standards of achievement, which do not always coincide with those of their managers or the company. When they make career decisions, they seem to be guided most by an internal inventory of their personal and professional needs, regardless of what might be organizationally prescriptive for them at the time. Their high career commitment does not enslave them to their corporations. The vast majority would continue working even in the absence of financial need. Many would choose a similar line of work but a context that would permit them even greater autonomy, independence, and career self-determination, for example, self-employment or consulting. Moreover, successful women managers, like the women of this study, are changing the face of corporate management rather than simply being assimilated into an unchanging male-defined environment.

The fact that fewer female than male managers sustain marriage and family could also be cited as evidence that women are sacrificing their needs for connection and intimacy for the sake of a corporate career. Of the forty interviewed, about half were married, twelve divorced, and seven unmarried. Eleven had children at the time of the interviews, six had them subsequently. Although these numbers conform to the common findings that about half of women managers (compared to 95 percent of their male counterparts)[12] are married with families, it cannot be concluded that these women have denied their affiliative needs in the service of their careers. The interviews reveal that these women have filial attachments and emotional lives outside the workplace, regardless of whether or not they are married. Some examples include a woman who cared for her sister's children and two women who became single parents because of their strong desire for their own children.

To attribute female managers' lower marriage rate solely to the necessity of coping with a demanding corporate career is to oversimplify. It seems more likely that their lower marriage rate is just one part of a complex of factors that distinguish the psychology and lives of male and female managers. Most male managers represent a traditional life pattern that includes conventional marital roles. In contrast, female managers are by definition unconventional; their needs and motives distinguish them not only in the workplace but also in their social relationships with men. The assumption that these women unequivocally want marriage may itself be unwarranted. A career-oriented woman who does seek a marriage partner has a far more complicated task than a similarly situated man. Like our other institutional structures, marriage is still set up along traditional lines that support the male career with women primarily responsible for household care. This is changing slowly as young men and women become more alike in their life goals, both desiring demanding careers in fields that have been traditionally male and both wanting spouses and children to be high priorities in their lives.[13] Because traditional roles are recalcitrant to change, women, as opposed to men, continue to be faced with the challenge of an integrated life. More young men, however, are beginning to encounter the conflict of a future of family and career in a society that has yet to accommodate such prospects for both marital partners.[14]

Women of this study manifested motives and behavior similar to those described by Hardesty and Jacobs; their focus was more on learning, performance, and the rewards of mastery than on career planning and politics. However, other interpretations are offered here that do not presume the operation of inherently female needs for connection in the corporate context. It is certainly the case that corporate women are functioning in an environment constructed by males and therefore perhaps most suited to them. If females are dissatisfied with corporate life, it is not because of frustrated expectations for interpersonal need fulfillment but because of extant corporate structure, which assumes a white male populace and a military model that permits a unitary life focus.[15] In this study we will look at women's testimony about their career paths and see how that testimony can be interpreted in line with traditional notions of female traits or, alternatively, according to a synergistic view of individual and social change.

Women who entered the business world in nontraditional ways did not have formal or scholastic preparation for management. There was no single or typical career path followed by the women of this study. They began work at different times in their lives and came from varied backgrounds. Not all started their working lives in business, and those who did commonly lacked specific training for corporate work. The relatively few who had training in a technical area were not usually prepared in business management. Hence, women developed their skills and potential as managers through work experience.

Most women of this study have straddled conventional and countervailing messages about life direction by gender and are therefore in an excellent position to demonstrate the dynamic interaction between individual psychological development and social change. In contrast, women who prepare for business careers in college presumably have experienced socialization shaped by and consistent with the forces of change; they have not had to wend their way through shifting social ideologies about female identity. Thus, their experiences yield less insight into the reciprocal contributions of social context and psychological processes.

In this study, as in those of Gilligan and Hardesty and Jacobs, women's own testimony provides the empirical data. We can learn about female "traits" as well as behavior, and about the relationship between the two, from what women tell us about their evolving selves in relation to work and family. Tracing the personal and career paths of these women elucidates not only the fact of change but, most importantly, the processes by which individual psychological development shapes and is shaped by social change. In the process of individual development, change involves a dynamic interplay between the psychology of the individual and the ideology of social structures.

Attention to women's words and their meanings can shed light on the nature, depth, and process of psychological change and how it relates to both new and old social contexts in which women live. To elucidate female psychological development in light of social change we need access to women's perceptions of their work[16] and private lives.

Social Change and Working Women

The context in which most social change has occurred is that of employment. Women have entered the paid labor force in an unparalleled way. Census takers tell us that their numbers account for approximately half of those gainfully employed. Forecasters project that white males will constitute only 15 percent of new entrants to the labor force by the end of this century. Women show no signs of turning their full attention back to home and hearth.

In comparison to the public sphere of work, the private one of domesticity is less changed. Women are still marrying and having babies. After a period of declining birth rates, we are now witnessing what some term another baby boom. Although the new parents of the eighties differ enormously from those of the 1940s, the lion's share of domestic responsibility still falls to the female. Though some books have been written about the "new" father and his role in his children's lives,[17] most literature has been concerned with what has been primarily a woman's challenge: the balance between work and home, family and career, self and other.

Women's participation in our society's paid labor force has a long and complex history, which will not be chronicled here.[18] Suffice it to say that we can no longer believe that women work simply for reasons of economic necessity or to mark time until marriage.[19] Certainly, there are such women, but the more compelling finding is that women simply want to work and be paid for it. Even those whose first jobs were motivated solely by economic need have had their heads turned. They like gainful employment for reasons other than money. Often those reasons have to do with meaningfulness and self-fulfillment. It is not only men whose needs transcend the personal and interpersonal realms of life. We can no longer believe that the sole or even the primary source of female satisfaction lies in caretaking and relationship. Many women want to work; indeed, they must work if they are to feel that they are worthwhile human beings.

Although women now account for about half of the labor force, most hold positions with low potential for what workers have called the elements of job satisfaction; their jobs provide little opportunity for autonomy, independence, or decision making. Despite low wages and little advancement, women still find satisfaction and reward in their working lives.[20] Working for both economic and existential reasons, women find that job satisfaction, however, increases commensurate to the skill level of their positions.[21]

Not all women are located in the underechelon of employment. A small percentage are sprinkled among the middle and upper ranks of the occupational hierarchy. How small the percentage is varies with the type of occupation; we see more women on the upper rungs of the ladder in social and public service than we do in the scientific and private sectors. It is not surprising that women at these levels are currently a minority, given that society's changed viewpoint about women's place is barely two decades old. Presumably, women thirty years old and younger grew up with significantly different assumptions about their roles and futures than did those ten years their senior. If our relatively new assumptions and their underlying social and political supports continue to hold fast, we might expect to find many more women preparing to climb the higher rungs of employment ladders.

We know that very few women currently hold high positions of executive responsibility in our corporations. On occasion, "women at the top" are featured in front-page stories or magazine articles. Fascinating though their stories may be, they are few in number and remote from our experience. In this study we learn about the women in the middle, those who wear neither blue nor pink collars but white collars with three-piece suits. Though still in the minority, there are many more women at the level of "middle manager," and we have little close-up information about them. We may know their numbers and their demography, but we do not know their persons.[22] By listening to their own voices, we can learn much about their personal and professional development and about ourselves and our organizations.

This study represents a beginning. Longitudinal data could contribute to our knowledge in new and exciting ways, but we also need more cross-sectional studies of the type undertaken here. In-depth interviews with a larger and perhaps a more stratified sample of women as well as with male middle managers would yield an understanding of personal and professional development, commonality and diversity, that we can only begin to imagine from our present vantage point. We look forward to others continuing from this beginning.

▫ I ▫

PROFESSIONAL
DEVELOPMENT

This study is divided into three parts. The first traces women's professional development from their early participation in the paid labor force to their becoming managers. Most of these women had not planned a career path and did not enter on a managerial track, although thirty-one held college degrees, eleven of them advanced degrees; thirteen of these earned degrees were in business-related fields. In chapter 1 we learn about how involvement with paid work shaped these women's motivations and aspirations for more professional responsibility. Job experiences influenced not only their work history but also their developing notions of themselves in relation to career.

Despite diverse and circuitous routes to the business world, the women interviewed began to discover the gratifications that accompany emerging competence. These women defy stereotypic notions of what is important and motivating to females. At work their primary focus is on successful accomplishment of the task at hand, not on people and interpersonal relationship. In contrast to a kind of filial loyalty that might characterize those assumed to be affectively oriented, these women demonstrate intense commitment to work rather than to a specific person, employer, or company.

Chapters 2 and 3, on career planning and mobility, focus on women's learning processes as they develop a career-oriented self. The varied and unorthodox ways in which they became involved in work carried implications for their abilities to map a career. Chapter 4 documents women's evolution as managers by illustrating how they were influenced by their own managers and how they perceive themselves in a management position. Women chronicle the changes they must make in relation to the workers as well as to the work. Transition to manager is particularly complicated when a woman comes from the clerical ranks or when supervision of former peers is now required. A separation of the personal from the professional and ascendancy of the latter are important achievements for these women, who again contradict traditional views of female nature.

□ 1 □

Work

Why do people go to work? What keeps them motivated at their jobs? Beyond financial necessity, there are many human needs that are met through participation in the work force. [1] People commonly express a preference for their daily toil even in the absence of financial need. That is, people would choose to continue working even if income were otherwise forthcoming. That the transition from employment to leisure frequently is a difficult one testifies to the many social and emotional functions that work serves in addition to its economic one. We become more aware of those needs in retrospect when we witness the emptiness that can accompany retirement. [2]

Humanists and social scientists have written about work and its meaning from pragmatic and spiritual vantage points, but for more than half of this century the work that was described and analyzed was understood to be "men's work." "Women's work" was unpaid, pertaining to the household and to caretaking. [3] Women who worked outside of the home were either single or obliged to do so for some unfortunate reason, usually financial necessity. [4] Men were expected to find primary fulfillment from their work away from home and only secondarily from their families. [5] Women's fulfillment was expected to come solely from their lives within home and family, and their activities there were not even called work. [6]

This rigid dichotomy between men's and women's lives and their separate sources of self-realization stemmed from an ideology that did not wholly account for or dictate reality. Its failure to construct females who thrived only on domesticity is exemplified by the women whose stories are chronicled here. Strongly motivated by work and its intrinsic sources of satisfaction, these women overcome both psychological and actual disadvantage through work experience made available to them by social change. A look at the separate-spheres ideology will show its effects on women who enter corporate organizations.

Gender and the Meaning of Work

A close examination of women's actual participation in America's paid labor force reveals a reality that does not closely conform to a separate-spheres ideology.[7] Women, in fact, have always contributed to the production and economy of this country. Even in the 1950s, with its image of the happy housewife providing the support systems needed by her employed husband, at least one-third of all women worked, and half of them worked full time.[8]

Although women have always worked, in and out of the home, for production of goods or wages, the idea that women do not belong in the paid labor force has become a pervasive piece of ideology. That notion had its origins in the nineteenth-century "domestic code" whereby the purer sex, female, was to preserve the home as a sanctuary in the midst of a competitive society.[9]

Even when families shared domestic and production work of an agrarian economy, women had been denied full legal and political community participation. When employed in the postindustrial economy before World War II, they were clustered in occupations that duplicated their customary "female" tasks of the preindustrial economy. A predominantly white male labor force met the threat of displacement by female workers with the formation of unions that could block women's entrance to the trades and thereby perpetuate female occupational subjugation and segregation.[10]

The industrial economy redefined work and divided it by gender. New means of production of goods and services segregated workers from home and family. Although a market economy contributed to a separation of spheres, it did not necessarily dictate a separation along gender lines. However, an ideology that came to be called "the cult of true womanhood" relegated females solely to home and family and males to a workplace distant from home.[11]

A division of labor might have been dictated by necessity, given the time-consuming nature of domestic work before and after the turn of the century. We might expect, then, that the widespread use of home technology in the form of time- and labor-saving devices after the First World War would allow women more freedom. This, however, was not the case. Instead, married women gained greater access to paid employment primarily in times of war and societal adversity, the depression, for example. Otherwise, the fact of gainfully employed females was largely denied ideologically, and women's subordinate labor positions reinforced the peripheral nature of their participation. Even as numbers of the female employed climbed in each successive decade of this century, women's place was still believed to be at home. And home could be as demanding as it had been prior to technological advances. Labor-saving devices allowed household standards to be raised to higher levels of cleanliness, nutrition, and familial well-being.[12] Women were still to be primarily occupied and, moreover, satisfied by domesticity. Female forays into paid work, even when they were full time and of long duration, were seen as temporary stopgaps for an unfortunate family circumstance.

Long-standing assumptions about gender-linked sources of fulfillment have died hard, because more than fulfillment is at stake. A certain societal structure has been built upon those assumptions, with its attendant institutions, norms, and practices. Thus, women's challenges to a gender-based division of labor, where men dominate the public sphere and women are relegated to the domestic or private sphere, were unwelcome. By permeating our social structures and practices, that division of labor had taken on the status of "natural law."[13] When social scientists describe such family divisions of labor as a universal social pattern, they gain a credibility that transcends social custom and becomes a kind of gender determinism. That is, men and women were assumed to be naturally and inherently suited to their respective positions in the social order. Women who longed for career and men who wished to stay home were worse than unconventional; they were misfits.

The Effects of Social Change on Women's Work

Two decades of social change have not completely overturned the assumptions that maintained firm borders between men's and women's work. There are those, albeit less than half of our population, who

continue to consider a gender-based division of labor not only conve-
nient but appropriate and "right" for the sexes. With more than half of
American women in the paid labor force, however, people are forced
to reexamine their attitudes and beliefs.[14] Piaget has indicated that
action often precedes consciousness in human development,[15] and
therefore attitude change would not be commensurate with a female
employee influx. Changes in our beliefs might trail far behind our
behavior. Further, the beliefs and attitudes that need changing do not
belong only to men.[16]

Beliefs about gender differences that built and sustained our society's institutions and practices became an integral part of human
psyches. Surrounded by a culture of certain thought and custom,
people developed and internalized consonant beliefs. Psychological
representation of a culture parallels its external practice in depth and
breadth. The social belief system is psychologically assimilated to such
an extent that it can be likened to a kind of collective unconscious.
Shared by the majority of the populace and not brought forth for
examination or reformulation, the system's tenets are not active inhabi-
tants of conscious minds. Though deeply buried, they still shape individual and institutional direction. Paradoxically pervasive and invisible, they are not easily disinterred for scrutiny by either women or
men.

The gender-based division of labor was as much a part of women as
they were a part of it—hence their inability to articulate the sources of
felt dissatisfaction with their lives that Betty Friedan dubbed the mal-
aise with no name.[17] How could our basic assumptions about appropriate lives for each gender constitute oppression? Both men and women
resisted notions that threatened to erode the foundations of their
institutions and ways of being.

Dubiousness notwithstanding, women began to recognize themselves in descriptions and explanations drawn by outspoken feminists.
Though some were content with home and family as their center,
many wanted the freedom to choose. More striking was their surprise
when they met discouragement and even discrimination upon entrance to the workplace.

From the turn of the century until recent decades, women have
consistently occupied different jobs than men, jobs that "required less
skill, lower pay, and few chances for advancement."[18] Whether young
and single, as she was prior to the 1930s, or married with family, as she
was during the depression and Second World War, the employed fe-

male was perceived as a transient member of the labor force. Women who wanted to retain their jobs after the war were more than ideologically discouraged; bureaucratic practices actively denied them employment through withdrawal of necessary supports (child-care facilities, for example) and imposition of rules that resulted in termination.[19] Still captive of a consciousness with a double standard, women often did not recognize subtle and overt obstacles to their employment without considerable feminist commentary. Moreover, their own beliefs about themselves and their life directions were not overturned without substantial guilt. Motivated by economics, the "empty nest," or self-fulfillment, they were entering and remaining in the work force anyway.

Women who entered the work force for the first time in the sixties after being bred and raised as homemakers faced a sizable task. Their struggles were external and internal. A workplace that was neither formally nor informally governed by equal employment opportunity presented a formidable complex of external obstacles. The internal blocks, composed of the psychic representation of a social belief system that said women belong in the home, were private but gripping. Societal and individual "shoulds" dictated that women were to be content with home and family. It was unfortunate if necessity required their employment, but they were certainly not supposed to want to work. And if they did want to work, what would become of their children and families? Who would take care of them? By wanting to work, women were not only defying societal norms but shirking their responsibilities to those nearest and dearest to them. It was the unusual woman who did not feel the burden of prospective dire repercussions.[20] One woman describes the process of entering the business world after a home-and-family hiatus:

> I've had a hard time starting where I did, which was really starting over. I found it very hard to know where I stood, where I belonged. . . . I probably had a very low opinion of myself in terms of what I could do in business. I really felt as though I was the bottom of the ladder. . . . I had no idea what I should be making at that point with the background I had. And I only cared about working with people I liked. . . . So I did learn from that experience that that's hardly the way to begin a job. And of course, having been away for so long, there are all those conflicts.

"All those conflicts" here refers to the pull between a female family identity and the paid labor that was associated with men. This woman represents many who were caught between the traditional ideology of female domesticity and new messages of equal rights in the workplace. Her incidental entry into the labor force is characteristic of women who did not anticipate a job becoming a career. Indeed, an at-home wife and mother who took a job in the sixties often found herself unintentionally pursuing a career. Beyond financial gain, the personal satisfaction and challenge offered by work engaged her commitment. Moreover, social change enabled her to continue work pursuits in a more open-ended way than had previously been possible.

Work Takes on New Meanings for Women

More than twenty years have passed since the beginning of what we call the current women's movement. Undeniably, change has occurred. Our society is not as monochromatic in its beliefs and practices as it seemed to be in the 1950s. It is not unusual now for women to be working, to want to work, to be preparing for and engaged in careers.[21] Though most employed women are still in subordinate jobs, the proportion entering traditionally male occupations has increased substantially during the past decade. Careers and professions carrying power, prestige, and responsibility are no longer seen as an exclusive male preserve. It is presumably understood now that women might want to work for the same reasons that men do: achievement, personal fulfillment, and self-sufficiency. Women who enjoy their work for its own sake are not labeled "selfish" as readily as they once were.[22]

It is no longer assumed that all women want to marry or to have children. The traditional nuclear family with husband gainfully employed and wife at home full time has become a statistical minority. What constitutes family has changed dramatically even if our notions have not. Behavior change may leap ahead of belief revision, but the latter is gradually pulled along by community evidence, individual experience, and political reinforcement (for example, affirmative action regulations).

Today's working woman does not face as many obstacles as her sixties sister did. Internal and external impediments, though not wholly vanished, have significantly diminished, or at least changed shape. Women can and do openly express and advocate what would have been taboo positions thirty years ago. Some eschew motherhood while others embrace sole parenting. Many express their unequivocal intention to work, moreover, to have a career, not just a job. Several want "to have it all," family and career, but they have yet to specify the pragmatics, dual-career family literature notwithstanding. Children and their timing are particularly problematic for women already involved in careers that they do not want to relinquish or suspend.

Old assumptions about the divergent natures of men and women fade as we begin to recognize that within-gender differences exceed those between. Ambition and achievement are not solely male characteristics, and women can define work as central to their beings. Subsequent to participation in this study, several of the women responded to a questionnaire which included queries about work satisfaction. Almost without exception, all respondents indicated that they worked for reasons of self, that they would continue working even in the case of unequivocal financial independence, and that most would remain in their current positions or line of work.

Mary, a happily married woman in her late twenties, goes so far as to subordinate her marriage to work:

> Once again, you have to understand my values. It's work, and what I've done in work is what I'm most proud of and what I most clearly, in terms of my identity, identify with.

Nina, who in her early thirties has achieved managerial status in a large corporation and is now gradually pursuing a bachelor's degree, talks about a lifelong attraction to work:

> I've always enjoyed work, worked all through high school. Was not real serious about my college work, wanted to go out and work instead of going to school. So that's what I did. Just always got a lot of enjoyment out of working.

Ego involvement in work can be as strong for women as it has been assumed for men. However, women born more than twenty years ago did not ordinarily follow the straight line to career that characterized male development. Females did not grow up with the expectation that they would work for a living, their own or anyone else's. Messages to boys about their future as workers have been comparatively uniform and unequivocal throughout history. In contrast, women's variegated work history has had ramifications for the development of any individual female. If career expectations were part of a girl's socialization, they were likely to be either traditionally female or less specific, concrete, and inevitable than those for boys. Just as traditional ideology prescribed, females did not prepare to spend most of their lives in the paid labor force; their entries were therefore adventitious and amenable to subordination and marginality. In the absence of a straight and narrow career path, the women interviewed took whatever route they found accessible and forged others.

Random Beginnings

Women enter the work force at different times in their lives and for a variety of reasons. Their employment paths often do not follow traditional lines, and they begin to define directions once they have begun work. Nina, who preferred work to school, meandered through some course work until she discovered an interest in business that later was enhanced by the work itself.

> I was just taking liberal arts things at the time till I decided that I thought I wanted to get some business experience, so then I started taking some business courses. Then I joined DI [current employer]. At that point, that was not my intention to join them. I just was going out looking for a full-time job . . . wasn't even real sure what I wanted to do.

Even women with an abiding interest in work did not receive the strategic preparation that a male counterpart presumably would. If the prevailing ideology had changed such that females, as well as males, were to anticipate lifelong work, then the above characterization would not be as typical of females as it is. Women are known to talk about falling into a work situation or "things just happening to [them]," particularly advantageous things. In comparison to men, females had not been perceived by themselves or others as instrumental, as actively directing and planning career paths.[23]

Many young women today are thinking about "what they want to be when they grow up" and consciously planning for lifelong paid work. A sizable number, however, have not been coached along those lines, and they will fall into work through various, random means. Our interviewees provide examples of how paid work entered their lives without their actively anticipating it. Exposure to encouraging work experiences, however, then served to secure in women a commitment to career comparable to that of men.[24] Social change operated both by making opportunities available to women and by shaping female psychological readiness to profit from those opportunities. Consequently, random work entry could result in permanent career paths.

Some were influenced and encouraged by other women:

> My next-door neighbor was working for a company that was just beginning itself. So she convinced me to go to work there. So that was my first

exposure, which brought me into the field where I am now. And as the company grew, I grew.

A change in family status can precipitate a woman's meeting an extant need for work. Ursula, whose impending divorce precipitated work in her late twenties, speaks for many who "wanted to work anyway."

> And my first job was about five years ago. I'd been out of college for a while. I had a family. My marriage was breaking up. And going to work was really not as a result of that, totally a result of that. There was a need that was not being met. I would have gone to work anyway.

Others begin at the beginning, which formerly was the clerical ranks for women in business, and worked their way up:

> I started out two days after I graduated high school, at the age of seventeen. I started as a steno clerk. And in those days, the olden days, my goal was to become an executive secretary as quickly as I could. Maybe there are a lot of secretaries who have not had truly good learning experiences. I think I did. I had some excellent learning experiences. In fact, so much so that I very often say that everyone in a corporation should start— whether they're MBAs or not—as a secretary, and they'll learn one hell of a lot about being organized and prepared and meeting commitments.

With few exceptions, these interviewees did not have masters' degrees in business administration. They entered the business world by diverse and sometimes circuitous routes. Few described a straight career path where scholastic preparation for immediate corporate entry could dictate the way up the ladder. Locating the ladder and securing their footing would become these women's first tasks. In many cases, they would begin with scant business experience and, most crucially, with little knowledge about themselves and their skills in the business environment. They can articulate in retrospect their strengths and how they grew.

> I was thrust into a position without any formal training. I came with knowledge, and I came with the sense of knowing priorities. And I had the proper attitude. I also knew who to talk to and how to talk to them. So that's when I first came into the company, and learned more and more.

> That's another thing I brought to the office that I didn't realize: an ambition, enthusiasm, and street smarts. I read people well, know who to trust and who not to trust. And that's saved me a lot.

For Ursula, her life circumstance and the nature of beginning work heightened her vulnerability:

> There was no training program. It was a sink-or-swim kind of thing; some of us weren't going to make it. That was pretty scary. Plus the fact [of there being] mostly men in three-piece suits. I just remember men in dark suits and calculators and a lot of talk— . . . I really let myself be intimidated. And now I can listen to that and realize that half the time they don't know any more than I know and don't have really any more ability than I have. But it was a very frightening time for me. I was very afraid. I'm a single parent, and by that time I was divorced. I just really didn't feel like I wanted to be unemployed. I realized that it was very, very competitive, much more so than anyone had made clear to me.

Entering the paid labor force in random ways has its drawbacks. The absence of formal training and informal advance knowledge is experienced as a distinct, but temporary, disadvantage that women of this study overcame. In addition to a lack of technical skill, they suffer crises of confidence and doubts about competence. An unconventional career path can foster personal uncertainty and a need for validation even in those for whom work is integral. A woman in her early forties who was one of the most accomplished of the group in terms of corporate status, Hope, articulates the origins of this kind of humility:

> I think I've been heavily indoctrinated with the work ethic. I've worked all my life. And I've had a strange kind of career. There are times when I feel like I really don't deserve all this . . . because I've felt for a long time that I wanted to do something to maybe just reassure myself that my skills are legitimate. I think when you . . . come up through the ranks you haven't validated the fact, and maybe what it is is a means of validating it and saying, "Yes, I really do deserve to be where I am, because not only have I worked hard, but look, now I've proven in the great classroom that I really can do this, and I understand."

The need to prove herself goes beyond what is normally expected for anyone in a new position. Because she entered through the back door, as it were, this woman is disquieted by self-doubt despite concrete evidence of accomplishment. She wants the kind of legitimacy granted by formal institutions of training. A degree or certificate serves as permission for her to be on the path where she finds herself anyway.[25] Most women in this study did not start out with such a ticket but earned their way through on-the-job learning.

Developing Competence at Work

Even when the direction and specific content of their paths were uncertain, these women commonly expressed a desire to learn more and more. Their motivation seemed to come from within, as enjoyment of work produced eagerness for more knowledge and responsibility. When the work itself was not stimulating, women sought new avenues and assignments for fulfillment. Some describe how different kinds of learning worked to their advantage and advancement.

> I find that I was a very adaptable person, and I was always willing to learn. I always wanted to know more, even more than the job encompassed.

> I've always taken the initiative, most always. And it's almost like, "What can I do now?" "These are my suggestions," or "How do you see that I can get started on this project and then I'm on my own?" . . . I'm basically a self-starter and a self-initiator.

With learning and accomplishment comes an increased sense of competence. Willing to take the risk of accepting assignments and positions for which they might have felt unqualified, they rediscover their abilities again and again. Those discoveries spawn motivation for further achievement. The process of overcoming initial doubt through accomplishment and thereby successfully taking on more affirms and extends confidence and competence. A sense of competence can serve as both a consequence and a prerequisite for this process.

> I've always regarded the fact that I'm competent [as] my big strength. I'm good, I'm competent, and I can do a good job.

Competence fuels confidence and an optimism that can turn problems into challenges. Nina, one of several women who began without degreed credentials, discovered her interest and strengths on the job.

> I'm kind of a real big optimist. There usually are never any problems. There [are] always opportunities. I won an award, and that I think helped me in that it allowed me to show them that I could do the job. And they in turn let me do some of the other things. I was very verbal; I didn't sit at my desk and do it. I told them, "Great, hey, I know how to do this now. Now what else can I do?" And it was a benefit to them.

Proving ability to herself and actively demonstrating it to others put a woman in a position to learn and do even more. Turning difficulties into a challenge and mistakes into opportunity can result in something bigger and better. Heidi, a woman who moved from sales to regional manager in her midthirties, likens the work to a creative process:

> Well, I think one thing that I learned [was] to quit worrying about making mistakes. Instead of worrying about doing something wrong, I

found that whenever you do something wrong you can always go back. In fact, many times it becomes a bigger challenge to make a mistake into something better than what you expected before. When I finally realized that, I put that application in everything that I do. I concentrate more on doing whatever I'm doing and not worrying about being wrong. And if something goes wrong, to date I've always been able to find a remedy.

The most significant learnings for women have less to do with the job itself than with their own capabilities. Certainly, they are proving themselves to their employers, but much more importantly, they are discovering heretofore unknown aspects of themselves. This is especially the case for those who have come to work in circuitous ways. Unlike other women and men who have had the rites of passage afforded by specialized education or training, these women learn on the job that they are up to the task and that they enjoy it to an extent that makes work an essential part of life. Not only is their competence great enough to stretch over errors, but they can begin thinking about an actual career path.

Looking Ahead to a Lifetime of Work

Learning more about the work itself and their own capabilities, these women begin to consider and formulate goals. Although such formulations at first may lack specificity and detail, they represent another step forward in the elucidation and clarification of a woman's career ambition. The presence or absence of definite targets for that ambition notwithstanding, interviewees consistently expressed an eagerness for more challenge and achievement that seemed inherent to their beings.

Work just constantly changes. I find that I'm not real satisfied when things get stable. And I don't think that's really unusual. I think you set a goal, you reach it, and then you want another goal. And I probably wouldn't like it if it weren't that way.

I keep accepting these challenges. I find it very difficult to turn them down, so there's something in my personality that won't let me do that. So, if I complain on one hand, I enjoy the challenge. I wouldn't want to ever get in the position where I was bored, but I haven't been in a place long enough where that's actually happened.

I was given a deadline. We have to have it done in two months. Get it done. I don't know why I didn't question it. I was proving myself, and I had to succeed. It was one of those things. Well, here it comes again. I've got to prove myself one more time. Proving yourself. Yes. I get a tremendous bang out of it. "Okay, give me something that no one else can do, and I bet I can do this." It's a challenge.

Unafraid to move forward and up in their organizations, these women defy stereotypic notions of what is important and motivating to females. They are instrumental rather than social-emotional in their orientation. At work their primary focus is not on people and interpersonal relationship but rather on the task at hand. A woman in her fifties, Esther, has wended her way through differing ideas about appropriate behavior for females at work:

> I couldn't stand the coffee-klatsch atmosphere. I think I was very straightforward and practical, and I wanted to get something done. I think early on, because I am from the generation that I am, I was concerned about hurting other people's feelings. It took me a long time to get over that.

Lisa, who is in her late thirties, has had a consistently unconventional attitude:

> I probably tend to be very cold when dealing with individuals in the sense that I'm not really interested or concerned about their outside-of-work situation. If it comes up in conversation, fine, but I certainly would never be accused of being a sociable-type person. I simply want to hear about the tasks and how we're going to get it done and then let's do it. . . . I don't have any social relationship with people that I work with . . . and I don't worry about what other people think. Or when I worry, I put it out of my mind, because that's not important—it's there, it's an irritation, it's a little scratchy—because I will move on, and they could move on if they wanted to. But if they choose not to, it's not my job to worry about them.

Career ambition has traditionally been the province of males. The women interviewed stand in contrast to that notion when they unabashedly express their desires for leadership, for the win.

> in this job I'm really—I guess what they call it is quarterbacking. I've got the plan in my head. I enjoy it when I'm sitting back and watching what I saw in my mind's eye actually taking place. And I really like that . . . there's a real zing in there for me. And I'm also very, very competitive [in] that, even had I lost, I don't think I would lose that desire to really have to perform. There's a need there, and I can't explain it really. But I get a real charge out of it, out of seeing that things are really rough and winning. I like to win.

> And I think that what I enjoy a lot is influence, and power, and leadership.

> I like being the boss. That's just the way it is. I found just since I've been in the business world that that is the aspect of the job that I like. Once I learn something, and I learn how to do it, then I feel that, "Well, I can do this well enough that I can really supervise other people."

As workers, they are conscientious, ambitious, and achievement-oriented. They speak of long hours, substantial overtime, taking work home with them. There are times when work not only dominates their lives but constitutes their lives. They are giving their all not for money or company loyalty but rather for reasons of self that may not always be articulated and that have not been traditionally associated with females.

According to Hardesty and Jacobs, these women could be in the "proving-up" stage of corporate work.[26] Their sights are fixed on the challenge of the work rather than on where assignments can take them in more tangible terms of promotion and money. Because the rewards women seek, having to do with the intrinsic nature of the work itself, do not coincide with the corporate reward structure, such women are predicted to cling to their companies waiting for recognition that does not come. In this study, however, women's attachments to the satisfactions of work are temporarily associated with the particular companies of their employ but ultimately transcend them.

Company Loyalty

The company that employs these women benefits from their diligence, but for the most part their ambitions transcend company boundaries. Their strong sense of responsibility to the company is in force during their employ, but it does not preclude a broader perspective.

I've always been professional-loyal, not organization-loyal. I mean I'm pretty clear about the work that I like doing in this world. And I just happen to be doing it [here] right now.

I have never felt married to the company that I work for, and as long as I feel that they are treating me well, and I am doing the best job that I can, I will stay. But if I ever see that things change, I would be the first one to move.

I left that job because I had a better opportunity. I'm not loyal to any company. I want interesting work, challenging work, and I want to be compensated for it. And if something better comes along and can provide those things at a higher level, then that's where I'll go.

and the realization that business is so much the same everywhere. I'm very cynical about people that have to work for their company because they believe their company will take care of them. I don't think that happens.

The relationship that develops between a woman and the company that employs her is a delicate and complex one. Our interviews provide ample evidence of these women's devotion to work and commitment to company. They demonstrate a professional sense of responsibility not only to the work itself but also to the company's purposes and goals. Their adoption of the company's mission as their own enables them to do whatever is necessary for success. Their success is the company's, the company's theirs. The time spent engaged in work, which can range from sixty to eighty hours a week, alone attests to the commonality of company and individual purpose. Whatever the company's particular form of production, these women are working long and hard to promote, sell, expedite, or foster it.

Yet they express an absence of something that they call company loyalty. Despite the apparent commitment that their hard work and impressive yields represent, they have not married their companies. That is, they have not decided to stay for life. Their commitments are intense but temporary. They give their all in a way that spells dedication, but the primary devotion is to work rather than to a particular company. A woman's devotion to work spreads to the company context in which it is found. To retain her, a company must meet the woman's needs for stimulating work, recognition, and advancement. In the absence of those provisions, women will begin to seek employment elsewhere. Though such change does not come easily, women can forsake their companies before they can relinquish their own needs for satisfying work.

□ 2 □

Career Planning

Women find work satisfying. Motivated less by money than by the challenge and stimulation that work can provide, the women interviewed derive pleasure from the nature of the work itself. Work has long been recognized as contributing both pleasure and pain to individual's lives. A source of conflict and frustration, alienation and even illness, work is nonetheless a staple of human existence for far more than its pragmatic value. It functions as an existential mainstay, a source of meaning and mastery that holds psychological implications for one's sense of self. This is as true for women as it has been for men.[1]

Positions requiring responsibility and granting autonomy have special attraction and staying power for many people, including the women in this study. They thrive on jobs that allow them initiative and independence. Many of the women depicted here hold professional positions without the customary credentialed preparation. Passengers without tickets, these women face internal and external obstacles as they pursue their unfolding careers.

In the first chapter we saw women take unconventional routes to business and overcome the uncertainties that can accompany the absence of official credentials.[2] Formal preparation focuses on more than work's substance, however. Skill development is balanced by attention to the structure of a career. One learns about the evolution of career paths and strategies for their promotion. Thus, finding satisfying work is but one step. For satisfaction to be sustained, job changes and mobility may be required. Knowing when and how to move takes planning, another critical job skill that many of these women acquire informally.

How do they find fulfilling work? What do they do when the work ceases to satisfy? Does their devotion to mastery of the work itself overshadow their learning strategies for tangible corporate success? What influences their decision making? In this chapter we will examine interviewees' experiences with career planning and the processes that prompt their thinking about how and when to make a job change. In describing the evolution of their jobs into careers, these women demonstrate the interaction between psychological development and social change. Their views of themselves and their life paths shift in line with the structure of opportunity. In turn, as notions of female self and career change, women move toward structuring more access to opportunity for themselves. Because most women of this study reckon with old and new messages about women's lives, they are in an excellent position to demonstrate the processes by which psychological development affects and is affected by social change.

Job Information for Women Only

Most of these women grew up at a time when being female was not commonly associated with career aspiration. Their formative years of childhood and adolescence were spent within a social context of clearly defined role expectations for males and females that seldom crossed. Thus, young women who sought advice about preparation for professional careers in their high schools of twenty-five to thirty years ago met discouragement and gender-linked warnings. Having witnessed her own mother's unpreparedness for assuming sole support of the family, Sharon, for example, knew that she would want to establish herself economically as an individual, that she would want sources of achievement apart from interpersonal and familial connections. Unsure about specific career direction, she sought information from a seemingly appropriate source:

> I remember an incident when I was in high school and I went to see a guidance counselor, and I was interested in becoming a dietician for some reason then. And she just said to me, "Oh honey, you don't want to go into that field, you'll never meet a husband." So at that point I said to myself, "Well, I'll certainly never go and talk to this woman again."

The strong incentive of independent identity through career became essential when job information was censored by normative expectation. Even in the midsixties, when an entrenched gender-based division of labor had begun to face scrutiny, there were memorable encounters:

> I can remember really wanting to go to medical school and trying to find out what courses I needed to take. And the counselor told me what courses but said, "Well, number one, it's very difficult to get in; number two, it always louses up your life as a woman, and you have to be really dedicated. And you'll never go out on a date, and you'll never have a boyfriend, and you'll never get married." . . . this was the picture that was painted. "But these are the courses you have to take, so it's up to you, but I don't recommend it. Just observe the few women that do go to medical school; they all look like men, they're all ugly," and on and on.

The conduits of social ideology clearly conveyed to females that their life path was to be domestically defined. A female's primary job was marriage. Paid work for homemakers was undertaken in the case of financial exigency and, as such, was almost always unforeseen and therefore unplanned, as in Heidi's case:

> I was thinking maybe two weeks in advance, early on. I have never been a person that really sat down and thought about what was going to be happening. A lot of it has just transpired. I just get married and live happily ever after, and then the bills are due, and we didn't have enough money. So I started working. It was just a matter of what was happening at the time. And even when I started working, I don't think it was until maybe the last three years that I really started thinking long-term. Now I know that I will be working. I want to work. I want to continue to work.

In this case, as in several others, the satisfactions of work prompted a new lifelong commitment to it. Many women interviewed did not begin with carefully considered notions of career in their futures. Marriage and its attendant roles were primarily anticipated by some. Several had vague ideas about work, apart from and in addition to wedlock, and a few foresaw work as central to their lives.[3] But even those who were contemplating work for the better part of a lifetime could not be described as actively forging a career path. Betty's comments typify what has become associated with females' "falling into" satisfying positions:

> I like working, and it was always my intention to continue to work no matter what else happened in my personal life. I was always looking for something that would be in the way of a career, somethat that I could devote myself to doing. . . . I just fell into it. I happened to fall into a little by-water that interested me.

A dearth of career planning among women has been alternately attributed to nature and nurture.[4] On the one hand, psychological traits assumed to be characteristic of females—for example, passivity and a primary concern with interpersonal connection—have allegedly stood in the way of the assertive, instrumental, apersonal behavior needed for the setting of a career strategy. On the other hand, sex role socialization has been called to task as responsible for women's lack of career preparation. Unambiguous examples of that socialization were seen above in the gender-directed advice given by 1960s high school guidance counselors. Even now, with an ever-increasing majority of women, married or single, working, females continue to be seen as having a choice about work that men do not have.[5] If this is the case, an ambivalence could interfere with both the individual woman's career planning and corporate acceptance of women as a permanent part of the professional picture.

Women have been more work-oriented than traditional ideology has allowed. Even prior to the current women's movement, some were determined to enter the male-dominated business world. In the 1960s few mechanisms were in place to prepare women for business careers. Graduating from high school in the late sixties, Marie saw opportunity in business, particularly for women, and she pursued relevant academic preparation. With a liberal arts background and a somewhat more specialized, but not business, graduate degree, Sharon's inclinations also ran toward business:

> I would have to say that ever since I was sixteen years old [around 1961] I always knew that I wanted to work in business. But I didn't know particularly what that was going to involve.

The psychological development of these women does not conform to the social influences of their time. Ideology rarely subsumes everyone, and individual variation in relief can anticipate more collective change. Prior to large-scale change, however, the structures and practices that would teach women about career were absent. That they could even have business aspirations at that time belies female passivity regardless of their ability to take the next step of planning. Women's thinking about business careers was truncated not by their unsuitable natures but rather by the absence of societal guideposts for females to take such a path.

If the question is to work or not to work, it is clear now that women can anticipate spending much of their adult lives employed. Perhaps they have less of a choice about work than they do about career. It makes sense, however, that if women must plan to be self-supporting, a career, as opposed to a job, would be the preferred route.[6] Although the women interviewed may have been tentative in their initial employment explorations, they developed the ambition that transforms a job into a career relatively quickly.[7]

Job versus Career

Though the distinctions between job and career are several, central to them is a significantly different way of thinking about and approaching work.[8] Given that many of these women did not anticipate working for the long haul, it is not surprising to find them stumbling into jobs without considering careers. Although an intrinsically female passivity might account for the absence of planning, it is just as likely that social context could prevent or promote an instrumental work orientation. Thirty-five-year-old Camilla attributes her psychological transition from job to career to the context of her employment. In addition, her coming of age in the early seventies was surrounded by a societal shift in consciousness about women's life paths.

> I worked just because I enjoyed working. It was something to do, get paid, enjoy what we were going through during the daytime. So I was just gathering skills at the time. I never realized how important that would be.

Describing a job change from a nonprofit to a profit organization, Camilla says:

> once I went into Stars Corporation, every word could have . . . a political overtone. So it was a change. I had to clean up my act. Well, that focused my career. All of a sudden I became career-oriented, and it became more important. I think I planned more. I have to sit down and think ahead, and I work less by the seat of the pants. I was older too, and I was also divorced, so those little interventions focused my life a little more. It just sharpened all of my skills.

Camilla describes several factors that shifted her perspective from enjoying a job to focusing on a career. Although she worked throughout her marriage, the unmitigated self-sufficiency of divorce combined with a turning-thirty maturity in a new seriousness. Shifts in her personal life are secondary, however, to the influence of a job change. Camilla's remarks target a corporate climate that required a new astuteness as primarily responsible for her career orientation. It is probably not simple happenstance that Camilla assumed that kind of position when she did, that is, when she was more developmentally ready for it. The combined influence of job experience, personal life factors, and societal opportunity moved Camilla to new meanings in her work and a new sense of self. Professional and personal changes often parallel each other.

Knowing that one is pursuing a career seems requisite to planning its course. There are many reasons why these women were not imbued with a sense of career planning. Some did not expect to work, never mind have a career. For many, entry in business was almost a random event. Early work in social service or other nonprofit organizations may have led to a business choice in contrast. A woman's employment path might also be shaped by other circumstances in her life. Abigail, for example, found jobs where her husband's work took them. As long as her work was secondary to his and her jobs transient, she could not entertain career prospects. Only when able to settle into a position could she perceive career possibilities. The psychological shift in her perception comes in the context of opportunity offered by a stable, continuing position.

> I have had to pick up and move off and not really plan. But I don't think it was until I saw that indeed there are opportunities for me to have some growth and real potential on the long term that it became important. I don't believe I ever thought I was a candidate for that kind of professional mentality.

Circumstances that keep a woman out of the work force for several years compound her difficulties with career planning.

> I think starting over at the age I was was difficult for me to work through—just because I really didn't know how to work a career path; I had no background in that. And I still don't have it all worked out.... But at least I'm understanding a little bit more about the areas I think I'd be comfortable with, and how you do move within an organization. I've never had a long-term situation. I really can do a lot of things, but where do I really want to go? And I'm not sure I know that even now.

It is not that females eschew career planning; it just comes as a surprise to them. The life path of many of these women took an unexpected turn for which no preparation was provided. An altered societal context that allowed women more career opportunity was still not structured for their direction; both the individuals and the institutions lack provision. Untutored and inexperienced, women grope for a map that has yet to be drawn and that they must then learn how to read. Devoid of clues, this woman's search bespeaks not psychological antipathy to career strategy but rather the tabula rasa that both she and the organization face.

Even when business was a first and uninterrupted toehold, few interviewees had formal training preceding employment. Instruction in the form and content of business is likely to include strategies for analyzing and planning the development of a career. Technical expertise represents, therefore, only partial preparation for corporate employment. Knowing how to plan and implement a career path may be equally important. Women who lack such knowledge sometimes assume that men do not. Although females' shortcomings in mapping career strategy have been amply described, there is little documentation that most men naturally do this and are effective at it, as commonly assumed.

With her mathematics background now applied to marketing technology, Mary, for example, would seem prepared.

> One of the toughest problems I've had is really thinking about my career. It's just scary sometimes when you read articles about how men plan their careers—they know where they want to be in five years; by April they're going to reach this step; they've got them all mapped out. They know whether they're ahead of schedule or behind schedule. It's just [that] we've never been trained to do that. In a way, everything that's happened to me has happened to me; I don't know to what extent I really went after it.

The kind of training Mary refers to is not solely scholastic. Instruction in career planning includes learning how to do it and also how to know that it has been done; analyses after the fact are an integral part of the learning process. These women attribute their lack of foresight to a deficiency in training rather than in themselves. Another woman concurs that males are socialized to plan careers and females are not. Undergraduate preparation in economics and business and hundreds of professional workshop hours still leave forty-three-year-old Gwen in a quandary.

> The stock question I had thrown at me all the time was, "Gwen, what do you want to do?" And I say, "I really don't know." Because I hadn't been socialized to think in terms of what kind of career goals do [I] have, what should I strengthen, what are my weaknesses, what are my strengths? And I used to get very intimidated because I felt like, "Oh, why don't I know what I want to do?" I mean, look at all these fabulous guys coming in with MBAs and what-have-you, and they seemed to get channeled into all these fantastic jobs—six months here, twelve months there. And suddenly they

find out what their niche is. They're on the right track. It just wasn't coming together for me . . . then suddenly, out of the blue, someone said, "How'd you get into management?" And I said, "I backed into it like all of us," at least in my age category anyway.

These women are aware of the handicap presented by the absence of career preparation, both formal and psychological. They attribute that handicap not to traits endemic to females but to the lack of opportunity structured by former social convention and sex role stereotypes.

The Development of Career

In the absence of active and conscious planning, how do the women interviewed develop careers? Several of them describe a path that evolved through experience. Their successful performance at a particular job gave them access to other jobs and functions wherein they repeatedly proved their capabilities to themselves and to others.[9] Increased opportunities followed successful experience. Based on what she has found useful, Bonnie, a thirty-one-year-old sales representative for a large, diversified corporation, advises other women:

> The key is to get into the organization. And then do a good job. Learn as much as you can. . . . Go in with an open mind. Be selective in the information that you give out. Sell yourself. And get that first job and then work like crazy. Do the best you can. Then, from there, select what you want from within that company. If you've already demonstrated that you're good and you have a track record, you are going to get that opportunity.

Betty's advice is reminiscent of Bonnie's:

> I believe that if an opportunity comes along you take it, take your chances. Otherwise, you get stagnant.

These remarks, which come from women who worked their way up from secretarial beginnings, represent a mixture of messages. On the one hand, women appear to be passive with regard to opportunity, taking it if and when it comes along. On the other, they also talk of making and choosing chances, putting themselves forward and taking risks. Given the history of female exclusion from the corporate world, an incontrovertible first step is, as Bonnie suggests, securing a toehold in the organization. Beginning with a gender-linked uncertainty about their position that transcends ordinary newcomer status, women must ascertain standing before plotting strategy. They do this by proving themselves through diligent and consistent achievement. Initially, the amount of energy devoted to proving themselves precludes simultaneous strategizing.[10]

In lieu of advance decision making, the pattern of women's experiences maps their careers. It is possible that these women's abilities were impressive enough to preclude their having to plan deliberate directions. Immersed in work and moving rapidly from one position to another, they view their paths in retrospect, and then their careers seem to have happened almost without their deliberation. Several attest:

> Career, what's that? Everything had always come to me. . . . I never had to think it through.

> I've never thought way ahead. It just happened. I've just rolled with it, and things have always gone positively. So I've never had a problem where I've had to really think about [the] long term—do I want this or whatever?

> Things seem to happen to me. Up to this point, I don't think I've really made anything happen for myself. I've made [it] known that I would like to be in management, which I am now. But as [for] the subject areas of the particular orientation that I wanted to find myself in, I always found it happening to me. It has been good up to this point. I've been lucky.

These observations speak to more than women's lack of career planning. They could describe what psychologists have called an external locus of control, a tendency to attribute successes to factors external to oneself and to assume the blame for failures.[11] An external locus of control had been found to be disproportionately distributed among women and minorities, although this is less so when the status and, therefore, the power of these groups are enhanced.

Personal powerlessness has been associated with female social standing. Women are bringing that psychosocial history with them as they take an uncertain place in corporations. When women's place in business is as firmly established as men's, we might expect them to display more belief in themselves as determiners of their fates, including their career directions. Psychological change comes with social change, but not without a delay. A shift in self-perception comes with living a different way over time. For example, a large, diversified media corporation offers Dorothy opportunity to develop in human resources management.

> I woke up somewhere about thirty; I'm thirty-seven now. I'm doing something I never expected to do. At that point, seven years ago, I'd found

a company where I really was beginning to move. But there was no real direction. After I got into this process of moving ahead and new responsibilities, it suddenly occurred to me that I was in the middle of a career. I did finally say, "Where am I going with all this work? Where do I want to be? How long do I go into something?". . . . I still don't have any training; it just evolved. . . . Career planning [will be] a very difficult exercise for me, because I don't have the ambition to be the president of the company. What I want to do is use my potential as far as I can go with it, as far as I feel comfortable with it, doing the best possible job I can; I will never do less than that. So to sit down and say, "In five years I want to be the general manager, and in ten . . ." That's not the way I think; it's not comfortable for me.

Comments like these lend credence to their designation as "accidental careerists." Not expected to work in the first place, women struggle to make sense of the job before coming to grips with the concept of career. The full realization of what they are involved in functions almost as a throwback to an earlier psychological place. When work is first reinterpreted to mean career, women are back at the starting line. Accustomed to the work itself, they must now contend with a new perception of it. That they are untutored in career planning is reflected in an all-or-none thinking whereby they are either immersed only in the work or striving for the company presidency. The in-between process of career planning is an elusive enigma. Suddenly, they are out of place again, not knowing where they stand or where they should be headed. The doubts about themselves and how far they want to go represent another expression of a fundamental questioning of women's place in the corporate world.

Taking the Reins of a Career

Not always forethoughtful about their career direction, women later become aware of influences that have moved them one way or another. While the work itself is engrossing, an awareness of its meaning in relation to organizational structure gradually unfolds. Women who are untutored in the plotting of a career are also unaccustomed to the informal communication that can shape direction and opportunity. At first, others in the organization might be doing the engineering for them. Susan says:

I don't think I had set any objective or was thinking in terms of long-term career goals. I was still trying to figure out what was going on and what avenues were open to me, what the system was all about, and what it involved to get into different jobs. . . . I had absolutely no understanding of what a mentor was all about, what your supervisor was supposed to do for you in terms of pushing you out into different jobs, and those kinds of things. Even though that had happened to me, when I moved into the professional position, I don't think I really put two and two together and understood everything that was going on, because so much happened behind the scenes.

Women whose careers were unanticipated began with a focus on the work itself and later attended to corporate climate and structure. In retrospective reflection they realize that forces aside from their performance propelled them on their paths without their full awareness. Susan's observations about covert planning by others are echoed by Rebecca, a contemporary whose technical training prepared her for a more straight-line path to her current position as systems supervisor in transportation. Content with her direction to date, Rebecca wants to become more actively instrumental in her career path.

> I've come to the point in my life that I've got to start really planning my career out for myself. I know that they have a lot of things in mind for me to do as far as advancing into management. And it seems very planned out by my supervisor. Although I've really enjoyed the experiences that I've had so far, I've come to the point where I'm questioning if this is really where I want to be. The other question is, if it isn't, where do I want to be? And I think I'm still kind of sifting through all of that.

Women are still in the process of discovery. The first discovery is that they can work effectively in the corporate world. Once the newness of professional employment in business has worn off and they are established in relation to the job itself, they learn that they are entitled to plan a career path that stretches beyond the task at hand. Making this cognitive leap takes time and experience, which includes interaction with others who prompt and stimulate it. Some women, for example, are encouraged to enter a dialogue with a superior, exploring possibilities for career direction. Gwen's description of this process reveals her awareness of the possibility of different agendas and levels of communication.

> We used to talk about what I wanted to do with the rest of my life, so to speak. He knew that I was serious about wanting to advance further. And he was responsive to it; he set up all of these meetings with various people. But he'd always come back and say, "Well now, Gwen, you have to think about what it is you want; we can't do that for you." And that used to get me very frightened, because I really didn't know what I wanted. I had no idea where I would fit. The whole general feeling I was getting while I was

going through this is that he is just placating me. I thought, "Oh boy, I'm being had here. He's giving me all these opportunities to go around and talk to these people, but I wonder really how sincere he is about it." But at the time I couldn't even in my own head articulate it as well as I'm doing now. I remember feeling a great deal of frustration, but it was inward then. I was saying, "Gee, see, it is my fault. I don't know what I want; I'm a typical woman. I keep saying I want this, and I want that, but I don't know what I want." So I would always turn it around on myself.

At forty-three, Gwen recognizes that both her frustration and self-blame reflect a female stereotyping by society that became a part of her. Her superior's help strikes a disingenuous chord because exposure to choices is insufficient as long as she lacks information about them, about the larger organizational structure, and, more importantly, about herself in relation to them. The choices are foreign to her; they can become meaningful when she is able to see some degree of fit between what they offer and the person she has become.

Gwen, like other accidental careerists, is in the process of revised self-perception simultaneous to her negotiation of a career. Social ideology about women has been dramatically altered in the course of her development, and she finds herself with one foot in each camp. Though her behavior is in line with the new female image, her attitudes about self and life direction lag behind.[12]

When early socialization is contradicted by later social change, a reconciliation between old and new ways of being takes effort and time. Women involved in this process may be mistakenly seen as captives of female traits because they still display traces of their conventional socialization. The temporary duality between a traditional sense of self and "liberated" behavior represents a psychological transition made by women in conjunction with social change. Their very struggle toward new self-definitions and career directions attests to the strength of social forces in shaping psychological development.

Women who have grown up in the context of a consistent social ideology do not manifest this duality. Their tasks are more linear in that business is not complicated by a competing belief system about self and career. Evidence of career planning is found among women whose paths could be termed straight-line. Recruited from campus to management training programs, they are able to analyze and plan their path through a company. Having held several managerial positions in the financial industry, thirty-year-old Cathy has been exposed to a variety of functions and knows what she must do next:

I knew that at some point I had to dig into a certain function, product, or area . . . that I needed that successful experience under my belt for both my own perspective and my sense that at some point I had to start becoming an expert in something, and not just generally knowledgeable about what was going on in the company, or about what might be going on in the economy. . . . I really had to carve out a specialty that I can then walk away from at some point.

Cathy's clear-eyed view of career advancement is unfettered by complications of conventional female traits. Compared to Gwen, Cathy is psychologically free to focus squarely on the topic at hand without reference to conflictual thinking that stems from opposing social ideologies. Her perspective stretches into the future even so far as envisioning departure from an area that has yet to be developed. After broad exposure within the company, Cathy knew what area she wanted for more depth. It would be one that would prove her worth to the company and its other employees. To secure the "blessing" of that area would make her "one of [them]." She would have gone through the "sort of baptism of fire that everyone goes through." She can then project beyond that position:

Once I get through this next job I'm in, I have enough of the mixture of skills that I think is necessary to get to the next level . . . I'm interested in. So I would like to do that. I would like to then leave [her current company] at some point because I don't know what it's like to work for any other organization.

Cathy's intentions to prove herself have a purpose beyond just that. There is no sign of her passively expecting recognition and reward for her accomplishments alone.[13] Rather, a specific position serves the function of proving her ability, and the more far-reaching one of providing her with the skills necessary for advancement. Moreover, she does not expect to reciprocate any rewards she might receive with company loyalty. She sees her current company involvements as a stepping-stone to advancement and to other organizations.[14] She plans further formal preparation for her clearly articulated career goals.

I'm thinking about going back to school for something that's more specifically oriented to where I believe that my career path is going now, which is . . . at a general management level.

Planning a Move

Time spent within an area or function is ordinarily an important factor in gauging progress within the corporate environment. Women invariably use time as a benchmark. Movement within an organization almost always implies short time periods at any one function. Marie, who has both technical training and an MBA, speculates about future prospects within a temporal framework.

I'll stay in this position another year to two years. . . . I'll use those two years as a real learning experience and then possibly, if I stay with [her company], go on to a more responsible position within another department. I'm certainly not married to the corporation, and if something else that was more worthwhile and gave me better experience came up, I would certainly go. It's been very worthwhile for me there so far. There are a lot of things along the way that you have to think about and decide whether you want to do it.

While concentrating on the job at hand, a woman reflects upon the value of her current position and where it might lead. She assesses the relevance of her learning to other areas and functions, using their requirements to assess gaps in her knowledge. She estimates her abilities in light of the requirements for advancement and the time needed to make the match. Even women who are not actively working these equations notice the passage of time in one position, a common corporate yardstick of progress. Thirty-five-year-old Stella shows signs of disaffection with her high-technology employer.

Certain things happen on the job. . . . you see responsibilities going to people that have been there a shorter period of time than you, or you find out that somebody that's only been there two or three years—and you've been eight—is making the same salary as you. I became very depressed, and I really knew I had to seriously consider doing something.

Lisa, like Stella, previously held various clerical positions and now keeps her eye on opportunities that her employer, a *Fortune* 500 company, does or does not offer:

If it takes them too long [to promote me], I will simply make other arrangements for myself. If I don't use [my experience] at DI, I will use it someplace else. . . . I will still have twenty-five years to work, and I don't feel any big ties to any company. I've worked for several. I would be afraid to make a change, but I certainly would do it if I thought it was the best way to go.

Most of the women interviewed, even those who had been with the same organization for a relatively long period of time, had made frequent job changes. They might occupy a position for a year or, at the most, two before moving on to another. The moves often represent advancements, promotions, or at least the employer's recognition of their usefulness to the company.

Movement within a company has its advantages. It gives a woman familiarity with a variety of functions and, therefore, different perspectives on the company as well as enhanced visibility. Broad exposure, however, can mean superficial knowledge. Women move on before they are able fully to consolidate the skills associated with each position. Worse than a feeling of having barely mastered a task, however, is boredom. Not only are women standing still when their position is unchanging; they are bored. And boredom is surely the kiss of death for women to whom work represents challenge and engagement.[15] Established in public relations and now in her fifties, Esther has identified but not yet solved the problem.

> I'm beginning to think I'm getting a little bit bored in my job. And I hate that. I've never been bored in a job . . . so that's why I keep looking to see if there's something else I could do [to make her job more exciting]. . . . I don't know whether I've gotten to a point where I'd say, "Let's deal with it day by day," or "Let's deal with it in a long-range plan," make a decision tree. I haven't decided how I want to tackle it. Obviously, I must want to tackle it if I'm thinking about how to do it.

A decision to make a move within or outside the company of one's current employ is not easy. Awareness of dissatisfaction and its sources, be they external events or internal feelings, may be long in coming. Once that awareness dawns upon a woman, she may consider and analyze her dissatisfactions extensively before deciding to initiate action toward a move. Awareness of dissatisfaction and decision to move are two separate stages. Feeling underpaid and bypassed, Stella describes the process of moving from awareness to a decision. Talking with other people affirms for her the decision she had begun to make.

> I had to make myself realize: is this the field I want to be in or do I want to change jobs, or is now the best time to change jobs? Are you happy in your job? I knew that the wheels had started turning, and I knew that somehow I would make some change. I think what really got me out of the rut of that eating away at me is I just made up my mind that I had to do something for myself. I could not sit around and wait for something to come to me. I think that those couple of things [people with less seniority getting more responsibility and higher salaries] triggered the [decision to] do something about my life . . . and talking to other people about career— some of the changes they have made in their career—made me realize that it's not too late. I think that's when I really said, "Okay, I'm going to do it."

Corporate women have been portrayed as reacting rather than planning.[16] Although Stella is reacting to events on the job, she speaks of taking action rather than waiting for recognition. Benefiting from the example and experience of others, she is moved to positive action on her own behalf. The thoughtful and interactive process that she describes does not seem to be gender-confined. Both males and females resist change, especially when it involves overturning stability. A stable, continuing position offers advantages that are not easily relinquished. A decision to move can entail giving up things of value. Monica has never had to face this equation before. With an advanced degree and experience in human resources, she contemplates leaving the large, diversified conglomerate where she has worked her way up the ladder.

> [What] I'm facing, where I'm at with my career, is probably the most difficult decision that I've ever had to make, and I haven't entirely made it yet, but maybe in a way I have. The company I work for is a very nice company, and it has the golden handcuffs: where I've got ten years of seniority, and I'm well respected, and it's comfortable, and I have a lot of friends. That is beginning now to be a trade-off. Am I willing to give all that up to get a job that has more earning potential and more responsibility? . . . I've kind of hinted that I'm not. I told people, "I'm not going to be happy in this job forever so you'd better realize that," but I've never really set a timetable. I think I'm now starting to focus, in the last few months, on a timetable. Maybe I'm getting more frustrated.

Several of the women interviewed had become aware of the need to make a change in their work lives. They approached the notion of change with careful consideration; they were not given to impulsive decisions or behavior. Their deliberations were almost always couched in temporal terms, as they gauged their circumstances and chances within the context of time as well as opportunity. None entertained unemployment, that is, leaving one job in the absence of another. Most were willing to give their current companies every chance to make available suitable prospects for advancement. A lack of organizational support for a woman's function, however, is likely to guarantee her disillusionment and eventual defection. Failing to find either formal or informal recognition of her consistently outstanding performance, Ina finally makes a firm decision to leave her current employer.

> The bottom line is this—I sold $500,000 in three months. This was 500 percent over the budgeted amount. So here I am, I'm going to get a review. It's really going to be good, and I've been wanting a title change. . . . I was fighting for it. I didn't get the title change [or a raise commensurate to her performance]. . . . that was the icing on the cake, and the kiss of death for the company, because I'm leaving. I am definitely leaving. I won't leave without another job. I pay the rent, so I definitely will have to have another position.

Women have been said to resemble men in talents but to differ from them in motivation.[17] Proclaiming less interest in salary and title than in growth and recognition, a woman is assumed to be working for psychic rewards that corporations rarely offer.[18] Unrealistic goals such as intangible recognition for individual excellence are met ultimately by disappointment. Men's goals of money and power coincide with what the corporation offers.

An examination of Ina's perspective on the reasons for her departure reveal a more complicated interpretation. Her motives seem to include both the psychic ones attributed to women and the tangible ones of salary, title, and advancement opportunity. Anger at the absence of recognition in various forms prompts her realization of this company's limitations.

> It was not just the not getting the salary or the title change. I saw CEOs come and go, and I saw how they maltreated people. And I also saw the culture. The culture is very different [from] a culture I want . . . and I just don't want any part of it. There's also not enough capability for me to move up the ladder, even if I wanted to be part of it. So it was a combination of a number of factors. But I just don't like the way things are handled.

A woman's recognition of her position's disadvantages can be confirmed by the observations of others close to her. When Ina tells about one of her business coups, her friend mentions the lack of less tangible forms of appreciation.

> In this very calm voice at the other end of the phone, "And what are they giving you, Ina?" "Nothing." "Well?" That was the other voice. It was like a little angel in the back of the head going, "And do they even take you to lunch?" No. "Do they even send you a bouquet of flowers?" No. "And what have they done? They've done shit for you."

Exposure to other kinds of companies and to other corporate women can spur new perceptions of one's own company, its opportunities, and, most importantly, one's abilities and potential. Her participation in the management program led to Lisa's realization of her company's shortcomings and her own strengths.

> Being up here last year, and being away from the work environment . . . made me realize that I was probably underemployed. I still am. I probably did not realize how much I could do, but listening to other people talk and realizing that I was just as smart or just as talented as some of the other people, and they have gone further, makes me realize that probably the work environment or the company or something there is holding me back,

so that if I want to move on I need to make a change. I never felt comfortable with [staying at a level for a long time], but I thought I didn't have a choice, and now I realize I do have choices. And I'm not as afraid as I was before of making a big change to another company or of moving to another city. I would do that now, I think, because I believe I have the skills to do it and that I could handle it.

Lisa, a thirty-seven-year-old single parent who has worked for the same *Fortune* 500 company for a decade, now sees herself in a new light, and she has also gained knowledge about opportunity outside of her company. The influence of context is apparent here. The demands of business foster an immersion not only in the work but within the corporation. The culture of other companies and what they offer women are unknown. An individual's prospects are shaped by her company until events or substantial exposure elsewhere precipitate a new perspective.

Enhanced self-confidence and new learning can change one's perspective. These changes may be longer in coming for women who entered business without the traditional credentials. Beginning from a deficit state, they first must overcome their own and others' misgivings about their ability to handle the work itself. Once they have been functioning effectively, their awareness must catch up with their success in order for them to stand back and look fully at the larger picture of planning for advancement and opportunity. A lack of confidence can certainly make a difference in what women think that they can do, but only up to a point. Then the structural obstacles take over. Once women begin to attribute their lack of progress to factors outside of themselves, they are able to think more flexibly about plans and moves. Contextual factors in their immediate and larger social environments can serve to stimulate or corroborate thinking along these lines, but women must be at a point of psychological readiness to assimilate such information.

The nature of a company alone can motivate the search for a new job. It is a change in thinking, however, that is pivotal.

I think most of [the change in perspective] has come from a building of self-confidence in that I know I can get a job if I want to. And so I'm more seriously thinking about moving. I was worrying about it last year, but not enough to do anything about it. But this year I would.

We have seen some of the factors that precipitate women's thinking about career moves. The climate and culture of a company, its lack of apparent appreciation for a woman's performance and accomplishments, and boredom in a position can each account for thoughts of change. What do women look for when contemplating a change? If we know what prompts women's restlessness, we can anticipate what would attract them. The last four years have left Leigh dissatisfied with the lack of progress offered by her comparatively young organization.

> I would want to go into a company where I could certainly grow as fast as other people, where there would be some kind of track, some sort of development. [In her present company] there's really very little career development. There's none.

Advancement, the potential for growth, and development are commonly cited as desirable, perhaps essential. Lisa, who claims to have been in one position too long, wants to avoid that pattern.

> I would only move if the area was growing and expanding, where you could move to other things in a short period of time.

Women do not want to climb a career ladder just for the sake of upward mobility. Movement and change must be associated with the intrinsic rewards of work articulated by Elena, who has spent five years in personnel programs of a large chemical industry.

> For the last year I have been thinking about it [leaving her current position]. First, it was sort of in the traditional sense that, "Hey, you can't stay in one job too long. You have to move up in the organization; otherwise you're a failure." And the more I think about it, the more I realize that that's not for me. Career moves just for the sake of advancement are not what I'm into. There has to be something else. There has to be some challenge, some degree of personal satisfaction derived from what you can accomplish in the job. And there has to be some intellectual challenge. Otherwise, I vegetate.

Women's desire for satisfying work has been interpreted as ultimately self-defeating. Those who are compelled more by task mastery than career planning are out of step with corporate politics and procedure and eventually suffer disappointment.[19] The need of women in this study for challenging work is juxtaposed to the desire for extrinsic reward.

These women do not quickly or easily decide to leave their companies for another. While disclaiming company loyalty, they usually give their employers every opportunity to offer them what they need in the way of challenging work and commensurate compensation. Sometimes a dramatic event turns their sights elsewhere; more often, it is a prolonged period of time in an unsatisfying position that prompts their consideration of alternatives.

Except in cases of flagrant abuse, most women are reluctant to leave their companies. If and when they do go to another company, it is usually after considerable weighing of advantages and disadvantages. The fact that their positions hold both contributes to their caution regarding change. Their decisions include careful consideration of conditions in their own companies compared to opportunities else-where, larger economic factors, and what might be most suitable to their personal circumstances. The next chapter will explore mobility further.

□ 3 □

Mobility

I think sometimes people get so involved in a job that they don't realize there are opportunities other places. They think, "This is the only thing I could ever do." And that's why people stay for long periods of time. I've gone through that phase in my life, and I realized that it isn't very healthy to have that kind of an attitude. Not only is it smart from a business perspective to always be aware of what's going on in a marketplace, but sometimes you just move because there's more money or more opportunity. The job serves as a way to get money to have a better life and as an outlet for your need to work and create and control and resolve or whatever. And you can do that in lots of different places.

A woman's interest and immersion in work usually precede her career planning.[1] Once acclimated to the content of corporate life, she turns her attention to its structure and her place within it. Women have been characterized as passively waiting to be chosen rather than actively steering their career course, as men theoretically do.[2] Moreover, women's addiction to task mastery rather than career planning and their familial-like attachment to the company of their employ presumably combine to keep them in a job too long.[3]

Although some women interviewed felt at a standstill, most had experienced considerable mobility. Hope's remarks at the start of this chapter suggest that women's immersion in a particular job to the exclusion of other skill development accompanying career mobility is temporary. The premise here is that women's job immersion is a function of their adaptation to a social context that has only lately admitted them, not of a peculiarly female myopia. Moreover, women's lack of career planning can be attributed also to socialization that has precluded their anticipating a lifetime of work. Once their relation to work becomes unambiguously career-oriented, women do surface from the task at hand to assess the form as well as the content of their professional development. Women can and do decide to move on the basis of opportunity for advancement and financial gain.[4] Hope's perspective seems contrary to a female need for personal connection through work and a primary concern with mastery as opposed to money. For Hope, the job is currency toward a better life outside of work as well as a means of satisfaction intrinsic to work itself.

In this chapter we will see how women respond to job changes in light of their presumed psychic needs for connection and preference for learning over advancement. The women of this study did express ambivalence about mobility when rapid changes prevented their full mastery of a job. While this could be interpreted as a female addiction to task mastery at the expense of advancement, it might also reflect women's incomplete assimilation of common corporate practice, which moves people rapidly with little concern for skill mastery. Still outsiders, women could serve as change agents for long-unexamined practice that ultimately works to the corporation's detriment; from our women's testimony, we do see at least one instance of a company putting the brakes on mobility when its pace compromised performance.

That women have influenced the shape of thinking about effective management can be seen in current literature proclaiming a consonance between most productive management and what have been characterized as females' styles.[5] A collaborative mode that promotes employees' autonomy and team building is now preferred to an authoritarian one. While this serves as recognition of women's contributions to corporate change, it also perpetuates a gender division that stereotypes managerial style.

Although women resist moving prior to skill consolidation, they balance mastery considerations with promotion opportunities. They do not sacrifice promotion for the sake of mastery; they are as interested in one as in the other. Moreover, their investment in mastery is not merely for its own sake but to better equip them for assumption of the increased responsibility that comes with promotion. It is curious that learning and task mastery have been set up as contrary to corporate advancement. Too much investment in the challenge and growth of the work itself hinders promotion. This opposition works against the development of competence and would seem to be detrimental to corporations as well as to individual workers.

When and how to make job changes that build a career is a common topic in management literature. It is generally agreed that some moves, given that they are the right ones, are strategically sound whereas too many could brand one as a "job-hopper" who lacks commitment. Rather than falling into the latter category, women have been faulted for clinging to a job beyond its usefulness for career progress. Tendencies presumed female include getting stuck in a position as a result of passivity, resisting change as a function of misplaced loyalty, or being compelled more by learning than advancement.

The Meanings of Change

A human resistance to change is not new; most of us have witnessed reluctance to change in ourselves and others. People ordinarily feel ambivalent about change. Simultaneously feared and desired, its frequent occurrence has become synonymous with stress.

Though our group of women would seem to share such commonly held concepts of change, they also recognize the idiosyncratic meaning of change within the corporate context. Change signifies mobility, which implies an upward direction. Women want frequent job changes to avoid boredom and to further their careers. Given a modicum of stability and security, women can embrace change in business, knowing that it means advancement. Rebecca, who has held four positions in six years within her company, depicts the mixed emotions of fear and excitement that accompany change:

> the usual things that most people go through in a new situation, whether it's business or personal life, when it's a foreign environment you're going into, and you feel that you're lacking. I felt I was lacking technically, and I went through all kinds of different feelings and emotions. A lot of fear, a lot of anxiety, confusion as to why I would be chosen to go into this particular area. But on the other hand, I felt excited. I enjoy change. I have to enjoy change. It looks like this is supposed to be a one-year assignment; so I don't know what's coming up again.

Common psychological reactions to change are juxtaposed to its new meanings as defined by the corporate context. Independent of gender, anxiety and self-doubt are ordinarily experienced in anticipation of a new assignment. These women are able to shift psychological gears and adapt to a revised meaning of change such that resistance is superseded by eagerness. Thus, a social context that radically revises the meaning of change similarly shapes the psychological perspective of individuals within it. Change is seen in a new light as a means of advancement and gratification.

The women interviewed wanted varied and engaging work, and corporate change represents a rescue from the routine of a well-worn position.[6] Many had been with their current company for several years, having held various positions within it.[7] Though few apply the term "fast track" to their paths, the pattern they describe could fall into that category. Spending not more than a year or two in a particular position, they move from one area to another, learning about different company functions such as product, manufacturing, sales, marketing, operations. Sometimes they are in charge of a specific project and are transferred upon its completion. With each transfer, they face their own lack of knowledge; a new area necessitates new learning. They are "green" and fearful, but the positive aspects of change are more compelling than its risks. Contrary to human inclinations to resist change, Cathy expresses the sentiments of many other interviewees when she speaks of seeking the dissonance of change:

> I don't know if I do this to myself intentionally or not, but it seems as though whenever I'm reaching a real comfort level in my job, all of a sudden I get put in a situation where there are at least four or five variables. Now I'm back in this position of having one little area of competency and all these other areas that I'm going to play a lot of catch-up on. I think it's going to be fun. It's challenging, but I always wonder if I'm really doing this intentionally, or I just keep saying, "Well, the timing is right, and it's right for me to move now." I think perhaps, deep down inside, to me comfort is boredom, and once I reach that level, I'm probably looking for something that's a little bit more interesting.[8]

Inertia may be a prevalent human inclination across many of life's circumstances. Within the corporate context, however, change attracts and perhaps even addicts people. Mobility, for all its risk, becomes irresistible. By her late twenties, Susan had held positions from data processing to production management in a technology corporation. Her reflections show how usual responses to change are turned upside down.

> In six years I've had about eight different jobs—a lot of exposure to different ends of the business. I think that the whole mobility thing really

worked to my advantage, because if I had had to stay in some of those low-level jobs any longer than I did, there is no way I would have stayed with the company. . . . [Now] I've been in positions that have been something I can really put my teeth into. In terms of costs, just as soon as you get comfortable with people, set up your ties, understand the systems, and generally feel comfortable with where you are at, the rug is pulled out from under you and you're moving on. [But] once you get accustomed to that, it's very hard to go into a position and stay there for any longer than a couple of years. I really believe that if I had to do a job now for more than two years I would go right out of my mind.

Once they begin to move, women do whatever is required to keep moving. Susan recognizes the cost of rapid movement in terms of loss of connection, comfort, and interpersonal relationships, but, contrary to conventional expectation, she readily relinquishes those in favor of mobility. Rather than reflecting female relatedness, her psychological needs in this context correspond to what is offered by corporate culture. One's own and others' expectations for performance are repeatedly raised and met with each new assignment. The cycle gains momentum from the continuing challenges it offers. Generally, what is required is a high level of performance in terms of both quality and quantity. Dorothy's version of what happened to her represents the experiences of several women. Moving up within the area of personnel, she has held four positions in her seven years with a diversified media employer.

I have moved very quickly in my career in the last five years. I haven't had a chance to get bored in any job, because I've been in it and then I've been promoted and then promoted again almost before I felt I was ready to—before I had learned it completely. I just began to feel comfortable, and there I was—off again. I felt, "Oh, my God, I'm just not ready." I was scared to death. It [her current job] really is a buck-stops-here kind of thing. . . . I guess I got more accustomed to the fear—I don't know if it went away or not.

Ready or not, Dorothy moved to a management position requiring her to make final decisions that were not to be routinely reviewed by a superior. How she coped with her anxiety is a familiar theme of the interviews.

but I was always very aware that the buck stopped there, and I always wanted to be sure that I made the right decision, and I always wanted to be sure that I thought things through completely from all different angles. It was an opportunity for me. It was certainly high visibility. I didn't want to make any mistakes. . . . I was working probably an average of fifteen hours a day. And I got myself into overdrive, and I just stayed there. I would not allow myself to let down and relax, because I was afraid if I got down I wouldn't be able to get back up again. But it was one of those mind-over-matter [things]. You just have to do it. At least that's the way I perceived it. I had to do it.

Having overcome resistance to change, these women seem to have made a psychological reversal that has abolished tolerance for the routine. Whether they call it comfort or boredom, they cannot allow themselves to be lulled into sameness. Hardesty and Jacobs might associate this headiness about mobility with a "proving-up" career phase, which entails considerable energy expenditure and fast movement.[9] According to those authors, proving up is followed by disenchantment when women's diligence and performance are not matched by corporate recognition. This failure is, in part, attributable to women's focusing too much on the growth that stems from learning rather than the tangible growth of promotion. Although the women of this study emphasize the importance of interesting work, they also attend to opportunity offered by mobility. They desire continued learning for two reasons, its intrinsic value and its application to more responsible positions. For these women a balance between the tangible and intangible rewards of work is sought.

Change and Company Loyalty

We have seen how women's desire for challenging work has been interpreted to preclude adequate attention to advancement. Presumably naive about politics and power in business, women allegedly expect to be rewarded solely on the basis of performance. Moreover, women are assumed to stay with one company for reasons of psychic connection even when commensurate reward is not forthcoming.

Lest we lose sight of performance as a primary criterion for promotion, a study that investigated the views of American and British senior executives found "that regardless of the country and the sex of the person . . . the criterion that was rated important most often was performance." Other criteria such as memberships, education, traits, and personal data received lower ratings in considering promotion of male and female managers. The establishment of competence must be foremost.[10]

Satisfying work was a priority for the women interviewed, but not to the exclusion of career opportunity. Mobility was a way of securing both; in fact, the nature of corporate work seems to require job changes to fend off boredom. Although mobility frequently occurred within one company, women would look elsewhere for a faster track, more money, or more fulfilling work.

The subject of a company switch arose in reaction to feelings of dissatisfaction either with the work itself or with opportunities for advancement. Women rarely changed companies for the sake of mobility alone. However, they recognized the advantages that such a shift offered. They might seek advancement within their own companies first but find that they could move faster by changing employers.[11] Bonnie, who by her late twenties had worked primarily in sales for four different companies, describes experience with job mobility across organizations:

> I moved faster by changing jobs than I would have by trying to work my way up in the same organization. In fact, I probably wouldn't have been able to work my way up had I stayed with [her former company]; it took the change to do that. . . . Don't take a lower job and hope you can get up there; it doesn't work. It didn't take me long to learn that you ask for the money up front too. You don't say, "All right, I'll start at this and wait." Because I changed jobs that often, I learned to get commitments on day one. Unfortunately, my nature is to get with the company and stick with it. I would really prefer to do that.

Bonnie's comments imply an inclination toward company loyalty that may or may not be gender-based. In chapter 2, we heard several women disclaim company loyalty in favor of career progress. It is possible that women, more than men, might cling to a company because of psychological needs for connection, but it is at least equally feasible that one's identity, male or female, can become tied to a particular organization. In addition, the desire to build a career where one has become knowledgeable, known, and habituated does not seem to be confined to gender. Certainly, men have been found to stagnate in dead-end corporate positions. In fact, rising executives have been disdainful of these male colleagues.[12] Having resolved the psychological pull between staying with a company and going outside of it, Bonnie has learned to secure the tangibles of a position, money and standing, before diving into its substance.

Conventional corporate wisdom says that movement from one company to another can carry significant benefits. The benefits usually cited, however, refer more to a job's extrinsic nature (primarily money) than to its intrinsic nature. Money was not a prominent topic of our interviews. Women spoke of it infrequently and in passing, in the context of broader work considerations. Unmistakably, a certain base-line of material compensation was required, but beyond that, money was seldom a primary consideration and never a singular one.

Women's laxity about money has been taken as evidence of their naivete about the real currency of corporate power. By not talking about money first and foremost, women give the impression that it is insignificant to them. The women interviewed cared about salary, but it became an issue for discussion only when it fell below an acceptable threshold. In studies of job satisfaction, money is not a primary factor for men or women. It assumes more importance with job dissatisfaction. In fact, people are rarely able to stay at a job that offers only financial satisfaction, and if they do, it is at significant psychological expense.

Money became a significant issue when expectations for appropriate recompense were not met. That is, when women perceived employers to be negligent in their formal and informal acknowledgment of performance, they turned their attention to material aspects of the job, including money and advancement. They felt an imbalance between what they were giving and what they were getting. In the absence of an imbalance, they were likely to continue as they had been.

On the other hand, extrinsic rewards alone cannot carry the day for these women. They need work's intrinsic satisfactions to sustain them. Challenging work that engages one's interest is essential. In fact, an emphasis on the nature of the work itself outweighed monetary concerns in the interviews. These women were not able to accept material reward as a substitute for engaging work. Too much comfort and ease prompted them to think about change. Perhaps another kind of imbalance existed, then, whereby the compensation seemed inordinate to the effort required. Nonetheless, women rarely mentioned money when talking about the nature of the work and what they needed from it. Again, this tendency is in line with job satisfaction literature that finds aspects of the work itself rated as more important than its monetary value for men and women.

It may be that the usual elements of job satisfaction do not apply in business. That is, success in the corporate context may require a shift in the weight of concern from work's interest to its tangible gain. If so, such a shift would be ultimately detrimental to both the individual and to the corporation.[13] External reward alone is not durable and does not sustain people at their work. Disinterest and boredom give way to bitterness and alienation, such that a person's dissociation from the work is to the disadvantage of both. Business managers and executives know that "bottom-line" productivity results from keeping employees happy in terms of the work itself as well as recognition for it. The importance of a participatory management style, which keeps workers informed of their contribution's meaning to the organization and provides recognition for it, is a common theme of current corporate literature.[14]

In these interviews we find women framing a delicate balance between the intrinsic and extrinsic aspects of work. Though women's focus is undeniably on the staying power of the work in terms of its substance and stimulation, they also have an eye on career progress according to the usual criteria of money and promotion. There is evidence that, contrary to conventional expectation, women are "making money a priority," as well as appraising a particular position's experiences for their application higher up the ladder.[15] Women's interest in the work itself and their careful consideration of job changes in terms of both tangible and intangible sources of satisfaction do not seem to be gender-bound. Moreover, there is no evidence here of underlying female needs for interpersonal connection as opposed to straightforward work satisfaction. And work satisfaction is surely composed of both the substance of the work and its pathfinding capabilities.

Thus, women are as interested in the intrinsic satisfactions of work, the sense of personal mastery that comes with it, as men are. Their learning extends beyond the job itself to the nature of its context—women learn quickly about mobility and what it means in terms of both interesting work and tangible reward. A sense of mastery for women in business, like their male counterparts, stems from both competent performance and the recognition expressed by money and promotion.

Resisting Mobility

Presumably more passive than men, females have been expected to get stuck in positions whereas their male counterparts actively steer career paths. Here, as elsewhere, reality contradicts stereotype in that passivity surely exists in men and activity in women.[16] As opposed to staying in a position too long, we find women moving rapidly. In some cases, we see them resisting mobility when it threatens to sacrifice competent performance and thereby work to their ultimate disadvantage. Women may appear to acquiesce to assigned, as opposed to chosen, job changes, but a closer examination of their thinking reveals a dynamic interaction between following and taking charge.

Mobility carries challenge as well as career growth and advancement. Presenting opportunities for new learning and fresh intellectual stimulation, transfers are commonly associated with promotions or at least increased responsibility that hints of further advancement. The women interviewed were learning about various company functions and the interrelations among them. At times a broadened perspective derived from job mobility seemed to be at the expense of skill mastery. Women felt themselves to be moving on before consolidation of newly learned skills could occur. Having moved through seven marketing and distribution positions in eight years with the same company, Carla talks about mobility's major disadvantage:

> The main disadvantage that I see for me—and it would happen to anyone else who has moved around—is that you don't get a long enough period of time in each position to totally grasp it. I've commented about this: . . . "Hey, sometimes I feel really inadequate. I don't feel like I've gotten a good enough grasp." And upper management says, "Well, you never know it all. You never know enough." So you have to keep going.

When a woman is moved quickly from one position to another, she is assumed competent. Her employer is tacitly, if not overtly, communicating confidence in her abilities. From the managerial point of view, she has proven herself on one job and thereby shown potential for another. From her vantage point, however, she has barely mastered one task before being hurried to another. External indicators, in the form of a fast track, attest to her competence, but she is not wholly convinced. Having spent two years in each of two technical positions within the transportation industry, Rebecca attributes her self-confidence to an internal sense of mastery that may require a longer stay in a position.

> I've never really been in a particular area for that long. When I started to feel comfortable with that, I was thrown into something else. I'm always in a state of change, which I don't mind. I don't ever want to get in a rut and to feel so comfortable with what I'm doing that it becomes boring. But I would like to at least get to the position where I feel fairly comfortable with what I'm doing. And I think that has a lot to do with the self-confidence.

Women who acknowledge the drawbacks of a fast track will not eschew opportunity, however. They are motivated to move up, but they do not want to sacrifice the quality of their performance. They want to remain in a position long enough to master it but not so long as to become bored with it. Comfort, which could mean mastery, signals boredom to them, but they want to begin to feel some comfort as a precursor to another move. Their managers' judgment of their competence at a certain job and readiness to move to another does not always suffice. Their sense of integrity about the work can cause them to "bargain" with a boss.

> [Moving fast is] somewhat stressful, I guess. But it's always been my choice to move. In this last job I sort of reached an agreement with my boss. I said it's getting to the point where I want to stay at a job long enough to feel as though I really know it. I've never gotten to the point of being bored or feeling as though I still didn't have a lot of catching up to do. Maybe I just want to know everything about what's going on, and I'll never reach that level. But I really do think it's time for me to stay in this job for at least two years.

This reservation about fast movement, expressed by several women, stems from an internal desire for knowledge and expertise that is also instrumental. According to their managers, they do not need that internal sense of mastery to move. Nonetheless, they want it for the sake of their own feelings of competence. Moreover, consolidated skills would better prepare them for the next position. Not only would they feel more qualified; they presumably would be so.

Sometimes women are moved too fast. Company practices and sex quotas can combine to sabotage both the individual woman and the company's ultimate productivity.[17] It is not always the individual who slows change. To improve their economic picture, Nina's *Fortune* 500 company put the brakes on employees' mobility.

> There was always very fast movement in our company, which wasn't always good. And I think what they have done now is good, in that they want you to stay in your job longer, so that you can offer more to the company; you can develop yourself. Because one of the things that [the company] would always do, and especially with women is: "Okay, I have a woman. We've got to get her up here because I've got to meet my targets." And she'd fail, because they put her here for a year, then put her here for a year, then put her here for a year, and it's not enough time.

Thus, women are attempting to strike a balance. They want to move fast enough to avoid boredom but not so fast as to preclude the development of expertise. Their sense of competence and confidence is derived from their own feelings of mastery within various areas of the company; managerial votes of confidence do not necessarily suffice regarding their readiness to move. It is not that women turn down transfers and promotions, but whenever possible they do try to exert some control over the frequency and direction of their moves.

Women's career mobility within their companies seems to be directed by forces outside of the women themselves, that is, their managers or other vague entities called "upper management." Women frequently describe being approached by their superiors with a proposed change of assignment before it was anticipated or, in their judgment, warranted. Despite personal reservations, women believe that in most cases they must respond favorably to the offer. Women are aware that a proposal may have several layers beyond the ostensible one of the particular assignment in question. A career path may have been drawn for them by upper management, and it is revealed neither overtly nor explicitly but through transfers and promotions one at a time. Thus, a woman analyzes each suggested move not only in respect to itself but also with an eye toward possible projected meanings and ramifications.

Frequently, however, a superordinate plan does not exist for a woman's career path. A woman can be in a position where her company "doesn't know what to do with [her]." Astute in estimating her position in relation to opportunities available within the company, a woman knows when she is boxed in with no clearly discernible path. Through attentive observation, she can assess management's perception of a path even in the absence of her own. Feeling slated or not, she does more than wait passively for a move to be offered. Women who have a career path planned by themselves or by their superiors, as well as those who do not, actively put themselves forward. They turn chance into opportunity.

For example, a boss who provides little or no guidance is actually furnishing these women with opportunity to expand their skills. Such circumstances could just as readily foster floundering and failure in an employee, but these women thrive on autonomy and seize the chance to prove themselves. Their willingness and ability to take the ball and run with it attest to these women's talents and extraordinary acumen. Taking advantage of just such an experience that could have gone either way, thirty-four-year-old Jill reveals her perceptions of how and why it worked in her favor:

> I was working for a high-level executive in employee relations, and his approach to training was almost nonexistent. So I was left . . . to my own intuition or ability to sort out how things were done and how I was going to perform this job with very little guidance. . . . I'd either sink or swim, and I

just had to do it because I wanted to be successful. And as the time wore on, I realized the opportunity that I had gotten was really terrific because he was extremely well accepted in the company by all levels. So the exposure was there, and I was in on the top levels, being able to see it all, which was a tremendous opportunity.

Having an opportunity is the first step, but not everyone sees opportunity in a given set of circumstances. It is conceivable that many would not interpret the laissez-faire attitude of the supervisor described above as constituting opportunity for an employee. It was the nature of these women as workers to capitalize on freedom, not to be daunted by it. They were given little script and an unencumbered stage on which to display and develop their competencies. This they interpreted as opportunity to prove themselves and to make their abilities known. Visibility is the key to further opportunity; established competence must be seen.[18] Like Jill, Cathy's visibility is promoted by a superior:

> It was he who would mention in passing to people in different departments that he has this person working for him that knew about this and knew about that, and if they wanted information, to contact me directly. So through him I was able to get a lot of exposure.

Whether a boss is spotlighting her or not, a woman continues to be aware of the importance of visibility and can secure it herself. These women typically monitor what they are currently doing and how it is registered within the corporation at the same time. Nina's focus is on both her managerial responsibilities and her visibility within the larger corporate environment.[19]

> In a large corporation and at the level I'm at, because I'm really a first-line manager, it's hard to get, not the recognition, but the visibility to other areas to let them know what you're doing. I've been able to do that, because I've gone outside the group. But you can very easily just stay in your own group and not want to bother with anything else. . . . So it's really what you want to do to get it.

It is a given that hard work is likely to yield a greater return when it is seen than when it is not. Rather than passively waiting for recognition on the basis of performance alone, these women take action on their own behalf by repeatedly bringing their labors' effectiveness to the attention of superiors. Monica, who moved from secretary to human resources manager in six years, expects her willingness to assume more responsibility than required to pay off, and she has gradually become comfortable with the stage fright that accompanies increased visibility.

I'm not going to sit back and say, "Well, since I don't have the pay and I don't have the real true authority, I'm not going to take it." That's not the way I've operated. I've learned that, at least for me, there's been a payoff to putting in more effort—[in] some organizations it doesn't pay; in ours it's paid. I remember going into my first meetings—this was way back when I first got promoted, and I had this knot in my stomach—and thinking, "My God, am I going to make it through this?" After a while I found that I really liked being visible. And, again, by being visible I had an opportunity to have more and more people come to me.

According to these women, what distinguishes them from others in their organizations is their willingness to surpass expectations. They extend themselves by taking initiative, expending extra effort, and assuming more responsibility than others do. They perceive and manufacture opportunity where others do not. They produce and take advantage of visibility to insure recognition, which is requisite to advancement. These behaviors, coupled with their ability, are likely to precipitate success. However, the organization itself can make a difference, as Monica acknowledges that her modus operandi might not produce the same results elsewhere. Moreover, her remarks demonstrate the impact of experience upon her personal, as well as professional, development. Her early stage fright is replaced by an eagerness for the visibility that performance brings.

Diligence and capability can move many of these women to the forefront. In addition to working hard, they develop strategies to enhance visibility and further their progress within their companies. Bonnie's advice to others is based on what has worked to enhance her visibility:

> So I would tell those women to do something that would make them visible. Put [a suggestion] in writing. Go to a high-level manager and ask for an important assignment. That's been a real key to opening somebody's eyes: "My gosh, that's unusual. Somebody's asking to do it." And being careful not to insinuate that I don't have enough to do. . . . Show a real interest.

Visibility notwithstanding, Bonnie does not wait to be chosen. Thirty-one years old and in sales, with no degree but with exceptional vitality, she actively pursues promotion opportunities:

> There is a lot of exemption, and it's hard to break out of those categories. You have to make it very, very [clear] that you do want to step up and get out. I think back on some of the promotions I had. It wasn't because they recognized the ability and added my name to the list. It's because I did it via writing, and also a confrontation across the desk, and said, "I want to

be added to the list of candidates." Make sure that you do get the opportunity. Don't sit back and hope that you're added. Ask for it, and you'll be respected for it, and you'll certainly [reap] more benefits that way.[20]

Visibility and exposure go hand in hand. With mobility, women gain both: they become visible at different levels of a company, and they are exposed to different company functions. Their knowledge broadens. More people know them; they know more people and more about the company. Thus, a woman's learning and professional development increase. These experiences not only enhance skill but promote commensurate psychological change personally and professionally.

Women's mobility exposes them to new learning and with it new opportunity. Assuming more responsibility, they deserve and want commensurate promotions. The promotions are not only for the sake of recognition; they serve a utilitarian purpose of facilitating the work. By her late thirties, Teresa had been working for eight years in a product area for which she had undergraduate and graduate training. She explains how the trappings of promotion will enable her more effectively to accomplish the research, marketing, production, and sales of her company's product.

> The authority, number one; that's one of the reasons I want the promotion. I honestly feel [that] if this is the type of job they're going to have me doing I'll be able to do it better with that promotion. Because people are impressed with titles and offices . . . stature. . . . With a lot of companies, offices are important—physical location and size of office. That's something that I resisted for a long time, because I don't like to feel that in order to be effective I have to have an office with a window. I know people who hesitate to come in and talk to you unless you're in an office with a window in it. And it affects your ability to do your job, which is terrible. Because it does, I have to accept that it does and therefore do what has to be done. So I used to be very free and easy about that. But the last time my boss and I talked about my promotion I said, "And by the way, tell them I want the office to go with it too." I hate to even hear myself say that, but I know why I'm saying it. I've learned to get a little more comfortable with it.

Teresa recognizes what must be done to enhance her effectiveness within the corporate context. While she may be personally opposed to certain ritualistic trappings, she ultimately adapts to them for a higher priority, professional efficacy in that setting.

What begins as an adaptation to the corporate context can evolve into psychological change. Women learn about themselves and their degree of fit within the organization. They also learn about what changes they can and cannot make in their companies and in themselves. Without sacrificing their integrity, they follow a course of psychological development that accommodates and, wherever possible, bends business practice.

Learning, then, encompasses far more than the content of the work. Women learn about the complexities of their organizations, the interrelations among functions, and what facilitates effectiveness. By moving from one area to another, they become increasingly aware of their expanding knowledge and abilities. Their confidence grows with their competence. They are offered and they fashion opportunity to develop their careers further. They seek and are chosen for promotions. They become managers.

No mention of geographic constraints on mobility, marr. + family issues

□ 4 □

Managing

Not all of the women held managerial positions at the time of their interviews. Some suspected that they were slated to become managers, given their history and current position in the company and the fact that they had been chosen to attend the management program. Others occupied positions that carried managerial-level responsibilities, but they did not yet have the title. Many were managers and expected to move even higher within the organization.

Beginning work without a notion of career and in nonbusiness settings, the majority of women here did undergo a reorientation of their sights in the course of their work experience. We have seen jobs evolving into career pursuits, as corporate exposure taught women not only about business but also about themselves. In this chapter, their transition to manager is traced by looking at how they develop in relation to others' and their own managerial styles. As they tell us what they made of various experiences with their own managers we see their psychological development shaping the kind of managers that they become. We begin with managers with clerical roots because they represent the prototypic experience of current social change for women.

Becoming a Manager

We have seen how these women's abilities and inclinations for work have precipitated their opportunities. Even those who began in clerical ranks experienced rapid upward mobility. Their stories run contrary to conventional corporate wisdom about how difficult it is to transcend a nonexempt status to enter an exempt one. We expect tales of women getting "stuck" within the lower ranks but do not find them here. Instead, we are told that where one begins in an organization is unimportant. What is important is performance: demonstrated effectiveness, initiative, and responsibility, as well as a propensity to take on more than the job requires.

Although a clerical beginning may not hamper mobility, the course may be more lateral than vertical. New positions with increased responsibility may be secured, but complete clearance of clerical underpinnings can be harder to achieve. Women of this study are unwilling to accept responsibility without corresponding authority for too long. Leigh, forty years old and just four years in the business world, struggled singlehandedly to free herself of clerical vestiges and move from a support position to a managerial one.

> I'm now in a manager's position whereas before I was really support. I had a lot of responsibility, basically, but not authority. Had to get out of that. And it's been hard. It took me a while to learn that I really had to get [out], because every time I moved to another department or was promoted somewhat financially I was still always within the same kind of situation. A year ago I realized that I have got to get out of this, and no one's fighting for me. I really had to fight to be moved out of that situation [to one] where I had no clerical responsibility.

The transition to manager can be a complicated one. There must first be an opportunity for the promotion. One can have substantial responsibility but remain in a support position with a superior credited for projects accomplished. In addition, senior management must recognize the potential of employees; they must be willing to look within their own companies for prospective managers. At Gwen's company, a diversified conglomerate that began with a product, management's sights were turned around under the influence of an executive's newly acquired knowledge and a social context supporting affirmative action.

> The opportunity opened up for a junior-management-type position, brand new function in the company, never existed before. And initially they went on the outside looking for men managers, and either they were too expensive or they didn't find anyone that met their specifications. Then they started looking at women outside the corporation until a gentleman, our executive vice-president who had just returned from the Harvard program and realized that affirmative action was coming into focus, asked the very simple question, "Is there anyone inside of the corporation, specifically a woman, that could possibly do this job?" The

consultant who was brought in to help form this function responded very positively. So then they went out on a hunt within the organization; I think they selected about fifteen women that they thought fell into this particular category, and I was one of them.

Gwen provides an example of an external, societal impetus for change within the corporation. The company had been operating in its usual fashion to fill a managerial position when an executive suggested implementation of a new procedure precipitated by social change outside of the corporate organization. External forces of change were mandating a revised process within the company that would give already employed women, albeit in subordinate positions, an opportunity heretofore unavailable to them. A revised social context, however, must be matched by individual readiness to meet that change.

An offer of promotion, once made, may not be immediately embraced. A woman may go through a process of internal questioning with respect to her qualifications and the risks involved. Gwen, a single woman who had occupied several clerical positions on her way to manager at age forty, continues:

> And so I was promoted into my junior-level management position with much apprehension on my part—a couple of things going for me. I knew I had reached the point where I wanted to do big[ger things]. I could not see myself as an executive secretary and administrative assistant the rest of my life. And they knew I wanted to work; I wasn't really a hausfrau-type of person. I just didn't know what I wanted to do, and I thought, "Well, if I fail, and there's a very good chance I may, I'll just leave the company. The very worst thing that could happen to me is I'd have to go back to being a secretary." So I said, "Why not?"

When social change offers opportunity in new directions for women, they are both ready and not. Gwen was part of two social contexts, societal and corporate, and both shaped her self-concept. Her emergent career identity fostered by a widespread social movement remained in amorphous form as long as her company did not tether it. Thus, her notions of career direction began to change in line with new societal messages, but their actualization awaited a corresponding opening by the corporation. Given that occasion, she is only partially prepared; she is ready for the opportunity but uncertain about its fulfillment. Once in the position, however, she is able to consolidate both her skills and her new identity, and each feeds the other.

Gwen's direction parallels that of the society and corporation in which she lives. Social change does not occur in blanket fashion, however, and considerable variation among institutions and individuals can be found at any given time. Beyond her own reservations, a woman moving out of a clerical status may face considerable censure by her peers. Gwen's story demonstrates how sources of support and rejection shift over time and in conjunction with her establishment as a manager.

> At that time [mid-to-late seventies] I was the first secretary, the first non-exempt person to move into the managerial ranks. And I really thought [the other secretaries] would be happy for me, but they rejected me completely. I was no longer one of them. A lot of little gossipy things like, "I wonder how she got that position," which really hurt me very deeply. The men, particularly the senior-level men, have always been very supportive. They never made me feel like "You were a secretary and therefore you have nothing to give me." The middle-manager men in the beginning were extremely supportive—went out of their way to be nice to me, sometimes a little bit on the sexist side . . . but nevertheless very supportive. About two, three years after I was into the managerial ranks, I started getting promotions, and the tables started turning. I started going out and taking my show on the road, so to speak. That was the turning point where suddenly they saw me in a role as a professional holding a meeting and sitting there with . . . the presidents of those companies and/or their bosses. And the fact that I knew what I was talking about, I was confident at what I was doing, [resulted in] very good acceptance. I think the women have finally accepted me. The interesting thing is, the more I move up the ladder, the middle-manager men subtly have turned. That bothered me until I realized what it was, and it was obvious that they feel a little threatened although I still don't understand why they should feel that way. "Boy you're—aren't you lucky you're a woman today?" Or, "The women today, they've got it made. Baby, you got it made."

Acceptance by women who had been her peers was obviously important to Gwen, but not to the extent of sacrificing her career direction. As former female co-workers became accustomed to the psychosocial shift themselves, they were able to appreciate a woman's managerial competence, and rejection of Gwen and the social change she represented gave way to acceptance. Moreover, Gwen may have become a role model for her former peers, whose sights were raised by her example.[1] The reactions of current male peers, however, demonstrate the tenuousness of social change that is not accompanied by commensurate psychological change in both genders.[2] It is interesting to note that discussions of psychological barriers to management positions for women most frequently refer to those associated with females and rarely to male psychological barriers that need changing.

Gwen is not alone in wanting to maintain favorable relations with former peers. The transition to manager is made more complex when one must then supervise heretofore peers. Coming to a large conglomerate in her late thirties as a data processing consultant, Renee describes the difficulty:

> I think I always have been people-oriented. The evolution further down the line was trying to relate to people that I had worked with on a peer level who were suddenly working for me, and at first feeling awkward with the distance that I was supposed to feel between myself and them, but still wanting to be friends with them on a one-on-one level.

According to traditional ideas of gender difference, interpersonal relationships take priority for females. Women who are managers certainly prefer good relations to poor ones, but they also recognize the complications that position can impose on interpersonal relationship. Comparing leadership styles and behavior of male and female managers, Chapman finds that "practicing female managers do not have a significantly higher need for fostering good interpersonal relationships than do their male colleagues."[3] Although women try to maintain positive personal ties, there is no hint of sacrificing the professional for the personal here. Gwen's main concern as she assumed a managerial position was development of her professional self.

> I just was so busy working at becoming knowledgeable about what I was doing and building my own confidence level. I was more introverted at that point, working on myself. . . . if they [her former clerical peers] didn't want to accept me, well, that's it, what could I do?

Part of the transition from peer to manager involves new learning about what is possible and preferable in relation to subordinates. Liking gives way to respect as a manager's priority. Colleen, who entered management in her forties, describes the change in her orientation when she became a manager.

> I think the roughest thing for me was my initial step into management. You have a different mind-set about things. Initially, I had gone into management thinking, "Oh, now the best thing is to just have everybody love you." How wonderful that would be. If they love you, everything's going to get done, and everything's just going to be real cool. I learned a lot from that experience. Consequently, what I try to do now as a manager is earn respect rather than worrying about whether people like me or . . . don't like me. If they do, that's fine, and if they don't, okay, that's a choice too. I come at management from a different perspective now than I did when I first got into it six years ago.[4]

Nina, who had worked in the same area of training and instruction for eight years before becoming a manager, recognizes that she must make similar changes in herself. The personal difficulty in readjusting oneself is only the initial part of the process, however. She must also prepare staff for her different behavior and for the changes that will be required of them as a consequence. Those being supervised adjust their work habits and their perceptions of the person who has become their manager. Nina is specific and forethoughtful in setting goals which she then executes gradually:

> I've had to fight with my inner feelings a lot and really concentrate on the goals that I was trying to set out. My staff had a hard time dealing with it. I tried not to make the change quickly . . . it was an adjustment period. It was about seven or eight months [before] my staff felt comfortable with me, because I worked with them before I was their manager. I think that's a very hard transition to make, because you're chummy buddies with everybody, and then all of a sudden you're their manager. It's "Hey, take me seriously. I really am the manager, and I'm responsible for this, this, and this." I've come to a point where it's not all the way there, but this year I feel that they really do respect me as their manager. They're willing to do what it takes to get the job done.

For women to be taken seriously as managers several conditions must be met. First, the organization, reflecting larger societal trends, considers women as candidates for these responsible positions. The engineering of structural social change must be accompanied by individual psychic change on the part of the female manager as well as her co-workers and subordinates. Since all of these changes are not ordinarily simultaneous, we witness the interactions that foster them and their processes in various stages. Once the positions are opened to women, perceptions of peers and subordinates, for the most part, are revised as a result of shifts created by the woman manager herself.

Management Fosters Personal Change

Whether one is supervising former peers or not, moving into a managerial position requires change. The job has changed, and so must the person. Not only must a manager deal with the work differently, she must also develop new interpersonal skills. Since managing people is not the same as working alongside them, women find that they must change their relationship to the workers as well as to the work. Such change requires them consciously to revise their self-image as well as the image others have of them. As Nina, a self-proclaimed optimist, becomes less nurturing, she is better able to help her employees develop themselves through honest performance appraisals.

I'm becoming less nurturing—not that I don't care. I have always been a very nurturing person, and I have a reputation for being that. Trying to break away from that reputation, especially in a work situation, is very hard because then they expect it from me all the time. . . . It's always very difficult for me to deal with conflict. This year I've been better able to step back. . . . I can take constructive criticism until it comes out the ear. I realized that that was because I didn't take it as being personal to me, but as a behavior that I was exhibiting. So I learned to keep that in mind as I started to use some more skills in [performance appraisal]. . . . that's one of the biggest changes that I've seen in myself, in that I've tried to step back a little bit and become—it's not less sensitive, because I'm still very sensitive to my people and their needs—but to really focus in on what the situation is at the time instead of always trying to make it hunky-dory all the time.

Nina is able to retain attributes central to self, an awareness of workers' needs, for example, while developing others necessary for success as a manager. Though most women interviewed did not cite personal sensitivity as a hindrance to their job performance, some did have to overcome customary reactions. Circumstances can exacerbate those reactions, as in the case of Gwen, who suffered rejection as a female pioneer moving from clerical to management ranks.

I, like most women, tended to take things personally, and if the secretaries rejected me, obviously I took it very personally. If something should happen . . . between my boss and myself or he got angry, I took it very personally. It took a long time, and I don't know that I'm 100 percent there, I don't know that I ever will be. But I take things a lot less personally today than I did then. That's a very big thing. If you really want to survive in life, let alone in management, you'd better become very—I won't say thick-skinned, but I remember [a friend] saying, "You're too thin-skinned, you better shape up, or you're going to be miserable." And he was right.

Business requires one to separate the personal from the professional. As both recipients and dispensers of performance reviews, women learn that judgments made about behavior are not to be viewed as direct reflections upon one's person. Hence, within herself a woman must distinguish between the personal and the professional, and she must also, as a manager, separate herself from her employees. For most effectiveness, management seems to require at least a modicum of distance between supervisor and subordinate. The nature of managerial responsibilities, potentially deciding another's corporate fate, requires conscientious "objectivity"; personal preferences are not permitted expression. Realizing that she now occupies an executive position of power and control in the financial industry, thirty-year-old

Marsha, already professionally credentialed in her technical area, develops a new professionalism whose hallmark is objectivity.

> for the first time I had control over someone else's life, which is pretty scary if you're not used to it. It created a little conflict internally, trying to make sure that you remain objective, for one. Try not to get very personal, which is something I think you have to learn rather than being taught. I just can't see anyone teaching you to be objective and [to] look at things on a purely professional basis without personal feelings mixed in. It took a while to get to that level, but I think I've finally got to the point where I can sit back and separate the person from the professional and try to be objective in evaluations and things like that.

Thus, managerial professionalism requires women to make distinctions within themselves and between themselves and others. The ability to make such distinctions has been traditionally associated with one gender and not the other.[5] Compartmentalizing the professional and the personal supposedly comes naturally to men, whereas women are characterized as imbuing even the most cerebral activities with emotion. It is a well-established idea that an emotionality traditionally associated with females renders them unsuited for business.[6] Despite repeated findings that managerial skills are indistinguishable by gender, the myth of female emotionality lingers.[7] Some have attempted to transform this alleged female liability into a strength by redefining what constitutes an effective managerial style: a facilitative rather than authoritarian approach that is sensitive to people's needs.[8] Other writers have asserted that the manifestation of executive, objective distance is surface behavior that contradicts women's "basic impulse to relate to and to nurture others."[9] According to this theory, many women who change in line with the demands of business are ultimately betraying themselves. In any case, to assert that women qualify for management on the basis of female traits perpetuates gender stereotyping and functions to keep women in their place, even outside of the home.

The women of this study speak frankly about personal change prompted by profession, but these changes become assimilated as part of their own psychological development in reference to a particular social context. Chapter 8 reveals that they can remain true to themselves while allowing different aspects of self to surface depending upon the context. Females are not ruled by emotion across all circumstances, just as males are not universally cerebral.

The women's testimony shows repeatedly the process of change in themselves and in others. That change is interactional in that people's perceptions and behaviors are gradually reshaped in line with new contextual configurations in the workplace that parallel social change. Women's revised behavior as a result of managerial requirements frequently represents the discovery of latent aspects of themselves. It is not that women have adopted behavior that proves ultimately contrary to their true natures but rather that the demands of a new situation call upon parts of themselves that had not had opportunity for expression before. Rather than adopting behavior that is at odds with themselves, they learn more about who they are, thereby refuting the idea of fixed personality traits and supporting the importance of context in shaping not only behavior but what we may become.

A distinction between behavior and identity is prompted most immediately by Hardesty and Jacobs's thesis that corporate women adopt behavior that ultimately betrays the "innate 'relatedness' at the core of a woman's being."[10] However, the debate about what part behavior and less visible processes, such as the unconscious, play in constituting a person has a long history in psychology. Freud and subsequent psychodynamicists have postulated the roots of personality and motivation as largely hidden even from the person herself, whereas behavioral theorists maintain that behavior, which includes actions, thoughts, and words, is not merely a surface manifestation but the essence of identity. They, like developmental psychologist Piaget, seem to subscribe to the idea that behavioral change is eventually assimilated as a shift in consciousness.

Thus, women discover heretofore latent aspects of themselves and their abilities as they escalate to management. In addition to the reshaping of self-perception, women learn to re-form the perceptions of others as they draw yet another line of separation to establish their authority in a new position. In the process of so doing, Martha discovers her own assertiveness in supervising mostly men in a production-line situation.

> again, it's establishing an air of authority. . . . That was very important. These people had previously viewed me in a service position. . . . another difficulty was that I didn't know anybody [in the area she was now supervising], and they didn't know me. But it was a totally different world, and it's a totally different kind of personality. I learned that I had more moxie in that job than I ever would have dreamed I had.

When a woman becomes a manager, she is sometimes challenged by subordinates to prove herself worthy of the position.[11] Despite a disinclination to assert her authority explicitly, Karen, a coordinator of high-level planning for a retail corporation where she has worked for five years, finds that circumstances warrant it.

> I have to do more learning to gain the authority; I don't like to just give orders to people. I like to explain why we need this thing done and hopefully get their cooperation through that. . . . and you come in as a newcomer and as a woman. I've found it difficult to deal with those types of people who hold back information from you and all this sort of thing. I guess I've gotten more to the point where I start to really put my foot down and say, "Look, I'm the boss."[12]

In conjunction with her new managerial position, a woman's psychological development progresses to a point of authoritative certainty that can be explicitly communicated to subordinates and peers. As the perceptions of all involved shift, so must their approaches to the work itself.

Delegating

A woman's authority as new manager may be questioned, but her ability to do the work is not. Women have made their reputation within the company on their task performance, diligence, and concrete accomplishments. They face a turnaround in their priorities when they move from worker to manager. Their task, as manager, is to stop doing so much of the work. Paradoxically, the strengths that elevated a woman to manager are transformed into shortcomings within that position.[13] Women who have always done more than their share of the work must learn to relinquish the substance of tasks to their subordinates. Reluctance to do so may be motivated partly by a desire to protect underlings from possible failure.

> I guess learning not to do everything yourself is another major thing. I've always had a problem with being a perfectionist, this feeling of, if-you-want-it-done-right-you-have-to-do-it-yourself, and working yourself to death. I still put too much pressure on myself.

Like Karen, Ina's first response was to do the work herself. As her job expands, however, her singlehanded undertakings are no longer feasible, and increasing task demands require her to be firmer in her expectations of employees.

> I used to be much more passive, much more, "It's okay. If you don't know how to do this, I'll do it myself." . . . So if they were confused over something, [instead of] saying, "Okay, I'll give you more time to do it," I

would take it out of their hands and say, "It's okay. I'll do it. I'll find time to do it myself" or "I'll show you right now." I [still am] much more understanding. But now I'll be more demanding because more demands are being put on me.

Women often try to maintain the work patterns that characterized them before entering management. Just as the new position requires a reorientation of their interpersonal relationships, it also mandates a change in their work habits. Responsibility for a much greater work load can cause a revision in their treatment of employees and the work.

The thing that really changed was just me being able to manage that much work and responsibility. It was just the magnitude of the work. I'd always been the kind of person that would sit and listen. But when you have twelve people you don't have time to sit and listen all day. That was one point that didn't go over real well, but I would have to, at points, tell them, "I can't talk to you now. Can you come back at a different time?" . . . They would always be dependent on [my nurturance], and they didn't need me. They knew what they were doing, and they were doing a great job. And they shouldn't have had to come in and get a little hit every once in a while to go on to the next thing. So I had to wean them away from that, because it wasn't helping me get my job done. And it wasn't helping them grow and be able to do things on their own, take a whole project and go with it.[14]

By treating her subordinates as though they were capable of more independent achievement, this woman promotes a revision of their self-perceptions as well as actually furthering their abilities. Their changes complement her own; as she assumes the tasks of management, their responsibility for the work itself increases. Both manager and workers grow in new directions that make for a more fully functioning unit.

To be absolutely certain of work quality and completion, women have relied solely upon themselves. They enjoyed a kind of independence as workers that they, ironically, cannot retain as managers. Now they must learn to trust their subordinates to do work that ultimately reflects back upon them as managers. Their workers' productivity becomes a test of their own. Although the magnitude of the work load provides strong incentive to relinquish direct task involvement, women discover another source of reluctance stemming from a perception of subordinates as fledglings in need of protection.

I thought I had arrived; I haven't arrived yet. And this surfaces in my reluctance to fully delegate. I very willingly delegate when I know the person is ready to accept responsibility. I'm now at the point in my career [where] I'm getting all this additional responsibility, where I'm going to have to relinquish a good part of the function that I originally started. And I think it's going to be hard for me to let go of my babies and let them hang out there on their own. I feel a sense of responsibility; I don't want them to get out there and flounder, not know what to do. I'm going to have to cut the apron strings and let them go.

Using the example of one of her subordinates, Gwen explains the reciprocity of success or failure that she shares with him.

If anything happens and he should fail in some way, number one, I would feel badly for him. I would feel some sense of responsibility in his failing. And the other side of it, it's a reflection on myself. If something goes wrong, regardless of who does it, I'm still the ultimate person that is responsible. And I guess I'm afraid of that. I don't want to have any failure on my scoreboard—not to imply that I haven't had any, but I really would like to have [a] very low set of failures. In the beginning I'd fill that stereotyped viewpoint: I should not make a mistake; I must prove to the world, and I must seek their approval. Now I don't care if they approve or not.[15]

Coming to management at age forty from a clerical background, Gwen is describing a series of stages in her development of a managerial self. She recognizes that her perfectionism and fear of mistakes surpassed normal expectation during the "proving-up" phase of her career. A victim of gender stereotyping, she believed that her record had to be flawless whereas male counterparts would be allowed some leeway. Whereas a man promoted to manager may be granted acceptance at the outset and must prove himself undeserving, acceptance of a similarly situated woman is withheld until she has proven her worthiness.[16] Her approval seeking represents a dependence upon others' estimation of her worthiness as an authority figure. She has come to a more balanced view now wherein pride in her work remains high, but her sights are focused less on gaining approval and more on the ramifications of her subordinates' performance abilities for their own and her success.

Evaluating subordinates' readiness to assume responsibility for a job is undoubtedly a learned skill that comes with managerial experience. In addition, delegating includes another component that again entails a process of separation. Employees' preparedness notwithstanding, women must extricate themselves from assuming total responsibility even in the face of unreasonable demands.[17] Dorothy, who comes in her late thirties to human resource management from clerical begin-

nings, agrees with Gwen that women tend to take on what men separate themselves from.

> I think I would have been a lot less hard on myself if I had a staff that I
> could have fallen back on, but I felt so much as though I didn't, that the
> only other place that it could fall was on me. That's probably a very
> typically female thing to happen. You just have the feeling that no one else
> can do it, or if you don't get it done, it's—men are much more likely to say,
> "Screw it. I can't get it done, that's just tough." And I don't approach things
> that way.

Women are able to follow their inclination to assume what might be
inordinate responsibility until their job's expansion renders it impossible. In order to delegate, however, a manager must trust subordinates'
competence. Even when they have confidence in their employees,
women may still have difficulty surrendering recognition for task accomplishment, particularly since this functioned as the foundation of
their success. Moreover, women's enjoyment of the work itself may
obstruct full delegation. Although this could be interpreted as an
addiction to task mastery that stands in the way of female assumption
of authority, it might also be a simpler matter of a need for new
learning.

To delegate, therefore, one must withdraw from direct involvement
with the work itself. A woman's sense of competence and her good
reputation within the company have been grounded in her firsthand
accomplishments. The modus operandi that built her success cannot
sustain it in her new managerial position. She must learn new ways of
working through others whose competence reflects upon her. Developing people and her trust in them becomes a major focus.[18] Stella,
required to coordinate several constituencies in overseeing publications for a high-technology corporation, refrains from imposing her
methods on others so that their own abilities are fostered.

> you can't work alone. I had to delegate, in other words. I had to set
> priorities. I had to sit back and not try to do everything myself. I had to rely
> on the other person's expertise. The main thing I learned is that every-
> body doesn't do everything the same way. I tend to try to push my way of
> doing something on other people, and I found that that just doesn't work.
> That's really been a great learning experience for me, because I want so
> much to say, "No, why don't you do it this way?" I've learned to accept the
> fact that people are different. It has helped me a great deal to learn that I
> just can't do everything alone, and I can't do it by myself—that people are
> important.

Once accustomed to managerial challenges, most, but not all, women are able to transfer their enjoyment from the substance of the work to its management. Working through and with other people can mean surrender of control and independence. Additionally, women must acquire skills of interpersonal assessment and communication.[19] For some women, like Roberta, developing the abilities of others is more work than doing the job herself. Her proclivity for doing the work rather than managing the people may be seen as a function of individual difference rather than gender, however.

> [Supervising others is] definitely not one of my strengths. I have a low tolerance for it. It just takes an inordinate amount of time. I'm a task person. I can't . . . be bothered with wondering about how I'm going to convey or communicate instructions or being concerned about what's going on. I much prefer doing it myself. And I always had a tough time delegating because of these very strong feelings that I have.

Considerable new learning is required when a woman assumes a managerial position. In order to relinquish her hold on the work and delegate both tasks and responsibility, she must develop her employees' abilities to the extent that she can trust their effectiveness. The effort involved in developing employees' skills, building and orchestrating a collaborative team, and communicating effectively in all directions is considerably greater than doing the work itself. While women were becoming task experts, they were also learning about management from their own managers.

Learning from Managers

As workers, the women demonstrated high degrees of autonomy, independence, and productivity. We cannot discern the extent to which these characteristics were inherent to this group of women, but it is clear that they thrived on environments that fostered and encouraged their exercise. Research generally has found successful women managers to display many of the attributes found among those of this study. They enjoy challenge, problem solving, and decision making. Women parallel men in their motivation and desire for advancement in authority and income. Moreover, they derive considerable satisfaction from the work itself, the intellectual stimulation of its process and accomplishment. Finally, female and male managers are alike in the relative values that they place on intrinsic and extrinsic job elements.[20]

As subordinates, their experiences with managers influenced them both positively and negatively and were later a factor in the development of their own managerial styles. Again, we witness their psychological development as workers and managers through their interactions with various styles of supervision. Aware of what had helped and hindered them, women took the lessons of their own experience with them when they crossed to the other side of the desk. Jessica expresses the sentiments of many in a description of what comprised effective management for her.

> Most of the managerial styles that I have appreciated and have enjoyed working under have been ones that lean toward autonomy. "This is what I need you to do. I don't care how you do it. Go do it." I haven't gotten along well with the management style that [says]: "This is what I want you to do. You take *A* and you put *A* into *B*, and then you take *B* and you put it into *C*." I mean, that drives me crazy. Another style that I have really appreciated is the notion that you don't feel like you're on the outside looking in. You know what the department goals are. You know how much money you [have] to spend to try to accomplish them. And you know what's going on. I also appreciate the fact that the management style allows you to grow and learn more. That could be internal, just in your one-on-ones with the manager, or it could be through seminars and programs—something that allows you to grow in your work, in the business world, all the different aspects.[21]

Through the freedom and license that certain kinds of managers granted, these women developed an awareness of their capacities for effectiveness on the job. In the absence of prescribed direction that can function to restrict, women discovered the breadth and extent of their abilities to be greater than anticipated. Not only can they do the job and more, they can forge their own paths through it. A manager whose expectations initially exceeded their own provided the right mix of autonomy and guidance.

> He gave me always a little bit more to do than I thought I could do; he held that carrot out there. He was a "provide resources" type of manager but not a hovering kind of manager. "If you need something, I will help you get it." Otherwise, "You're on your own. If you need to talk to me about it, that's fine, we'll talk about it. But otherwise I expect you to deliver what I've asked you to deliver." And so that . . . is the kind of manager that I prefer. I need independence. I need autonomy, but I need somebody to give me resources of whatever kind, if they're resources that I can't get for myself.

This manager provides just enough of a framework so that one's independent abilities and accomplishments are fostered. In contrast, some managers are so laissez-faire that women are left totally to their own devices without a hint of support. Once the initial fright is over-come, Gwen develops strategies for dealing with the job and her manager.

> When I got into the first level of management, I worked for probably the best person for me, because he was the kind of individual who said to me, "Okay, you got the job. You're on your own, kid. I don't want to see you. I'm going to put you in your own office ten floors beneath me; go to it; I don't have time for your crap, so just do the best you can, and if you have a problem come see me at lunch; you can buy me lunch." And I said, "Oh, my God, what am I doing?" Up to this point, in my personal life as well as in my career life, I had been in a subordinate role. You have a problem, you go to your boss, and he fixes it, right? . . . Making decisions on my own [was] very difficult when you're not used to making decisions that impact budgets and things like that. He almost terrified me at first until I just started getting underneath and finding out what his personality was really like. I think I was the first woman that he had ever managed, . . . and he . . . had difficulty managing, in the true sense of managing. So he was having as many anxieties as I was. And once I learned that, then I began to just kind of fight back a little bit—"You're not going to scare me anymore" type thing.

Gwen was moving from a subordinate role to a decision-making one. Feeling unprepared to assume such responsibilities, she had to over-come her anxieties and forge a working relationship with a supervisor inexperienced with women. Her first target was this frightening manager; she recognized that an increased understanding of the way he operated would be essential to her effectiveness. Her ability to accomplish this was as important as task mastery in preparing her psychologically for management. In conjunction with the change in her perception of this man, she gradually shifts her understanding of herself from that of subordinate to manager.

These women do not find functioning under fear conducive to effectiveness. Intimidation is not a major part of their own styles when they become managers, and they do not appreciate it in others.

> The man that was in charge of me managed by fear. He was incredible. He said things to me that I'm sure, if they were said in a group, . . . he would be highly reprimanded from the company. He criticized my dress; he criticized everything that I did. Not necessarily because I deserved it, but he wanted to make you so mad that you would do better. And I had problems respecting him. I've never been one that needed to be managed or hovered over or strongly directed.

Bonnie, a confident and independent worker, also has had managers like Gwen's who were unaccustomed to working with women. In Bonnie's experience, however, the communication gap was never bridged.

> I've seen other situations where the manager . . . stays away so much you don't know where he's coming from. And I attribute that to the fact that maybe he's a little uncomfortable working around women. . . . I don't know if he's intimidated or what, uncomfortable. . . . I've had managers that are so uncomfortable talking to me that nothing's been able to get accomplished.

The outcome of a superior–subordinate relationship is not governed by gender, however. It is the character of the individual manager, male or female, that can be instrumental in women's professional development. Good and bad experiences can be had with male and female managers alike.

> Up until the last two years I was working [only] with men and had no problems at all. Everybody worked well together. And in the last two years, I had a director who was a female who was, in my mind's eye, the stereotype of the hard-nosed ball buster. And her attitude was: that's how she got ahead, and she would not move any woman ahead unless that woman was of the same type. Since she was such a stereotype right down the line, most of the men assumed that she would be out there pushing and pulling for all of her women when it was really just the opposite. She was harder on the women, because they had to scratch like she did. Most of us didn't want that. We were managers of people and of technical stuff, and we didn't really relate to any of that. We had never had any problems with it before, and we certainly didn't expect it with her. And so the learning experience was just learning how to get along with her.

Renee's experience is in contrast to Colleen's:

> probably the people that I would look back on as being extremely supportive of me or what I wanted to do—both were females . . . I had the feeling that they were more interested in helping me grow. They're more interested in supporting me. I always had the feeling that I could really go in and talk to them about anything, and they didn't consider it either a bitch session, or whining, or complaining, or anything like that. It's just part of the business. That's the way they dealt with it. If they felt I was wrong, I was told I was wrong. If they wanted it a certain way, they came out and told me that. I always found that men will come out and do that, be that direct with you. . . . it was helpful; it helps you grow.

Direct feedback coupled with high expectations for success in the face of increasing responsibility is cited by women as contributing to their growth. Managers who provide challenging work and supportive confidence help women develop their strengths and self-awareness. Gwen was influenced by a woman manager, who also served as a model for the evolution of her own supervisory style.

> First of all, I think she's a fantastic role model for women . . . very, very bright. And very human. And very supportive of women, in a positive sense, not just because "You're a woman, I support you." Kinds of things that I learned through her are important management skills: Patience, number one, the ability to detach myself somewhat from my subordinates. It's healthier for them and healthier for me. Learning to delegate, very important. She did a lot in that area for me, because I tended to feel that I was putting a burden on my subordinates should I delegate some responsibility. Giving me a lot of visibility . . . broadened my view of [how] I saw this particular function moving. Challenged me to think, "Well, how about putting this in, how would you like to take responsibility for . . ." "I don't know if I can do it." "Sure, you can do it, it's yours," and that kind of thing. So I got a lot of visibility and a lot of exposure, and she just kept channeling me in the right direction just by giving me more and more responsibility and more of my diverse responsibilities.

What contributes to the development of women's managerial talent cannot be distinguished from general principles of effective management apart from gender. What worked for the women of this study would apply as well to men who were becoming managers. Of particular interest here is the process of internal change described by women accustomed to a subordinate self-perception, who were now functioning in a context that granted them authority if they were willing to take it.

Being a Manager

What are these women like as managers? Experiences as subordinates contribute to the development of their own managerial styles; supervisors serve as both positive and negative role models. Jessica, thirty years old and in charge of construction projects for a consumer product chain, provides one example of how women use experience to shape their behavior as managers.

> When I first was thrown in the managerial position, I didn't know anything. . . . I always try to remember what it was like when I was on their side of the desk. What things really turned me off, and what things did I really enjoy? I always try to give [subordinates] as much of the whole picture or the whole segment so that they can claim ownership, so that they will take pride in what they're doing.

Control of the work can be empowering. When people understand the reasons for an assignment and how it fits into the larger work context, they become more willing and effective workers.[22] Delegating means more than merely giving work to others to do; a manager must learn how to delegate so that subordinates are eager to do a good job. A manager of product distribution after eight years with her company, thirty-year-old Carla believes that people's sense of importance is enhanced when they know their work's meaning.

> I do delegate a lot of the work, because we are a very, very busy area, and it changes daily. I try to be as honest with my people as I can. To me that's very important. I try to explain to them the reason for doing things, rather than just say, "Hey, do this." And I say why I'm asking them to do things because nobody likes to be told to do things . . . the importance of it also, how it fits in with what we're trying to do as a department. Give an overview. Tell them the importance of their job.

Some managers go beyond providing reasons for tasks assigned and allow subordinates to contribute to decision making wherever possible. Even when they do not have the authority to choose the task itself, they can actively participate in discussions of how to do it. Currently supervising several former peers, Nina astutely tailors her managing to the nature of her group.

> I've got a strong group that are very strong-minded, very opinionated. . . . It keeps you on your toes . . . it's really very difficult. You don't walk into a meeting and say, "This is this, this, this," without some sort of response from them. So I've learned to be very participative in most things. And they really like that. . . . all I ever have to say is, "Hey guys, remember we met and this is what you decided to do." Well, you know, that was their decision. I found that it really does work, because when they've come up with what they want to do, how they want to approach it, that's what they really put their forces to go do.

Nina does not simply abrogate responsibility for decision making, but her approach is heavily influenced by an understanding of the people she supervises. One could view her as smartly strategic in gearing her style to what is most effective with particular subordinates. Crucial to effective delegating is a manager's ability to match people with assignments. Knowledge of the strengths of each employee and the most beneficial means of communicating with individuals and the group is central to an efficient operation.[23] Nina has been perceived, however, as overly people-oriented.

> some people . . . think I'm much too people-oriented, and I don't think you can be. I'm very sensitive to my people, to their needs. They know me

so they know that I respect them, that I trust them. I have full confidence in them. I always involve them in the decision-making things that they can be involved in; I should say that there are some decisions that I make arbitrarily on my own. But I always involve them in the process so that they buy into the process, because they're the ones that are going to have to ultimately do the job to get it done.

Another manager who relates her style to its context, Monica, a human resources manager for three years, finds supervision on a small scale amenable to individualized assignments. A relatively small number of subordinates enables her to match their strengths with the tasks' requirements.

I have a very personal style with people, and part of that is maybe because I'm not supervising a large group of people. But I get to know my people very well. I learn what turns them on, and I try to give them that kind of responsibility. I know what each of them likes to do, and so I structure the department around their own areas of expertise.

Within a people orientation, work is managed around persons rather than persons managed around work. That is, individuals are central, and knowledge of their personal strengths determines the delegation of aspects of tasks. Many managers are like Teresa in that they attempt to balance their people orientation with the establishment of authority.

My managerial style is participatory. I tend to establish friendships, so to speak, with the people I work with, to a degree. There's just so much of a friend I can be and still maintain the authority and the responsibility that I have to have. But I talk to my people and encourage them to talk to me. And I told them as much as I could tell them about what was going on in the company as a way to help them to understand why they were doing certain things. I never asked them to do anything that I didn't do or wouldn't do. And I never asked them to do anything that I couldn't tell them why we wanted it done. And when I couldn't tell them, I told them, "I can't tell you." I think it's just part of my personality . . . be as honest and open as possible and try and work with [them]. I've always tried not to separate myself from my people in terms of, "I'm the boss, and you're the . . ." And "I'm important, and you're not." I've tried to stay in touch, not to separate or elevate myself in their eyes. I try to be very down-to-earth. You had to establish, "I am the boss." I made sure that was established—but in such a way that I and they could become comfortable with it.

Women who are effective managers can establish their authority while retaining an interpersonal connection with employees that is within the parameters of a professional relationship. Their "people orientation" is in the service of the job; they are primarily concerned with effective managing, and attention to the individuality of their staff serves a task purpose. Further, the term "people orientation" seems to carry several different meanings. For some, it connotes personal knowledge and involvement with subordinates. Others use it with reference to employees' participation in mapping the work and making decisions. It can mean matching tasks to a particular individual's preferences and expertise. Regardless of differences in operational definitions, however, a people orientation almost always implies a manager's awareness of the feelings and predilections that a subordinate position involves. As subordinates themselves, these women sought expansion of responsibility and advancement. As managers, they see their charge as providing opportunities for subordinates' growth as well as fulfilling the company's function. Even those who do not characterize themselves as people-oriented express a commitment to develop their people. Colleen talks about her evolution as manager from one who desired subordinates' affection to one who combines attention to task completion with people promotion. In contrast to Teresa, who has advance-degreed preparation in her company's product, Colleen, postdivorce, worked her way up without degrees in a *Fortune* 500 corporation.

> I know I'm a lot better manager today than I was six years ago. . . . I'm a very task-oriented individual, and I'm goal-oriented. I feel as a manager I'm charged with a responsibility, that of getting the job done. It's also my responsibility as a manager, if the job can't be done, to go back and spell that out. I like helping people to grow. I think a good manager should have somebody, and maybe even more than one, ready to take their job. And I consider it my responsibility as a manager to train my support and help them grow and to get them moving. I don't want to see people sitting in the same job for seven, eight, nine years. I would be bored with something like that, or else you're milking it, one or the other. At least that's been my experience with watching people.

For subordinates to grow, they must be given the opportunity to discover and exercise their abilities. Conditions that generally have been known to foster development of competence include a balance of trust and support. A manager with confidence in a worker's ability can freely delegate while unobtrusively monitoring the safety net. On balance, the manager provides enough instruction and guidance to facilitate an employee's independent accomplishment. Jill, in personnel since her college graduation ten years ago, describes the balance she attempts to achieve:

I have learned from the negative perspective of some managers [who] don't communicate enough, and learned from the individuals who have a very tight hands-on approach. I don't like either. I really like to delegate to my subordinates and certainly know what's going on, but I feel that I allow them to accomplish a task on their own without getting involved where I shouldn't. I think sometimes the balance of training and stepping away is a very difficult one to achieve. I certainly never want them to feel that . . . I'm not interested in what they are doing or that I'm not around to help. But that balance, I have found, is one that takes experience just sorting out— because you want them to develop on their own and achieve what they want to achieve, as well as getting the job done and having it look the way I want it as a manager.

Employees who are accustomed to being closely supervised must learn to make and execute decisions. Marsha finds it necessary to wean her subordinates from a dependence fostered by a previous manager.

the guy before me . . . controlled absolutely everything. He made all the decisions. In my opinion, he didn't give the staff a chance to grow and develop. They had become accustomed to not making decisions, for one, not planning, because he did all the planning. And I'm just the opposite. Basically I feel that I should be there and know what's going on, but I should not be making the decisions. They should come to me with their own opinions, and . . . I'll agree or disagree, and if I disagree, I'll tell them why I disagree. And then we can talk it out. They weren't used to doing that. They were just used to coming to their supervisor saying, "This is the problem; tell me what to do." So that's taken some adjustment.

These managers strive for a balance between arranging conditions to insure success and granting autonomy to workers. They seem to agree that subordinates benefit from a participatory managerial style. Increasing acceptance of this style indicates that organizations are moving toward effective management for both the company and its employees, "a style of *good* management vs. one defined by sex."[24] However, it is not always feasible for employees to control decisions, and since these women pride themselves on honesty and fairness they make no pretense of involving employees when they are not. Abigail, who began to build a career in education and training in her midthirties, credits her employees with performance and strategic abilities that, under her skilled tutelage, produce effective teamwork.

I'm very good at getting other people to do much better work than I can do myself. And they know they're producing much better work than I can do, and they know that I know it. I've had some very real success in building quite effective teams of people. I don't play games. If there are decisions where their input is going to have an impact, they provide it. On the other hand, if it doesn't matter, I don't tease with, "Let's all get together and . . . see this thing through." I don't demand things of people that I don't do myself. I am very quick to respond to their problems, and [I] spend a lot of time troubleshooting. If something is inhibiting their activity, I will attend to it immediately. I'm very structured in my expectations of people. Management a couple of levels above me has been getting requests from people to be assigned to this team because they see it as a professionally growing experience. So that's been nice to see.

Providing opportunity and giving free rein do not suffice to develop people's competence. A manager must function as an overseer, ready to engineer conditions conducive to an employee's effective performance. Moreover, obstacles that hinder success may be anticipated, or at least recognized, so that a manager can clear the way for a subordinate's achievement.

As managers, the women interviewed commonly espouse a philosophy that implies a certain pattern of behavior. First, they arrange conditions that facilitate the development of competence. To insure the continuation of those circumstances, they remain alert to encumbrances that might function to the contrary. They do not wait passively for an employee to raise discussion of a difficulty; they themselves actively troubleshoot. The ensuing mutual knowledge and respect allow them to trust their subordinates to flourish. At base is consistently clear, open, and direct communication initiated by the manager. Whatever the message, subordinates can expect to receive it without bias from managers who are frank and direct like Colleen.

I'm comfortable with [my management style], because I think I'm fair. If somebody needs help, I'm more than willing to give it. I'll provide whatever is needed if it's within my realm to do it. I also have expectations for my people. And I'm usually pretty clear about that. There are no guessing games. When I give a review, no one is surprised, because they've had the prior feedback. They know what the expectations are. And some of the reviews I've had to do are not always so good. But I rely on the facts, and that's what I deal with. I deal with hard facts, not whether I like you or dislike you. I don't deal with that at all. I refuse to. So, good, bad, or indifferent, that's kind of the way it is.

The same process that fosters women's development as managers accounts for their subordinates' progress. They tend to give their people what was most effective for them as workers. What made for their success seems to work for others, who then build productive teams under these women's guidance.

Autonomy within a cooperative effort is vital for these women as workers and as managers. They need and grant independence but not without the support of a vigilant supervisor who monitors progress and problems. Effective functioning as worker and manager requires an objectivity that separates the personal from the professional. They need a reciprocity of trust with their superiors and subordinates. A balance between control and trust is necessary for worker and manager alike.

The past and present context of women's work lives provides a frame of reference for change. Women derive their managerial beliefs and behavior from experiences with their own managers. They use their past experience as subordinates and their previous managerial selves as measures of their own progress. Changes within women are registered in their behavior; awareness of their growth is confirmed by reactions of others.

> I think that I don't get emotionally involved. I'm objective about what I'm doing now. And everything isn't life and death. It isn't as if I have to convince everybody; also, things don't have to be my way. I don't have to win every time now. I'm not in competition with the whole world. And . . . people like to work for me.

Hope is calm and content with herself, and others are drawn to her as a manager. In relation to herself and to her company, she is successful.

□ II □

PERSONAL
DEVELOPMENT

The first part of this book was devoted to the professional development of women at work. We examined the work lives of forty women who had been identified as managers or potential managers by their corporations. Through interview data, we learned about their early interest in work and how that materialized in the development of business careers. Even in the absence of explicit career planning, these women demonstrated the ability and inclination to climb the corporate ladder. As they made their way from uncertain beginnings to a corporate career, we traced the interaction between their psychological processing of events and contextual influence.

In tracing women's progress in business, we used their testimony as focal point. Our information came from their own words; their perceptions served as our source. With access to their private conceptions, their introspective analyses, we gleaned how they processed what was happening to them. Thus, we learned about women's development in corporate contexts from their own constructions of meaning; the sense that they made of events and relationships brought new substance to our knowledge of women in business. Moreover, the internal vantage point allowed us an important view of the process of female psychological development as it is linked to social change.

In Part 2 we again use women's understandings of their lives as our primary source of knowledge. Here our subject matter is the personal, rather than the professional. A distinct dichotomy between these two realms of being is not totally

95

possible. Since interviews occurred within the context of participation in a management program, women's orientation was professional; they expected to be queried about their careers. Their responses to questions of a personal nature were ample but frequently were made with reference to a professional context. They might, for example, talk about changes in themselves and then relate those changes to their work environments or describe the impact of personal change on their careers. The nature and timing of our interviews were not amenable to obtaining complete personal histories, but the women's generosity with information about themselves allowed compilation of personal data of significant import.

Women were asked about themselves and their families of origin and procreation. How might they have been influenced by their original and current families? Has their career development been related to family background? What changes have they seen in themselves in a year's time? How might they describe their perspectives on the future; have they changed between the first and second interviews? Women's responses to these questions and to inquiries pursuant to voluntary personal disclosures provide the data for the chapters in this section. An examination of women's reflections upon themselves, their families, marriage, and children serves to further our understanding of their professional and personal development.

□ 5 □

Self

Women's accounts of their professional development are replete with references to the self. When they talk about their relation to work and how their careers unfolded, they naturally talk about themselves. In actuality, women's self-development is the topic of this entire volume. In Part 1, their self-disclosures formed the underside of a text whose main theme was work. Here we look at the self more squarely in its own right.

Information about women's self-development comes from interviews that were centered primarily on career. What we learn about the women themselves is drawn, therefore, from both direct and indirect responses. They were explicitly questioned about self-perception, especially with reference to experienced change. Additionally, they offered observations about personal characteristics, internal dynamics, and interpersonal behavior in conjunction with responses to a variety of other questions. All self-expression was welcome, and this chapter represents its compilation regardless of contextual source.

Women discuss aspects of themselves that are ostensibly most related to functioning in the workplace. Ambition, achievement needs, and notions of what constitutes success have apparent connections to work and to the development of a career. Although self-assertion and confidence are discussed within a context of professional growth, women readily acknowledge their wider ramifications. In fact, their reflections about personal attributes are often more broadly drawn than the confines of work might dictate. These women recognize that personal qualities contribute to professional development. Moreover, work experience can change an individual's attributes.

The idea that individual characteristics can be significantly modified through learning, experience, or various forms of changed consciousness runs contrary to trait theory, the traditional psychological understanding of personality.[1] Trait theory holds that an individual's personality, in place at an early age, is composed of enduring, relatively fixed attributes whose consistency warrants the appellation "traits."[2] In contrast, a more contextual view of personality formation and change holds that personal characteristics, displayed through behavior, can vary considerably across time and situational demands.[3] Personality can be understood as highly malleable in response to new learning and changing contexts over the course of development that continues through adulthood. Contemporary American women, for example, have displayed significant change in their perceptions of self and prospects for life direction commensurate with the current women's movement.[4]

Individual psychological change, then, can be prompted by the larger social context as well as by the conditions of one's personal life. In either case, women display diverse attributes, some conventionally associated with their gender, some not. Just as we can no longer portray women in stereotypic ways, we also cannot uniformly characterize women in similar career positions, as this would simply be trading old stereotypes for new.

An examination of the personal characteristics of women interviewed provides lucid evidence of individual variation. Women with equally impressive professional accomplishments express divergent views of themselves. A uniform description cannot be applied accurately to them. We do not find here a picture of an "organization woman" that would lend itself to generalizations.[5] We see instead a fascinating collection of people with different personal styles and attributes.

In this chapter we will look at the various ways women characterize themselves in relation to achievement and ambition as well as how they view success. Our guide is always their initiation of topics, and we find them frequently addressing questions of self-assertion and confidence. Finally, we will turn our attention to women's experience of change within themselves.

Achievement

In the chapters on work and mobility, a common sentiment among those interviewed was a desire for challenging and interesting work. Women frequently did not have a specific path planned for their careers, but they knew that they could not tolerate a position that became boring. Boredom was synonymous with comfort for many who found themselves moving out of a position prior to feeling complete mastery of it. Though reluctant to sacrifice learning for advancement, they could not turn down opportunity. New positions may or may not have represented promotions, but they certainly meant exciting challenges.

Management women's drive for mastery through new learning and their commensurately low tolerance for boredom are common findings.[6] Some theorize that this characteristically female orientation is responsible for women's ultimate disappointment with corporate employment, which is not structured to recognize and reward individual excellence.[7] Other authors contradict this notion and provide evidence of corporations' seeking and promoting people who exhibit high internal motivation for achievement in relation to the work itself.[8] Moreover, women are found to value and be motivated by many of the same job elements pursued by men.[9] There is considerable evidence that male and female high achievers, who are more psychologically alike than different, are concerned with both people and production.[10] Moreover, rather than being preoccupied with themselves or their status, high-achieving managers of both sexes are conspicuous by their concentration and investment in the work itself.[11]

Women of this study overcame their initial fears and repeatedly proved their capabilities with each assignment. In the process, they learned about themselves. These women became increasingly aware of how much they could do and how much they needed to feel gratified. A drive to do and be more, what psychologists call need for achievement, can exist even before a woman is fully conscious of it.[12] Through observation and experience, women like thirty-year-old Jessica, who has held five positions in six years, discover inherent needs that set them apart from others.

> There are people out there who are perfectly content with very run-of-the-mill, I hesitate to use the word "mundane," but they're just up to a level. They're working at their little peak or whatever, and they're perfectly content to stay there, and I'm not. And I have realized that I'm

different from a lot of those women. I think that was a long time coming for me.

Interaction with a social context can precipitate an individual's self-discovery. Watching her own and others' behavior at work precipitated Jessica's recognition of a quality unique to her. It is likely that her inner drive existed prior to her consciousness of it. But, then, articulation of a personal insight serves to consolidate its place within one's self-image. Once recognition of an individual characteristic occurs, understanding of self and others is enhanced. Jessica elaborates on the delineation of herself from others.

> [*What makes you different?*] I would think some of it is more education. I think another part of it is . . . there's something inside me that drives me. I think another thing is the desire to be challenged whereas they don't have that desire to be challenged. The desire to accomplish things in a business atmosphere that some of these other women don't have. It's been a very positive thing.

Lisa's realization that she was underemployed in her current company was confirmed through exposure to other women managers and their companies. She also distinguishes herself from other workers at her job.[13] She has not always been reconciled to differences in motivation among people, but she now accepts that others do not necessarily share her conscientiousness or achievement needs. She has adopted a purely pragmatic attitude of caring mainly about the work's accomplishment.

> I've changed in the sense that I now accept the fact that people are working for different reasons. They will not all be like me. They will not have the same drives I have. And that's perfectly okay. I think there was a time when I thought it wasn't okay. It's okay as long as the job is done.

The primary motivation for these women is not something external to them. Both women and men rank intrinsic factors of achievement, advancement, growth in skill, responsibility, and the job itself as more important than such extrinsic factors as status, salary, job security, working conditions, quality of supervision, and co-workers. In Part 1 we saw that women were not urged on by money, title, and position; these received attention only when conspicuously absent relative to the magnitude of effort and accomplishment. Rather, it is an inner drive or need to achieve in a continuous way that accounts for women's striving and mobility.[14] If they reach a point of coasting in a job, they become wary and restless. Though happily married and looking forward to starting a family at some future date, Mary claimed, in chapter 1, that she identifies most with her work accomplishments. Climbing up through four technical positions in as many years, she ascribes her achievement needs to internal standards of success that are independent of others.

> I was always looking ahead. It seemed very odd, because I was driven with the idea of moving ahead quickly. I continually wanted to be challenged, and I found myself mastering these jobs very quickly, very quickly wanting to move on to something else. Almost instilled this . . . sense of failure myself if I wasn't following this predetermined path in my head of what I should be doing.

Esther is another who monitors her progress against some internally constructed criterion. While others in their fifties might be coasting into retirement, Esther looks forward to making the next decade as productive as possible.

> I think I'm challenged by myself more than I am by other people. But I need an atmosphere in which things are churning. I don't like time. I equate the passage of time with progress. I feel as though if I've lived a year and haven't done something new or progressed a step, that it's a terrible waste. I don't know whether that's good or bad or not, but it's very much a part of my makeup.

Heidi's main source of motivation is her own sense of accomplishment, which is considerable as she moves from sales to management of an entire region for a growing manufacturing firm.

> I'm not as strongly motivated by the competitive aspect as I am just from the self-accomplishment. . . . I'm competing against myself, really. I don't think of it as competing; I just think of it as doing the best I can.

Such high levels of self-reliance and self-directedness do not necessarily imply greater competitiveness, but rather heightened achievement orientation.[15]

Thus, women display motives and achievement needs for work that have customarily been associated with men. Women of this study do not appear to be troubled by these motives; that is, they are not at odds with some other abiding aspect of themselves that would seek interpersonal connection or suppression of success as a primary force.[16] Carol Gilligan's descriptive theory would have women's development characterized by interpersonal connection and men's by independent achievement. We will see in chapter 8 that women of this study could be characterized by both, but in different settings. This kind of separation has been associated more with male functioning than with female, although it would make sense that females in heretofore male roles would function similarly. Spurred on by internal standards of achievement, these women clearly seek work that offers stimulation and challenge. Previous accomplishments have barely settled when they begin to look for the next source of achievement.

Risk

The other side of challenge is risk. With each new undertaking, women's success is potentially threatened.

> It didn't take me very long to come to the realization that, relatively speaking, I know a lot about what's going on in the corporation. You think, "Hey, I've got all these years ahead of me, and I'm already that far, and if I'm already that far, man, the sky's the limit." The positive is the sky is the limit. The negative is, "What if I can't make it? What if I can't do it?"

Wide corporate exposure allows Jessica substantial learning about the company and about her potential within it. By analyzing her path to date, she sees what is feasible for her future. The prospects both excite and frighten her. Nonetheless, it is likely that she will seize opportunity rather than shy away from it. Women are aware of the risks that mobility entails, but ultimately the urge to do and be more captures them. By her midthirties, Jill had worked for three different companies before joining her current employer, a firm that began with a consumer product and has since diversified. Jill's story illustrates the pull between risk and security.

> I remember envisioning that there is a big world out there and there must be an awful lot to learn. Although I had learned an awful lot in the time I was with [a previous employer], I thought the opportunities and growth have got to be greater in a large organization. I remember one individual talking to me about this—who had been with the company about fifteen years at that point, and he is still with them, and I'm sure will be with the company until he retires—saying, "You can't learn any more out there than you can here. We have such a great staff and such a great organization, we are so solid, that why take that risk? Why go out there? You could work for a major company and they could sell the division and you'd be out of a job." He was trying to discourage me from taking that step, and I decided that I really had to take the step, that even though it was still early in my career I could risk that situation if it didn't work out. I couldn't limit myself, the way he had, to one product company for a career and be satisfied with that limitation. So I left.

It was not unhappiness with the first company that prompted Jill's restlessness. Her curiosity and need for learning without the structural limitations imposed by a small organization weighed heavily in her decision to change companies. The risk of change was preferable to feeling that her opportunities and potential for growth were limited.

Women assess their prospects for fulfillment in relation to the particular company that employs them. They recognize the need to achieve within themselves, and the way they work is testimony to that need. Hence, its chances of being met are a function of the company context as well as of the person. Individual efforts notwithstanding, a company must provide recognition and opportunity for these women who analyze the consonance between their career needs and what is offered and valued by particular organizations.[17] Aware of her inner drive, Carla had to demonstrate her seriousness to the company. Her credibility was particularly tested in light of her youth and the fact that she was working in a traditionally male, natural resources industry in a less progressive part of the country.

> At first it was just proving to people that you were serious about a career, serious that you did want to work and you did want to continue in a job. I was single at the time. Everybody kind of takes you to be, "Oh, she's cute and everything but so what?" [In my mind I knew that] I can still be friendly, and I can still have very good friendship relationships with these people, but they have to know I'm serious . . . and it was just learning how "to live," quote, unquote, in an organization, because you do have to live there. You spend a major portion of your waking hours at your job.

Learning the culture of an organization and what it might offer is crucial for women who need to achieve. They may be fully cognizant of their own needs, but for satisfaction to prevail the organization must cooperate in continuing to meet those needs. Whether or not high achievement will bring the conventional rewards of success depends largely upon the organizational environment. "If the environment within which an achieving woman manager performs does not encourage (and reward) achieving behavior, she will find it difficult to succeed."[18] It is, therefore, the interaction between individual characteristics and the context of their occurrence that is pivotal. It is not simply a case of women's proclivities for satisfaction from the work itself, for mastery through new learning, being naively inappropriate within the corporate world. Rather, it is the fit between their individual propensities and those of a corporation to value them tangibly.

Thus, in both Part 1 and here we have seen women who manifest considerable achievement motivation. For some, this is functional across contexts and therefore seems inherent. For others, it develops in conjunction with an interest in work. It is not necessarily the case, however, that women have so much invested in the task that they fail to attend to the politics and pragmatics of corporate promotion.

Because most women of this study did not grow up with a career path in mind, they may have begun their corporate employ at a different stage of vocational development than many men and young women today.[19] Their being at the "exploration" rather than the "establishment" stage could account for these women's initial eagerness and investment in the work itself; it would be erroneous, however, to take what appears to be a sole preoccupation at face value. While learning about themselves in relation to this kind of achievement, they are simultaneously learning about the business in general and their corporation in particular. The fit between their needs for achievement and the opportunities offered by their employers is carefully monitored by the women of this study.

Women can and do move when the organization does not foster or recognize their accomplishments. Although their emphasis may be on achievement in relation to the work itself, women of this study simultaneously keep an eye on their vertical paths within an organization.[20] For them, satisfaction through the work and advancement in the company are linked. Although accomplishment of the task at hand is motivating, it alone cannot sustain achievement-oriented women who desire the challenge of new tasks that inevitably imply risk as well as career progression.[21]

Ambition

A distinction between achievement and ambition unfolds in our interviews. Articulated or not, women without exception demonstrate high achievement needs. Their initiative and diligence on the job, their willingness to do more than required, and their eagerness for new learning all attest to their strong achievement orientation. For all, an internal sense of accomplishment served as guide and motivation along their career paths. External and material trappings were secondary.

Ambition, in terms of a desire to climb the corporate ladder, was not a consistent part of the women's profile. Some were definitely aimed at moving up. For Monica, achievement is coupled with ambition. She has worked for the same conglomerate since college graduation nine years ago, at first as a secretary and later as a manager. Her management responsibilities began three years ago, shortly after receipt of a relevant advanced degree.

> A career is very important to me. I'm very achievement-oriented; that's a very important part of my life. I look at things now, and if something doesn't happen in two or three years I'm not going to sit here and and just say, "This is it." The thought of doing what I'm doing now for more than two or three years would be very boring to me. So to move up a corporate ladder is very important.

Others, like Dorothy, have a different notion of ambition. Older, with fewer degrees, and with a slightly lower level of responsibility than Monica, Dorothy's remarks reflect a more exploratory mode.

> I'm ambitious to use my potential; I am not ambitious just to climb the corporate ladder. I don't know yet quite where that is.

They may be uncertain about what direction to take for fulfillment, but they know satisfaction stems from functioning at the peak of their ability.[22] Holding a high corporate position does not necessarily guarantee gratification of internal achievement needs. In fact, Teresa associates upper-level positions in her company with unwanted stress. Equipped with a graduate degree, she has climbed five steps in product development with the same chemical company over an eight-year period.

> The point that I'm in now is just a gradual slope up. It's not a steep fast track, fast pace, ambitious, because I'm not that. I can see myself going one to two levels higher than where I am now and feel very comfortable with it, because as far as I can tell from my perspective, the higher you go up, the more responsibility, and the aggravation is there. I don't want that . . . I don't want to struggle anymore. I will do what I have to do to do a good job and to get rewarded for it. But I'm not looking to be the [top].

Knowing more about what she rejects than what she wants, Elena plans to reflect upon future possibilities.

> I don't have an overwhelming ambition to be president of the company or to necessarily move to every higher position. There are some things I don't want to do. I'm not sure of what I want to do and how I want to do it. But that's okay too. I've been pushing very hard for the last five, six years, and comes a time when you have to take some time out, figure out what it is you want to do.

The reflections of these women reveal that they are at different phases in relation to their career paths. Some have settled for themselves the nature and breadth of their goals; others are still exploring the fit between their work needs and what might be available to them within the corporation. A period of diligence may be followed by consolidation and further consideration of the extent of their own ambition. Women can reach a point in their careers where they are not necessarily striving for the next step, yet they feel content with the level of their accomplishment. Linda describes such a balance, now that she has been recognized for her four successful years in sales.

> I think [it's] just being in a position where I don't feel I have to be constantly reaching and striving for something else. I'm competent at my job, and I feel that competency. So that's sort of resolved: You don't go to work every day saying, "God, am I going to be able to get through this problem?" You have a set of experiences that you can bring to bear now and feel comfortable about those situations. It's not a constant learning thing as it was for a long time. . . . I spent so much effort on that, and I think just that balance and having that experience . . . allows you to refocus so when you go to work you're at work, and when you go home you're able to focus on some other things.

Ostensibly, high achievement need would imply ambition in terms of traditionally observable benchmarks. That is, we might reasonably expect women with strong urges toward growth and advancement to aspire to title and position. Certainly, these women want acknowledgment of their worth and accomplishments from their employers. Recognition does not always take the form of ever-escalating promotion, however. Criteria for success show the variability that characterized ambition.

Success

Women's ideas of success were almost always bilateral, referring to both internal and external criteria. Colleen's idea of success refers more to internal criteria. This may be because she came to a career later, after marriage and children, and has not been at it that long; also, the size of her *Fortune* 500 corporation may make the top even more remote.

> I don't care about being president of the corporation. That's nothing that turns me on. I'm more interested in really being happy with what I'm doing and feeling as though I'm contributing. That's how I view success.

Promotion and financial reward may be necessary, but they are not sufficient for these women. Doing worthwhile work and being significant contributors to an organization are important ingredients of success for them.

An internal drive that is manifested in reliable and remarkable productivity sets these women apart. They stand out in relation to peers and colleagues because of their effort and effectiveness. Employers notice the results of their labors and come to depend upon their consistency. Having opportunity is only a beginning; it is what women do with it that makes for their success.

Women attribute their success to hard work, dependable and timely production, and connections with people in the organization. The way they work almost insures visibility upon which they can capitalize. Bonnie, for example, used her earlier positions in the company to maximize learning about various corporate functions and the people connected to those functions. Her association with those people contributes to her success in subsequent company sales roles, when she must meet the demands of customers.

> I hired in at the corporate office, had all the very important people around me . . . and they have now moved on into different areas of the company. But I have that base with all those people . . . and it's really helped a lot. Not only has it helped me in terms of knowing people, but just learning the job, too. Now, if I need some assistance in that area, I know just whom to go and ask. I know how to get these people.

Despite variation in ambition, women realize the importance of putting themselves forward within the corporate context. Their noteworthy performance enhances their visibility, which in turn can yield greater opportunity. Once they have opportunity, these women know how to make something of it. No matter what their ambition, they must be thinking about and asserting themselves to secure intriguing work. Contrary to traditional notions of a female orientation to others before self, thirty-one-year-old Connie, one of the most accomplished executives of this study, attributes her success to putting self first.

> I'd always been very willing to do what is best for me and always put myself first. [In deciding about a job change, at first] what's best for me wasn't number one, because this [other job] was clearly best for me. I don't know why I was starting to play with "Well, what's best for my husband, what's best for [the company], what's best for my staff—how can I leave them?" . . . I don't know why I didn't put myself first, but [then] I stopped for a minute and leveled myself and started to think, "Well, what has happened to your career? And the reason that you've moved is that you've always been able to put yourself first." That influenced my decision.

The process that Connie describes illustrates the importance of context in shaping one's thoughts and decisions. Though women may be inclined toward connectedness, attachment, and nurturance in interpersonal relationships, they are equally able to adopt a different orientation in matters of work and advancement. In considering a career move that meant a substantial leap up the ladder, Connie found herself thinking about others first and then realizing that that was not the mode that had served her best professional interests to date.[23] If the primacy of interpersonal connectedness were generalized to women in all situations, that could become a "trait," which then dictates and confines who and what women are and can be. Without exception, women of this study do not confuse business considerations with those of an interpersonal nature (see chapter 8 for more on this). This is one of the few generalizations that we can make about these women.

Notions of success, however, follow the more common path of diversity here. Women vary in their criteria for what constitutes success. Some clearly and unequivocally want the traditional rewards and recognition offered by corporate careers; however, these are the minority here and in other studies.[24] More frequently, we hear women talking about intrinsic standards for success, those associated with personal satisfaction from the work and the quality of one's performance as well as the meaningfulness of contribution to the company.

Does this confirm Hardesty and Jacobs's analysis that women, unlike men, become hooked on individual goals of learning, mastery, and personal growth to their ultimate disappointment and spiritual demise within corporate settings that reward politics, not performance? Few women of this study expressed this kind of disillusionment, but it is possible that they had not yet progressed enough in their careers to have reached that plateau.[25] Perhaps women deny a desire for the traditional success of high executive position because they know that structural conditions continue to preclude their attainment. Or perhaps, as Hardesty and Jacobs suggest, women whose values remain incompatible with those of the corporate world know that they still do not fit and choose to occupy a compromise position. Or, finally, it may be that these sentiments are simply another extension of women's consistent tendency to underestimate their abilities, performance expectancies, and prospects.[26]

None of these explanations wholly accounts for what women of this study have said. Their awareness of their own capabilities and corresponding high expectations for further achievement contradict the notion of underestimation of ability and performance expectancy. Their testimony does not yet have the ring of compromise, as they seem to continue to strive to be and do more in the workplace. Feasible explanations include the idea that these women have not yet reached the level of disillusionment, or that awareness of structural obstacles keeps women from striving for what is still the impossible. A certain amount of time in corporate management has been associated with promotion to top positions; these women had not yet served that time.[27]

The stages of women's progress in corporations are reflected by the different themes depicted in the literature over the last decade. When they were entering and establishing themselves, advice and analyses centered on overcoming personal and structural obstacles to achieving managerial rank. At the close of the decade, the literature is replete with examination of obstacles to women's assumption of the highest executive positions.[28] Whether the majority of women, or men, for that matter, actually aspire to the upper echelons, the opportunity should be equally available to them.

It may be that, as outsiders still not totally assimilated within the corporate world, women do not readily adopt its norms and standards. Maintaining their own standards contributes to an integrity of self that has customarily been marked by a balance between internal criteria and external conditions. Several women articulate an unwillingness to climb the corporate ladder as it currently exists, with its attendant stress and consuming demands. Simultaneously, we are seeing a change in corporations' criteria for success and its rewards, as recent management experts call for an emphasis on the very standards of achievement exemplified by the women of this study.[29]

Self-assertion

Women recognize the need to promote themselves for the sake of career success, however that is defined. Characteristics commonly cited as necessary for corporate success include firmness, decisiveness, assertiveness, and an ability to calculate risks; these are necessary for both women and men.[30] When assertiveness was not a salient part of their personal repertoire, high achievement motivation required its development within the professional context.

The women interviewed display variation in their personal characteristics in conjunction with a context's requirements. Interpersonal sensitivity, as opposed to the primacy of self, can be a disadvantage in the corporate setting. Young, degreed and highly accomplished in financial operations, Marie is tough-minded about the company's money matters but believes that her caring about others can interfere with professional effectiveness.

> Probably the biggest difficulty, I would say, is learning how to be a stronger person in terms of directing other people and persuading them to do what you know has to get done. It's more than persuading, though; it's more a kind of taking a very strong stand on something. I know that one of my shortcomings is that I don't like to be very forceful with people. And in my position I have to be. At times it grates on me that I have to do that. Probably my personality has a lot to do with this—a sensitive person, feeling and considerate of other persons' feelings almost to a fault at times . . . and that makes it a little difficult in the business world. So that's something that I have to work on: to be thinking about me and what I have to do a little bit more than about everybody else's feelings.

In the first interview, Marie diagnosed obstacles within herself that could work to her professional detriment. A year later, a transformation was well underway. Perhaps part of the process of change is articulation of the need for it. It is likely that change has already begun by the time it is talked about. At the second interview, Marie offers a different description of herself:

> I've probably become more assertive in what I've been doing. [I'm] making a lot more decisions and really sticking with them and carrying them through to whoever I decided I had to carry them through to. I just made the decision that, well okay, you've got to do what you've got to do. You know, really kind of screw everybody else. You just have to tell everybody what you do and why you do it and why it's important to them, and then they have to develop some sort of confidence in you. So that takes a little bit of a while.

An anecdote depicts behavior that vividly illustrates changes in the self. By separating the personal from the professional, Marie was able to preserve a working relationship to her own and another's benefit.

> I had one situation where I was dealing with [someone who was not] accustomed to having to deal with me. There was something that had been a big issue. He was very taken aback that I would call him on the carpet. I said to him, "Well look, I don't know what the problem is here, but if you don't like me that's just too bad, because I don't really care whether you like me or not. We have to work together. I understand where there might be reasons why you might not care for me. I don't really care whether you do; you shouldn't care whether I like you." I think he was shocked that I would confront him, and that I would even say to him, "Maybe you don't like me." I think it showed him that maybe I had a little bit more guts than he gave me credit for. And maybe I had something to say. So that has been working out just terrifically ever since.

Marie's retrospective analysis of her strategies and why they were effective is illuminating. Paradoxically, knowledge of her colleague's personal background precipitated her adoption of a purely professional attitude. Through her assertiveness, Marie was able to preserve a positive working and interpersonal relationship. The change in her, however, has ramifications that reach beyond the immediate situation described. Her professional functioning has generally been enhanced. Most crucially, Marie's perception of herself has been revised.

> I figured he probably thought that I just didn't have the guts or the balls to do it. So I said, "Well, I've got to show him that I do." That's the only way . . . that I would get any respect from him, to show him that I could be as tough as he could be and that I wasn't going to sit there and start to cry because he didn't like me or anything like that. That's what made me decide to handle it that way, because I knew the type of personality that he was. And it's worked out really well; we get along very well. He calls me for advice on a lot of situations now. In that particular case, I was able to gain somebody's respect, [which] I would have totally lost otherwise. If I had remained quiet and docile, he would have never developed any respect for me, and I would have never been part of his organization, [or been] able to work with him at all. So, it's helped me a lot to function in my job. It's probably helped me gain a lot of respect for myself, too.

Change in what seems to be a singular personal dimension can have considerably larger significance. Although the nature of work may present the initial need for change, a person must be internally predisposed to it. In the case of assertiveness, a certain degree of belief in oneself and one's position is requisite to the risk of public disclosure. To subject to public scrutiny one's heretofore private views on matters of mutual concern requires confidence in oneself and in the justifiability of one's position.

Once change is begun, it reverberates back to the person. When an individual is moved to behave differently, others ordinarily notice and react. Those reactions can serve to shape further change in the individual. Thus, a dynamic interaction occurs whereby individual change elicits responses that can affect the direction of further change. This process is described by Marie:

> I've become more argumentative. . . . I was not argumentative at all before. If somebody said, "Oh I don't agree with you," I'd say, "Okay," and walk away. But I've become more assertive, more aggressive, more determined to stand up for what I believe in, even on very simple issues. People have mentioned it to me, and they thought it was great that I had become so much more aggressive, or assertive, or demanding in a sense. And I

don't think it was really a conscious decision that I made. I didn't say, "Well, this is something that I have to do." It's just evolved, and I suddenly noticed it in myself, and then when people started mentioning it to me, I said, "Oh my God, I think I had better quiet down a little bit." But they were really encouraging in that they said: "I think it's great; I think you should keep on doing whatever you're doing." That has made me feel a lot better also, because I have the type of job where I have to do that. . . . I can't be wishy-washy; I have to stick to my guns. And I think it has helped a lot.

Marie disclaims a conscious decision to become more assertive. To what does she attribute the change? The initial prompt comes from the job's requirements, but her self-assertion is reinforced and sustained by the immediate and the larger social milieux. Her assertiveness evokes positive reactions from those in her environment, and it facilitates her work. Further, she feels more general acceptance on a larger scale for being an assertive woman. When asked to what she attributed the change, Marie replied:

Partially, just out of necessity, because of my job. I really had to [be assertive] in this current job; it was either "do or die." If you didn't speak up and say what you had on your mind, then you would just drown. So that, I'm sure, is a big part of it. Society in general, I guess; it is becoming a lot more accepted for a woman to be in a middle management . . . position; . . . people don't look at you as strangely as they used to. You don't get that reaction anymore; people don't think it's strange for a woman to be in a position like that.

Other women have found themselves in environments that required them to assert themselves, perhaps more than they ordinarily would. A new position commonly calls for proving and establishing oneself. Given their considerable mobility, we might expect these women to be well versed in that situation. Jill, who had taken the risk of moving to a larger organization, now asserts herself as she assumes a controversial managerial position.

I realized that I was going to have to be much more assertive perhaps than I had been in the past. I had never gone into an environment that was mixed in terms of degree of welcome. I'd always had certain support. At first, I thought, "Oh dear, I don't know that I can do this." But I realized, of course, that [others], in different phases of their career, are in these conflict situations; why should I not be faced with it? [That realization] in essence turned . . . what I saw as something that caused a lot of anxiety into a challenge. [I] decided I was just going to do the best I could and take each day as it came and let the chips fall where they may. And [I] started to build a real enthusiasm and energy to try and show some of those other individuals that they were wrong.

The power of self-conviction and determination is strong in these women. In a sense their self-assertion extends not only to other people but also within themselves. On some level they assess an environment's requirements and how they will meet them. That process involves a degree of assertiveness even before their attitude and plans are operationalized.

The internal power of the women is, of course, pivotal, but their environments also work to influence them in various ways. A hostile environment can represent a challenge; an encouraging one can consolidate a woman's growing assertiveness. A woman's workplace can also provide examples of desirable behavior. Stella, who felt herself to be at a standstill in her career, finds models to emulate in her organization and other social groups.

> Exposure, and it's mostly women. There have been a couple of women they've brought into [the company] who are just super. I tend to be so gentle about hurting people's feelings; they're not nasty, but they have a way of expressing their opinion and getting their ideas across very firmly. And I really have learned from that. It's not just the people at work; there's been a couple of people at church. Just being around them, I think, has really helped me. It's not bad if you don't agree with somebody, whereas I always felt, "Oh, I don't really agree with that; I'm not going to say anything." I just wasn't exposed to people that much, or maybe I didn't let myself be exposed to people like that that much.

There is a certain state of readiness that precedes change. Exposure to sources of influence alone does not suffice to precipitate change. Personal receptivity must be part of the equation of developmental progress.

Thus, women develop assertiveness in relation to their environments. Personal growth and professional development interact and influence each other. The context of work, its requirements and actors, can foster and reinforce individual change. That change becomes part of the person not only in behavior but also in the enduring sense of self. In turn, personal change can revise professional relationships and enhance competence.

Confidence

Self-assertion implies confidence.[31] To declare oneself publicly in situations where it makes a difference is a risk. It involves putting oneself on the line with regard to personal acceptability and, in the case of these women, career continuity. However, to remain unassertive is perhaps a greater risk, since their work requires assertiveness. Although the work environment may instigate assertion's development, the women interviewed quickly discover the personal and professional advantages that self-declaration offers. Their effectiveness with tasks and people increases, and their self-images change for the better. They become more confident.[32]

What makes these women successful is a combination of competence, confidence, and self-assertion. We have seen how their approach to work, meticulous and responsible, contributes to their visibility and consequent opportunities within corporations. For opportunity to be made available to them, women's competence has to be noticed. Thus, they promote themselves and their capabilities; they must be assertive in order to accomplish the task at hand and to advance to others. For them to engage in the process just described, women have to believe in themselves and their abilities. They must have self-confidence. Being competent and not confident is insufficient, according to Dorothy, who earlier voiced uncertainty about her career path:

> I never really feel, until I've done the job for a long time, fully competent in what I'm doing. Or maybe it's not competent as much as confident. Competent yes, but confidence no. The lack of confidence—I think that has been the single most debilitating thing in my career.[33]

The sense one makes of experience, how it is interpreted to oneself, shapes not only its meaning but also its import. Although Dorothy had evidence of her ability, she was not able to incorporate it into an image of a capable self until she reached a point where experience combined with her readiness to do so.

> I think I have spent in my past an awful lot of time thinking I couldn't do it, or thinking I wouldn't be any good at it, or thinking I wouldn't like it, or something—even though I had examples [to the contrary]. But this particular experience . . . really helped me focus in on "Yeah, I do like it, and I am good at it." And maybe [that] just took me over a hump.

How do these women develop confidence in themselves? Their assertiveness grew through interaction with people and contexts that encouraged and reinforced it. Therefore, it is not surprising to find women's self-confidence developing as a function of experience and exposure to others' belief in their competence. Traditionally, there has been an emphasis on background factors in childhood and the early formation of self-concept in understanding people's career aspiration and choice. However, these formative factors may be less important as predictors of success when an individual's self-concept, needs, and values are modified by job experience.[34]

A sense of competence comes with task mastery. Each assignment successfully completed contributes to one's feeling competent and enhances confidence for the next undertaking. Nonetheless, new positions also evoke uncertainty. People do not necessarily know what they can do until they have done it. Dorothy summarizes a process that typifies many women interviewed:

> every time I've been put into a situation of organizing or running or managing something, it's always been preceded by fear, followed by an enormous effort, and then a lot of success.

It is not unusual to doubt one's ability to perform a certain task in the face of no evidence to the contrary. However, doubts are replaced by discoveries as women accept new challenges. The support and faith of a superior can facilitate a woman's explorations. Several women recall their confidence being boosted by employers whose belief in them preceded their own. A boss assumed what for Betty was still to be learned:

> The man I worked for started me doing things that I really didn't know I could do. He just assumed that I would do them, and I did them.

With another's encouragement, Connie, one of the highest-level managers of this study, learned to trust her own intuitions even when they were not yet supported empirically.

> I learned to have more confidence in my hunches, which I always assumed had to be proven before I went out and did something about it. It was really because this president and I worked very closely together, and he encouraged me more and more to "go with it if that's what you think. Do it." So I did—and more and more confidence.

A manager helped Heidi, who moved from sales to regional manager, to overcome self-doubt:

> The woman who hired me . . . gave me a lot of support, and she was in a management position at the time. I had very little self-confidence at that point, and she established and kept building the confidence in myself.

The person who hired her was an important figure for Beverly also. Just the fact of being hired can convey confidence in a woman's ability. Relatively new to the profit sector, Beverly manages a human resources area in a traditionally male transportation industry.

My boss, who was the one that had faith enough to hire me, kept saying, "Sure you can do it." He managed somehow to balance the challenges to me with the security of not pushing me so fast that I really did flub up. He managed to keep stretching me without ever giving me more than I could handle, and that was extremely important.

An experienced person's faith in a novice's potential is an important initial building block. Further, how that faith is registered can be critical to an employee's development. The balance that Beverly describes is fundamental to learning and accomplishment. A good manager assesses the employee's capacity for new material and paces its presentation to challenge but not to overwhelm or defeat.[35]

Even when women are confident about their job performance, they can be helped to see the significance of their work to the organization. Presumably in a position to see how the pieces fit together, a manager can communicate the meaning of an employee's part of the work to her. Under her manager's tutelage, Sharon's work gains larger meaning within the personnel area.

From my most recent manager what I received was a very genuine self-confidence—I think I always had self-confidence, in knowing that what I was doing was good, but he gave me the confidence that the organization's really interested in what you're doing. And he put a real value on what was important.

A previous manager's influence can remain vital and instructive across years of a woman's experience. Ursula, now in industrial sales, still carries with her an early manager's positive example.

There were many good things about our working relationship. He was a very positive person. I tended to go to him with with problems, and he was always able to turn any negative I came with to a positive. I now do a lot of the things that he told me I ought to think about doing there. He had a way of building on your strength. . . . And I've been in a situation . . . where people don't do that. [Now I am] able to stand back and say, "Wait a minute; who's saying this negative thing?" And start thinking about my strengths, and not let one person's opinion or one situation devastate me like it might have before. He was a very positive influence in that way.

Several factors contribute to the growth of confidence. A superior's belief in a woman's potential can begin a process of her self-discovery. Managerial support that balances guidance with license allows women to learn about their own abilities as well as the task at hand. Their competencies multiply, and their confidence increases. Through observation of their own performance, they begin to internalize new ideas about who they are and what they can do. A person must be receptive to the implications of those observations; she must be developmentally ready to absorb them. The experience of successful accomplishment expands an individual's competence and furthers her confidence. Success that involved overcoming substantial odds was a boon to Heidi as she moved from sales to a difficult management position.

> I think there's certainly an added amount of confidence in having dealt with all that I've done. I feel like I've established a great deal of credibility very quickly. Because a lot of people truly expected me to fail. . . . I don't think they thought anyone could [do] it . . . and it'll be a credit to me. So I think I have a great deal more confidence. I know not that I will succeed. I now know that I have and will.

Monica's basic confidence was increased through achievement. Beginning as a secretary, she earned an advanced degree and achieved managerial status in the human resources area.

> I don't think I was ever not confident, but I've probably gotten more confident. Making a change, and taking a little bit of a risk, has helped to increase my confidence level. I guess I knew I could do it, by just doing it, that's got to do something for you.

Others concur that risk and change often culminate in success experiences, which then serve to build confidence. Some comment on a gender difference in the progression from achievement to confidence. Women seem to think self-assurance about their aptitude for a given task is necessary prior to its undertaking. In contrast, men have few qualms about enterprises for which they are unprepared.

> "How did you know you could do that before you tried?" Most of the men I've known have looked at me and said, "Well, I didn't. You just go do it, and then you learn." And I'm starting to learn that. You just jump in and you learn, and it's okay. They expect that you learn while you do it.

Thus, women learn about the expectations and practices of others in their organizations. As they see their own strengths grow in breadth and depth, their perceptions of themselves and of others change. With an expanded repertoire of accomplishments accompanying confidence, previously foreign goals become attainable. Working closely with upper management in her corporate planning position, Karen begins to see that others are as human as she, and that she is as extraordinary as others.

> I guess it all goes back to confidence. Finding out that senior managers are human beings too. Watching some of what you might pick out as their

failings and saying, "Well, I could do this. I can do this job—maybe not today." But it all relates. I think confidence is probably the overriding thing.

Persuading others of their value is sometimes less difficult than convincing themselves. Women's internal standards surpass those that exist on the organizational level. Once they are able to put their achievements in perspective, women like Nina, the optimist who eschewed school and is now in instruction and training, can credit themselves and absorb their worth.

> I think we're our worst critics. People tell you, "You're doing a great job." "Well, no, I could be better." And it's not that I've lowered my expectations of myself, or lowered my standards, but I've just come to grips with "Hey, yes, maybe I am doing a good job."

Others' evaluations can boost one's confidence, but a person's self-appraisal is ultimately the most meaningful and often the most stringent. Confidence is fully achieved when one no longer looks to others for approval. Beverly describes the change for her.

> It was a lot of external strokes that made the internal okay, so that I knew when I was doing a good job then. What was neat for me was [that] I can now tell. In this job, I don't need people telling me all the time when I'm doing okay and when I'm not, because I really learned how to find that and identify it for myself.[36]

Change

When these women talk about themselves, they talk about change. Interview questions required them to take a somewhat longitudinal view of their career paths. Reflections on the evolution of their careers and what that entailed necessarily included references to self. Personal change was an apparent part of professional development, which in turn contributed to self-awareness and revised images. The two worked together: Change in one domain made waves in the other.

Although the women interviewed included observations about personal characteristics in the course of career discussion, we also asked specifically about significant changes they had seen in themselves within a year's time. Accustomed to introspection, women readily cited change in the areas of confidence, personal strength, and comfort with themselves. It is conceivable, of course, that the vote of confidence symbolized by being sent to a management program contributed to the changes described.

We have seen how confidence has been strengthened within the corporate context. Feeling more confident, women find risk taking easier than they did before. As the risks escalate, so do the stakes. Connie succinctly articulates her feeling as she assumes ever-higher positions:

> I feel a lot more confident. I feel more vulnerable at the same time.

Increased confidence can be accompanied by a feeling of comfort and belonging. Lacking these at the time of the first interview, twenty-five-year-old Alison had recently joined a new company after the brakes had been applied to her rapid upward mobility by a previous employer. A year later, she notices in herself

> greater confidence. I would say for about a year now I have been able to walk into a conference room, make a presentation, contribute during a meeting with a great deal of confidence. I'm just more comfortable in the business environment.

With self-assurance comes enhanced faith in one's ability to control choices and outcomes. More certain of herself, a woman knows she can better control her circumstances.

Confidence increased with women's growing awareness of their capabilities. Professional experience and success have contributed significantly to their knowledge of themselves; they know better who they are and what they can do. Greater self-knowledge helps to clarify goals. Having moved through seven technical positions in as many years since college graduation, Susan is now surer of herself and her direction.

> I think I've become a lot more sure of myself. I think my horizons have really been broadened over the past year so that I understand a lot more about myself, what my own needs are in terms of a career, and about where I can go.

After struggling with her own lack of career direction and contending with ostracism by former clerical peers when she became a manager, Gwen's experience provided a clearer notion of her identity and direction.

> I don't mean to sound immodest, but I think I've changed for the better. I really feel very positive about it. . . . at least I know who I am and what I want; I'm very sure about that. I feel very good about myself.

When women experience success at inordinately difficult tasks, they are strengthened in several ways. Teresa recounts various aspects of a changed perspective:

I think I'm stronger, if that was possible. Before this year I didn't think it was possible. But all the things that have happened to me, and to be able to still keep everything intact, took quite a bit. So I think I've gotten a little stronger, more tolerant, and a lot more patient. I learned, when things don't always work out right away, to just step back from it and say, "Take it easy, be a little patient. Things will change." And they do . . . Take it a step at a time.

The lessons learned from experience can be applied to subsequent situations, but perhaps their ramifications for the self are most enduring. Hope's accomplishments redound to herself.

The strength: I've always known I was strong, but I don't think I ever really appreciated it until this year. Calmness; less of a feeling of hectic tension in my life, but just kind of an inward knowledge that I can handle anything that comes along, and an appreciation for what I have handled with none of the emotional highlight of it.

Women identify change within themselves as associated with professional experience. It is not the experience per se but its translation into meaning for the self that makes for difference. Women reflect upon career developments for their personal as well as professional implications. Self-development is integrally connected to their careers. What becomes important is a sense of contentment with oneself and one's work.

We have seen that women bring a great deal to their work, and work contributes to them. They derive satisfaction and enjoyment from the work, and their achievements enhance competence and self-confidence. Through work, women learn about themselves, their abilities and potential, their needs and aspirations. Professional experience affects the way they think about themselves and defines what matters to them. Fears diminish as confidence grows. Enhanced self-esteem is manifested by Teresa's comfort with herself and others.

I'm just not going to be intimidated. And I'm not going to apologize for what I've managed to accomplish because somebody's not comfortable with it. Either they learn to get comfortable with it, or they continue to be upset. I'm not going to let them upset me about it. It's as simple as that. It all comes to [this: In] dealing with people that I work with, I'm more important. If I have a dilemma with them, fine; I don't want to have a dilemma with myself. I'm going to be honest with myself. I'm going to feel good about how I'm reacting. I'm not going to say, "Why did you take that? Why did you give in to that type of thing? Why did you allow someone to treat you like that?" Why, that's just not going to happen with me. I'm getting too old for that.

With experience and maturity, women develop professional acumen and personal assurance. What they learn about business is incomplete without concomitant self-knowledge. Ultimately, it is women's expanding self-awareness that enables them to feel at ease with themselves and their work. Recently settling into a continuing position when her husband's job no longer dictated her place of residence, Abigail has made effective professional use of her observations of self in relation to others.

> I have a better sense of what I'm good at—and less concern for what I'm not good at. Less worrying when I find that I am the best at something in a group. That can be a little jarring when you're suddenly finding yourself in a collection of people you thought much abler. I'm beginning to be better able to use it. . . . It takes me a while to be accepted by a group. And that's sometimes a very useful asset—maybe especially as a female. I've decided not to work on correcting that. I've learned that, eventually, with a little bit of contact, people who shouldn't be afraid of me aren't, and maybe those who stay afraid of me should. Politically, there's a lot of power in that kind of perception. People often leave you alone if they'd just rather not hassle with you.

Astute observations of their own and others' behavior are used to professional advantage and as a source of personal reflection. Women see themselves change in the context of their careers. As they become more aware of their strengths and needs, they are better equipped to facilitate their own contentment. To reach a balance where they are at ease with self and career, women monitor their own development and incorporate change.

Success is ultimately defined by the women of this study as being happy and liking one's life—"being happy in your own skin." As Hardesty and Jacobs conclude, "Being 'happy in one's own skin' may be one of the most difficult yet crucial challenges management women . . . have before them. Because, in the final analysis, there are no easy and ultimate answers; there are only individual choices. There are no maps to follow; there are only inner compasses to trust."[37] Evidently, the women of this study have succeeded.

□ **6** □

Family

In talking about their careers, women described themselves. Who they are and where they come from were undeniable parts of the interviews. Remarks about family crept into accounts of career path as well as in response to explicit queries. A woman's professional life was informed by personal learning and attributes. Similarly, her personal development was significantly shaped by career experience. Her identity was about both.[1]

Career was integral to these women's identities. They abided by contextual distinctions between personal and professional, but their analyses often joined the two. Able to relate diverse aspects of their experience to each other, women presented an integrated perspective on their lives and themselves.[2] It is not surprising, therefore, to hear references to family within a discussion of career. Identities were formed through family and profession.

Women were asked specifically about the influence of family on their career development. Because of the question's open-ended format, they were free to select which family to talk about: the family of origin or the family of procreation. Responses centered on family of origin.

That one's first family has a profound influence on identity formation and life direction has been a long-accepted tenet in psychology. The channeling of men's and women's lives into separate spheres of endeavor, corresponding to mutually exclusive personality characteristics, has served to confirm our theories of the socialization process and its differential application by gender. Exceptions to expectation have prompted special inquiry. Thus, when females claim a traditionally male domain for their own pursuit, psychologists become particularly interested in what distinguishes those females from their traditional sisters. Their family backgrounds are studied to determine the origins of personality characteristics and ambitions that deviate from gender expectation.[3] In seeking understanding of the departure that these women represent, such studies usually look for common themes among their upbringings that might account for nonconformity.

When women first began to enter traditionally male domains, their numbers were so small that such inquiries could be elucidating. We learned, for example, that pioneering female managers were often firstborn or only children who identified more with their father's enterprise than with their mother's caretaking.[4] Commonalities were sought and found, and psychology's wont for generalization again was satisfied.

As their numbers increased, females pursuing formerly male occupations could no longer be catalogued according to certain family configurations. In addition, a psychological focus on sex role socialization and family demography alone does not suffice as an explanation for adult identity development and motivation.[5] Factors of social context, including political and economic change, must be considered as shaping individual life direction.[6] Moreover, a fuller understanding of human development requires psychologists temporarily to put aside their nomothetic approach for an idiographic one.

In this study women's family backgrounds are examined for insights about the formation of their identities and aspirations. Commonality is neither sought nor found. In fact, what we discover is a diversity of experience and messages in families. For some women, mothers were perceived as most instrumental; for others, fathers; and a few indicated that their families had no influence whatsoever on their career development.

Early socialization is but one of several important influences in one's psychological development. Moreover, we have learned that development does not end at age twenty-one. Not only does it continue throughout adulthood, but it can be radically reframed in connection with a shifting social environment.

The families of the women here manifested messages that departed from traditional notions of the course of female development, even as they were living according to those notions themselves. We find, too, that people do not necessarily acknowledge the influence of social movements, even while they are being shaped by them.[7] The women of this study demonstrate both the early influence of family and the later shaping of identity in relation to social change.

These women, whose lives deviated from a traditionally female path, attended to the kind of sex role expectations that existed in their families.[8] Many focused on the roots of the independence that later served to distinguish them from other family members and female peers. Presumably, countless aspects of family life might have been topics for these women. Most salient to career, however, were parental expectations and familial perspectives on education, independence, and sex roles.

Parental Influence

It is common knowledge that a family's environment contributes significantly to the shape of an individual's future. That environment has both external and internal components. Outside of it, a family has several sources of identity within the larger society; its race, class, religion, and ethnicity inform a family's practices, beliefs, and opportunities. Cultural heritage and social access are largely determined by the sociological circumstances of one's birth.

Beyond a sociological rubric, factors operating on the individual level shape a person's future. Internal to the family is its psychological environment. Freud awakened our consciousness to the importance of early child-rearing practices for subsequent personal development. Whether or not they accept a psychodynamic framework, social scientists since have reiterated the significance of family in molding its members' psyches.

Notions of self, relation to other, and place in a social network originate in the family. Parent–child relationships are especially critical to one's growing understanding of identity and future. Self-image is subject to many other sources of influence throughout the course of development, but the first impressions emblazoned through the intimacy of family carry considerable weight. Our relationships within the family not only become the prototype for subsequent ones outside but also teach us who we are and what we might expect to do with our lives.

A family's instruction about children's personal attributes and future paths had varied by gender for more than half of this century. Males and females learned characteristics and directions that were separate and specific to their gender. Institutions representing various aspects of society fostered and reinforced gender-specific behavior, and children had firsthand models in their own homes. Mothers who served as family caretakers and fathers who went out to work were powerful role models for children's emulation.[9] Thus, males' and females' identities and destinies were overdetermined by internal and external contributors.

It is not just behavior of role models that influences a child's development. Parents' messages about their own and their children's identities can take many forms. Influence extends beyond behavior to attitudes. For example, the operative factor in the case of mother–daughter messages may be the mother's degree of satisfaction with her role. Thus, mothers who are at home but dissatisfied with that position are more likely to encourage their daughters to do something different.[10]

Lessons conveyed verbally and behaviorally are particularly influential because of their source and recipient. Children are in a formative process and are therefore malleable, especially by the most powerful people in their lives, their parents. Parents derive their power from their position: Children are totally dependent upon them for an extended period of time. Thus, parental teachings about the child's value and potential are of extraordinary endurance.

A division of labor according to traditional gender lines would find fathers in the work force and mothers in the kitchen. If role model imitation followed expectation, girls would identify with their mothers and thereby formulate notions of themselves and their futures around domesticity. Indeed, some women interviewed, like thirty-seven-year-old Dorothy, began with such notions, which were subsequently revised as a function of career opportunity and professional experience.

> my early socialization through my family was very patriarchal, and my mother never worked. It was understood that if I went to school it wasn't for any particular reason other than it was just something to do. But not any emphasis was ever placed on career for a woman; nothing was placed on learning for a woman. It was understood in my mind to become a mother and a wife, and that was it. So when I went to school, I never really took it very seriously; I didn't study very hard; I really didn't care. And my whole reason for being there—and what I think a lot of women in my position at that time were going through—was to find a husband.

Predictions of sex role imitation ordinarily follow same-sex lines: Girls are expected to identify with their mothers and boys with their fathers. Within a context of a gender-based division of labor, however, girls would have to identify with their fathers in order to develop the characteristics requisite to career aspiration. Females who did just that—identified with their fathers and subsequently became executives—were the subject of an early study, *The Managerial Woman*.[11] That study also supported the association of high achievement orientation with birth order, firstborn or only children getting an inordinate share.[12] Among the women interviewed here we find more variability in birth order, in which parent is cited as being influential, and in the ways influence is manifested.[13]

Social beliefs about gender roles vary with time and context. Children born after 1960 were likely to receive very different messages about gender-appropriate identities and directions than those born two decades earlier.[14] Social change spawned by recent human rights movements has affected our attitudes and practices regarding male and female traits and behavior. Revised beliefs and economic conditions have combined to allow women's development and occupation to extend outside the home. The families of the women here reflect social change in their communication to daughters.

Psychology has traditionally promulgated the importance of family background variables as foremost determinants of individual personality, including achievement motivation and future aspiration. Emphasis has been on identification with the same-sex parent, who serves as the primary role model. These early conceptions of sex role identification no longer account for the complexity of children's development. There is increasing recognition of the need to go beyond a theory of identification that considers only the influence of the same-sex parent. It is conceivable that each parent displays a combination of expressive and instrumental influence toward daughters.[15]

Moreover, this formulation largely ignores its cultural foundation. Gender-defined characteristics attributed to individuals are societally determined, but psychologists customarily have not focused on the social context of personality formation. Further, the psychodynamic tradition in this country has reinforced the idea of fixed personality traits dating from early childhood. Psychology's narrow vision had perpetuated the notion of exclusive male and female personality characteristics that suit them for separate spheres.[16]

When individual psychological development is placed within a social framework, our analyses change. Moreover, when that social framework is seen as actively contributing to individual development, perhaps shaping it as much or more than parental sex roles, we gain a deeper understanding of psychological development. The premise here has been that individual psychological development is affected by social change. Indeed, the women interviewed demonstrate the dynamic interaction between familial and societal influence on individual attributes and aspiration.

Instead of traditional sex role identification determining the life paths of these women, we find their development responding to social change. Acknowledging the influence of parental example and messages, they trace personal change in relation to revised cultural messages. Their parental messages incorporate some unconventional ideas about female identity and life path. In addition, concepts of self and life direction formed later in reference to changing social norms can transcend earlier development.[17]

Thus, women holding responsible corporate positions provide ample evidence of our changed mores. How were they raised? What kinds of role models did their parents present? How did they develop the personal attributes that we saw described in chapter 5?

We cannot generalize about upbringings and messages related to gender that those interviewed may have received. Since they spanned an age range from early twenties through midfifties, the time frames of their early formative years vary. Most childhoods predated the current women's movement; yet these women developed high achievement motivation for work and career. By looking at their families, we gain insight into the shaping of these women's aspirations.

Mothers as the Prime Movers

For several women, mothers were predominant. Sharon's mother stressed the importance of education, and at the time of the interview Sharon had already earned one graduate degree and was pursuing another.

> Absolutely from my mother. Nobody in our immediate family ever went to college, so being the oldest child . . . my mother always encouraged me to think about going to college. It was always to have a better job. There was a real big focus on having skills and being unique in that respect. And she was absolutely the prime reason. In that respect, my father was always encouraging but certainly not so much on a vocal level. It was definitely my mother.

Parents do not merely convey a "Do as I did" message to their children. In fact, mothers often use their own lives as negative examples for their female offspring. They want their children to have opportunities that they lacked. Alison's achievement orientation began early with educational strivings, and by the age of twenty-five this young woman had found herself already on the edge of managerial positions.

> My mother, from as early as I can remember, was pushing me. . . . I think she always felt cheated by the fact that she didn't go to college, and she didn't have a career and didn't have a way to be independent. . . . As long as I can remember, my mother was always saying, "Get a college education so you can be independent and never depend on a husband or anybody else." I bet I heard that once a week for my entire life.

Mothers, who had been socialized according to traditional gender dicta of female domesticity and dependence, found their experience wanting and preached the opposite to their daughters. Recognizing the limitations imposed upon them by economic dependence, they encouraged their daughters to increase the possibilities for their own lives. Leigh's mother did not mince words in her explicit message, but Leigh did not begin to build a career until she joined a growing manufacturing corporation in her midthirties.

> she had been a support when I was young, very definitely. When I was in college, she would say things like "Prepare yourself for a job." "But I want to take all these art courses." And if I had listened to some of the things she said, I might have done things a little differently. I don't know if I would have, but she had been through [it] herself and knew where things were. Very bright woman.

When mothers recognize the many options that could be available to their daughters, they often coach them about paths to pursue. Marsha's mother described the different destinations in which various paths would culminate. This tutelage in decision making and nurtured independence prepared Marsha for a direct path to a high executive position in finance for which she had solid undergraduate training.

> I have to give her some of the credit because she did a lot of talking. We were very close. We talked quite a bit. And she would bring up comparisons: "You either do this, and this is where you may end up. But if you do this, there's no limit to where you can go." So I have to say that she was the major factor.

The support of a close relationship is crucial to risk taking. Encouraged to make decisions and tutored in their consequences, a woman develops a strong self-image and many skills necessary for career success. Ursula, in industrial sales and a single parent by age thirty-two, also learned strength and skills from her mother's example.

> My mother was a very strong influence in our family. She was a very strong woman. . . . And I think I've incorporated—I've learned from her. One of the things that's helped me so much has been being persistent, not giving up. If somebody tells me, "No," how can I make them say yes? How can I change their minds? Or what do I need to change to make it work? And I really picked that up from my mother. My mother was not in business . . . But she was strong and took responsibility for a lot of things. And I think she had a lot of influence on the choices that I've made.

The majority of women interviewed had mothers who were not employed in business. Several had never worked outside of the home, and the few who had were primarily part-time employees. A mother's participation in the labor force did not define what and how she communicated to her daughter, however. For example, some employed mothers would have preferred full-time homemaking, and others who were at home would have preferred paid work. Daughters became aware of what mothers did, said, and might have desired. Their personal characteristics evolved under a mother's watchful tutelage, others from a more subtle model. Values and a general sense of personal worth, not tied to any specific undertaking, were derived from supportive maternal environments. Daughters also learned skills and attributes essential to career from mothers who managed not businesses but homes.[18]

Where Fathers Take the Lead

Ordinarily, neither parent dictated a particular path for a child to pursue. Instead, daughters were encouraged to develop so that they were prepared to take advantage of all sorts of opportunities. Like mothers, fathers had various ways of fostering development that ranged from specific expectation to general support.

Through intellectual challenge, Connie's father sharpened her thinking ability and stimulated her assertiveness. His style of coaching reflected his own strength, which served as both a formidable model and a dependable support. By her early thirties, Connie, who had always been a high achiever, was headed for one of the top executive positions held by women of this group.

> I was the oldest child, and I was given a lot of opportunity to experience things first time around. I think my father encouraged me to debate and

talk: "Why do you feel this way, and how did you get to that point, and why?" Interested in what I was doing. So I think my father was important, and my mother was very supportive. And I don't know that I'm through this stage yet, but I would be very secure and calm if I could go home and ask him the answer to a question, and he told me his version of it. Whatever that version was, I always felt that was the right story and that probably nobody else knew, because nobody else was as smart.

A father's authoritative expertise can work to a daughter's advantage when he not only lends her the benefit of his experience but also facilitates similar expertise in her. Connie learned that she could rely on her father as a knowledgeable consultant, but more importantly, she developed her own problem-solving abilities through his prompting.

Other fathers also emphasized cognitive skill in their daughters. To expand oneself through knowledge is useful for its own sake as well as for practical purposes. Scholastic study and achievement can promote a sense of accomplishment and self-esteem. Meanwhile, broad exposure acquaints one with prospects for the future. Through education, daughters learn more about available opportunity and about themselves and their aptitudes. Teresa's interest in school carried her through a graduate degree, which prepared her for escalating positions within her company. Her recollection of an emphasis on education is common to many.

> We had to go to school; we had to do our homework. That was just what you were supposed to do. And I always did well in school, and they kept encouraging it.

For Ina, who also held a graduate degree, the importance of education was an unquestioned given:

> [My mother's] idea of an education [as] security was the key thing that ran through my whole life—and my sisters' also. We all have professions. . . . And they always encouraged it. You got one B and all the rest A's. Well, next time try for all A's. Go for the top. And even still, my mother's very proud of my career.

It is not necessarily one or the other parent who promulgates education and high achievement, but fathers, more often than mothers, are perceived as demanding. The demand may be connected to scholastic performance or to achievement more generally. Without articulating particular expectations, Leigh's father still served as a motivating force for her, though it was her mother who had instructed her to prepare for a job when she wanted to take art courses.

I'd say my father was very demanding—a very demanding person. And it wasn't as though he was gearing me to go to work. But the person I had to succeed for was my father . . . he's been very successful, and a very bright person. And I had to prove myself to him. So I've always had to fight hard to do that, but it's certainly been a motivation. And I wouldn't have known that many years ago. I certainly know that now.

A father's admirable characteristics can inspire his daughter's emulation. Further, his qualities make his approval all the more desirable to a daughter who strives to prove herself worthy through similar accomplishment.

Nina, who had been more interested in work than school, can now relate her father's values to her own.

My dad's very goal-oriented. He's always instilled that in us—to get our act together and to have some goals and aspirations and to set them high, and . . . both my parents would always support us in that.

These women describe encouragement and support for achievement in a general sense. They do not speak of being groomed for a lifetime of work or career, never mind a specific occupation. Sex differences may remain, with families expecting boys to prepare for lifelong employment and coaching them toward particular careers.[19] Perhaps females born within the past two decades have received similar messages. However, the women of this study, who have spanned the old and new messages about women's lives, speak in the sketchier and broader terms of achievement.

Family Support for Achievement

Influenced by the spoken and unspoken, children are commonly unaware of the sources of motivation during their formative years. In retrospect, they can recognize family components that contributed to what they have become. The full meaning of parental example and instruction becomes clear when women connect their current selves to the past. Stella attests to the value of the interview question in stirring an integration for her.

I like the idea of you getting me to actually talk about [my family] and to relate it somehow. I never really saw a correlation between my feelings for my family and my work and the obligations and the things like that. I always thought that this is one thing and this is another and somehow the two paths never meet, but it's almost inseparable.

Several women interviewed acknowledged the influence and support of both parents in their development. Karen, who coordinates financial planning for a retail corporation, derived different qualities from her mother and father, and their individual strengths combined to enforce a belief in her potential.

> My father was very much one of these workaholic-type people. He was also somebody that you could never satisfy . . . and so I think I probably did a lot of stuff trying to please him but never quite getting that satisfaction. My mother was a very organized person. . . . I learned a lot of organizational-type things from her. I would say both parents were pretty strong. And I was never raised with any sort of feeling other than you could do whatever you wanted to do.

We see here the origins of the strong achievement orientation that was apparent in chapter 5.[20] Striving to do and be as much as possible begins in childhood in relation to a parent and continues in adulthood in relation to oneself. Personal attributes and concrete skills that contribute to professional success are initially acquired through family tutelage. Connie draws parallels between her behavior as a child in the family and as a professional in the corporation.

> I can remember always, as a child, having to do, to be, in order to please my parents, I would want to get all A's. Then I took up horseback riding, and I had to enter a contest, and I wanted to win, get the first prize. And immediately, when I got this prize, I turned and looked to them to see the smiles and the positive reinforcement. So it must have started there. I think that I play to the house when I work. I don't build a lot of relationships with subordinates, and I don't build a lot of relationships with peers. What I do is build relationships with superiors, and that's got to go back to wanting your parents' approval. . . . It's got to be a transferring of that. And then just being hard on yourself . . . if I have a chance of doing it perfectly, then I will do it. But if I only have a chance of being average, it's not fun anymore. . . . So it has to be that. It goes all over.

Even when women cannot trace career origins to family influence, they are aware of an unqualified support for their endeavors and for themselves. Renee's family is virtually ignorant of the technicalities of her work as a systems consultant, but she feels their pride in her accomplishments.

> My family per se has never had any kind of a part in my career. . . . she [her mother] never had any idea what I did for a living. And I can't blame her. If I were not in the industry . . . I cannot explain it to anyone else. So they really didn't have anything to do with it other than just being very proud. I would always get a strong sense of that.

Thus, families vary in the ways they exert influence and in the values they choose to emphasize. Some families' influence is perceived as negligible with regard to career. Most women interviewed nonetheless acknowledged their families in the development of a strong sense of self. A general emphasis on education and preparation for employment was an integral part of many women's upbringing, but critical to development was a global feeling of parental faith in daughters' worth. Not only did parents reinforce certain values, they believed in their daughters' abilities to meet expectations. Personal strength ultimately contributes to professional growth. Specific career assistance is less vital than the gift of self that Connie's parents have given her.

> My parents are not involved right now in coaching me or giving me tips on how to be more effective. They provide a lot of love and support and encouragement and interest—in that sense, helping me form a strong self-concept. I think they did that.

Sex Roles

An environment that both supports and holds out high standards can instill in a woman the belief that she is capable of doing anything she chooses. However, open-ended options are contrary to a gender-based division of labor that prescribes what roles males and females should occupy. Many women interviewed came from homes where traditional gender lines held sway. In some instances, the explicit message about a daughter's future did not contradict the modeled one. Monica, thirty-two, believes that her choices would have been different had her family not perpetuated customary sex roles.[21] Now a manager in human resources, she has earned a graduate degree since her secretarial beginnings in the corporation.

> in fact, I get aggravated with my parents, because my mother and father were very traditional. My father made the decisions. My mother was a full-time housewife. They talked a lot about girls do this and boys do that, though they always encouraged me. I did very well in school, and my father was very helpful to me [in] school work. There was a feeling that I should go to college, but it was for the wrong reason. It was because you'll meet a nice boy and get married. And unfortunately, no one ever gave me any other options. Had I to do it over again I certainly would have had a different view of things.

The larger cultural environment can reinforce family stereotypes of the preferred gender. The strength of inner conviction overcomes socialization that limits female potential. It is Hope's internal sense of self-worth that fully frees her.

> We had a very male-dominated environment. Boys—like they are everywhere, but specifically in the South—boys are the chosen kids. And everything centers around them. Girls are just second-class citizens. And so you never really get over that. The conflict comes when you realize that "Hey, I really am not a second-class citizen. In fact, sometimes I'm actually a better citizen than they are. I'm more capable, I'm more competent." And that brings another kind of conflict, because you don't have to prove that you're that. You have to come to terms with the fact that you're simply being as good as you can be—good, by your own definition, not good by someone else's.

Even when women grew up in homes that depicted traditional sex roles, they learned of other possibilities for their own lives. Parents, in the majority of cases, communicated prospects for their daughters that they themselves were not living. Jill reiterates an emphasis on education and values demonstrated by parents. The principle underlying specific lessons was that she could do and be whatever she pleased. Earlier, we saw Jill decide to risk leaving a small organization for the large one where she became personnel manager within a year and a half.

> Obviously, they have played a tremendous role in my life, as every family does. In my career development in particular, both parents contributed something differently. My mother did not work and has always been oriented toward the home and family life. My father has always directed all of his children, that we could do anything we wanted to, that as long as you worked hard, and were productive, and did your best, . . . it was out there, and you just have to try. And he himself was a very hard-working individual and very dedicated to whatever he went into, so his own behavior was an excellent example of what he had to teach us. I would say that certainly helped in terms of my career development.

Parents instilled in daughters the value of conscientious effort. Moreover, parents conveyed their confidence in women's ability to attain their goals. Daughters internalize both the beliefs and the confidence originally derived from their families; hence, they formulate and fulfill similarly high expectations of themselves. Susan, a twenty-eight-year-old production manager, can feel the full weight of her personal worth and professional success as a result of this kind of family interaction.

> The environment I grew up in was pretty much middle-class. My parents were very concerned with grades for all of us, and there was really no distinction in terms of who could do what, or who was supposed to excel at

what. My father's whole thing was that everybody should be a math major, everybody should be a chem or physics major. They were real pushy around achievement. I think that contributed a lot to what ultimately happened once I got into the work environment. The standards of performance that they expected became my own expectations somewhere in the later years of college. I didn't need them behind me anymore, expecting that. I expected it of myself. So they really played a critical role [in] developing those expectations and achievement levels.

When we examined women's work patterns and personal characteristics in earlier chapters, we saw them manifest high standards for their professional performance. Individual variation notwithstanding, they were impressively uniform in their desire to achieve all that they might, not necessarily in terms of material reward but in relation to their sense of self. One woman spoke for several in saying that she was more apt to improve herself due to constantly questioning "whether I'm as good as I should be." There is plenty of evidence that these women have high standards for their performance, and those standards seem to originate in families where expectations for children's development are gender-free. With a background in human services and currently working as a manager in a traditionally male transportation business, Beverly learned that she could do whatever she wished as long as it was at a high level:

> But he [father] was really influential in that he truly believed that I could do anything I wanted to do. He had none of the traditional ideas about what I ought to do and what I shouldn't do. He was also a real perfectionist and expected me to be a cut above average in everything always. So there was a lot of achievement pressure and a lot of performance pressure.

Janna's family also valued cognitive strength and encouraged her career:

> My father's major value system has to do with competence and intelligence. . . . reinforced for being bright. So I was never told that I really ought to consider being a nurse or a teacher. It was always expected that I would go to college; it was always expected that I would have a career. And I don't think that as a child or a young woman growing up in that family I was ever treated as a female.

The absence of a gender-linked socialization characterized Esther's childhood in the depression years.

> I can't honestly say that I was . . . brought up in an atmosphere that said women can't do this or can't do that. I just believed I could do anything I wanted to, and I never thought of it as being a woman. I did a lot of

reading when I was a child, and I had a lot of role models in my own mind—people like Marie Curie, George Sand, Amelia Earhart was a great heroine of mine, Clara Barton, Elizabeth Browning. They sound like such stereotypes, but they were the women that I really did relate to.

Whether women had female role models available to them in their immediate families or from other sources, they still developed the idea that everything would be available to them regardless of gender. An "anything is possible" notion came from parents like Nina's who believed that to be so for their daughters.

And my parents have instilled [in] us that we had the ability to do anything we wanted to and given us the opportunity to do that.

Independence

These women recall receiving both general and specific notions about themselves and their futures from their first families. For many, particular parental emphases on education and achievement were apparent progenitors of internalized high standards for their own performance. A family environment that communicated support and confidence in daughters' inherent worth was critical to their developing belief in themselves. Frequently coupled with such faith was encouragement for gender-free pursuits and a future of economic independence.

Socialization according to a gender-based division of labor would shape female identities for domesticity and economic dependence on a male. The majority of women interviewed had mothers without careers—indeed, without paid work of any kind—who spent their lives occupied with family caretaking. When their mothers did enter the labor force, it was often out of necessity as divorced or widowed women who had children to support. Daughters learned an indelible lesson from the experience of mothers who were suddenly abandoned and unprepared to fend for themselves and their families. Women whose primary occupation had been wife and mother were not equipped to take over as breadwinner. Witnessing what had happened to their mothers, women resolved not to repeat the pattern. Mary, who claimed work to be central to her identity, sees the link between her current independence and her mother's experience.

I think [what] influenced me most is I wanted to be independent. I would never do what she did. I would never ever want to put myself in a position where I would fall apart. I don't want to give up "I'm me" and "I'm going to support me, and I'm going to be independent." I'll give up some of my independence in other ways but not in terms of money and support and my identity.

Family tragedy exerts a powerful influence on psychological development. From the misfortune of parents' lives children infer what they must avoid in their own futures. Colleen learned early from family events and her mother's reaction to them.

> I always felt a need to be self-supporting. I never wanted to depend on a man to have to take care of me. I'm talking about financially. I think I got that because my dad died when I was young. My mother had to go out to work . . . and she was totally unprepared for that shock. The kinds of things that I saw her going through and the pain that she went through because of being totally unprepared for it was something that I never wanted to experience.

Rebecca, equipped with an advanced technical degree and a corresponding supervisory position by age thirty, drew very specific conclusions from a similar life history:

> The other significant thing was [that] my father died so young and my mother had to go back to work to raise me. I always felt that it was kind of a driving factor for me in being independent, and being able to draw on an educational background that was marketable. [I felt] that I could always draw on that strength, [having] that education behind me, that if anything similar happened in my life, whether I got married or not, . . . I would feel that I was not totally dependent on my husband and that income. And I think I've done that. As a result, I can never see myself not working. I don't abandon all other roles—I enjoy being a wife and hopefully a mother someday, but there's always that thing in the back of my mind that says, "Well, you know you have this identity. You know you're not going to give it up."

Environmental events and circumstances are formative influences in children's psychological development. In these cases, the lessons of adversity seem to extend to earliest recollection. Women talk of "always" having wanted their independence. The long-standing convictions formed as a consequence of family circumstance become part of their identity.

It is not only death or divorce that molds daughters' resolve. Absence of economic advantage confirmed Hope's need for financial independence.

> I think [there was] always the sense that I could take care of myself. I never wanted to be in a position where I had to rely on someone else and be at their mercy. I grew up without a lot of advantages. There was a lot of

negative stigma to the area that I grew up in, so I was constantly over-coming obstacles, and that has something to do with what goes on in the job. By the time I was fourteen, I was already into expressing myself and becoming my own person. Certainly I have my mother's strength. And when I left home, I left because I felt like I needed my own identity. . . . it got me started on the right track, because I became who I'd always been inside anyway.

Sometimes a family's main influence is not from direct teaching or parental example. Women define themselves and their aspirations in reaction against the negative model of a family's status. Stella received personal support, but inspiration for a different direction from her upbringing.

They've encouraged me in anything . . . that I want to pursue or anything that I feel that I want to do. But as far as making a decision about myself, an actual decision, I think it comes directly from me. The only thing that I can say is that I grew up in a very poor family, and I grew up knowing that I didn't want things to remain the way they were. And that was always in the back of my mind, that I knew in order to do better I had to rely on just me. Because I can't really say that anybody in my family influenced me. They were certainly supportive of everything I did.

The development of self-reliance may be a common outgrowth of certain kinds of environments. Where a family's situation, for whatever reason, precludes deliberate individualized attention to its members, children learn independence early. Thus, socioeconomic advantage is not a necessary condition to develop personal characteristics that fore-cast women's career and economic independence. Roberta's ability to fend for herself grew even in the absence of family guidance. Currently a consultant in a staff operation of a *Fortune* 500 firm, she finds herself working on degree completion and developing a career path in her early thirties.

Well, with all of us kids, . . . there was never much support in terms of what we were doing with our lives or with our schooling or anything like that. So I learned very early on to be independent and just to fight for myself as best I could.

A need to be independent is communicated to daughters in several ways. Many learn from the negative example of mothers unprepared for employment. Adverse family conditions teach children to develop attributes and abilities that will insure a different adult life. Mothers might communicate the virtues of independence even when family situations do not ostensibly precipitate it. Elena, a single parent who resists dependence, remembers receiving contradictory messages that she subsequently sorted out for herself.

> What I consciously know is that my mother was always very ambivalent about her dependence on my father. She said, "It's really important for you to take care of yourself." So that's something that I always had in my head. But yet, it was also very important to her that we should be feminine and that we should be attractive and that we should be looking for a husband. So, her whole message was always very, very mixed. . . . And basically what I learned [later] was that I could support myself, which was a very important thing to me, because I felt at that time that I didn't want to focus my whole life on finding somebody to marry me and support me. I couldn't possibly do it—what I was supposed to do. And that encouraged me to explore even more.

Regardless of whether they learn it as a function of early necessity or later experience, women are convinced of the importance of self-sufficiency in an economic sense. Fending for themselves, living up to high standards, and achieving gratifying work all become integral to who they are and the way they live their lives. They may become wives and mothers, but not at the expense of their identities as fully functioning independent human beings.

□ 7 □

Marriage and Children

Women have customarily grown up with the expectation that they would marry and reproduce some day. By so doing, they would be serving not only individual needs for adult family connection but also a crucial function of societal continuity.[1] The future of a society, of course, rests on procreation, and Americans have institutionalized that in the form of the nuclear family.[2] Although the romance of love and marriage is touted as central to adult family formation, it is the complex of higher-order ramifications that perpetuates a social system.[3] For societal purposes, individual needs pale in light of institutional structures. The unit that we call family, and other cultures call kinship, gives fundamental structure to economic, social, and political transactions.

The Development of a Gender-Based Division of Labor

A society's economy largely dictates the form family must take to support it.[4] The requirements of an agrarian economy, for example, were different from those of a technological one. American families that had been working their farms as a team were divided by the Industrial Revolution. A gender-based division of labor was more firmly established as men sought work away from the homes where women remained as caretakers.[5]

As paid work became more segregated from family life, the roles of males and females calcified. Even though the means of production had shifted from home to industry, there were still domestic chores to be done and children to be tended. Women were designated as family mainstays and men as breadwinners. Over time, custom was translated into ideology so that males and females were believed to be inherently suited to their respective roles and to no other.[6]

Thus, a child's gender largely prescribed its socialization. Females were to be groomed for a life of domestic caretaking and males for paid production. Little girls were to aspire to marriage and children, not to career, profession, or even paid employment. Should a female prepare herself for work outside the home, it would only be as a fallback in case of family exigency such as the incapacity or death of a spouse.

Despite ideology to the contrary, women had been members of the paid labor force throughout the twentieth century. Married women's full-time, long-term work was discounted as something extra and temporary. Women's primary responsibility was always the family, not paid labor participation. Social ideology shaped the widely held belief that each gender was intrinsically suited to its occupation, so that crossing the line into the other's domain would be seen as unnatural and societally traitorous.[7] An individual who did not subscribe to the appropriate gender path was a misfit who betrayed social obligation. If females eschewed marriage and embraced career, what would become of the family structure that allowed our institutions to function?

An Established Ideology Challenged by Social Change

The current women's movement, which opened doors of homes from the inside out, freed females to pursue explicitly paths that were not solely domestic. Women's exodus from the home challenged our belief system and constituted a substantial threat to the way our society functions. Both internal and external forces pressed women to "keep their place."

Institutions and the citizens who constitute and uphold them are known for their resistance to revision. People, including the women themselves, had internalized the ideology that circumscribed male and female roles; to change long-standing notions about the nature of women and what they were suited for required a major psychic overhaul on both the individual and the societal level. To overcome such massive resistance, the new ideas about "what little boys and girls are made of," and what is in store for them, must have hit a resonant chord in enough women to move them to change their lives and, in so doing, the shape of our society.

The kind of change that the current women's movement represented, therefore, could materialize only through the concerted efforts of many rather than the isolated attempts of individuals. The unit of change was at first individual and later institutional; personal and social changes shape and are shaped by each other.

We are witnessing this social change in process, as the full psychic overhaul and corresponding structural revision have yet to be accomplished. Hardesty and Jacobs provide evidence that the traditional expectations for women still exist, albeit underground. That the traditional ideology maintains a foothold within people's unconscious is illustrated by the male and female reactions to maternity cited in their book. Pregnant corporate women discover "basic male ambivalence about working mothers," when men tacitly agree that mothers should not be in the workplace. Women's ambivalence toward their jobs is manifested by their using childbirth as an excuse to leave less than fulfilling careers.[8] Pressed into a career that has not met its promise, they can use maternity as an "acceptable copout [that] allows women to let dependency needs surface."[9]

It is probably the case that men and women still harbor beliefs that fit a gender-based division of labor. That some men would be more comfortable with women at home and that some women permit children significantly to interrupt their careers are undoubtedly true. The picture is more complex, however, than the inevitability of custom arising from the unconscious. We also see women struggling to maintain their career paths while considering family. A majority of female college graduates are preparing for lifelong careers. Moreover, the Department of Labor reports 65 percent of new mothers are returning to the work force within a year of childbirth.[10]

The women of this study express an unwillingness to interrupt, never mind relinquish, their careers for reasons of family. They resemble high-achieving women who are found to have high expectations for both family and career.[11] However, those who do want children articulate the conflicts and dilemmas involved in simultaneously maintaining a career. Perhaps those women who do give up their professional positions to stay at home with their children find the struggle too difficult and solutions not in sight. When institutional structures do not accommodate individual life choices, it sometimes is easier to give up the institution rather than do battle with it. Women who drop out and the corporations that lose them are the casualties of the limits of change.

Whether or not people consciously identify with the agents and goals of social change, their lives are affected by it. Women who do not call themselves feminists still recognize domesticity's limitations and the importance of economic independence for females as well as males. In chapter 6 we saw parents who had lived their own lives according to traditional sex roles singing a different tune to their daughters; though marriage and family were still valued, the message expanded beyond that to "you can do anything you choose." Daughters also learned to develop financial independence from the experience of mothers who struggled because they had not. Without being active participants in the women's movement or even conscious supporters, these parents were socializing their daughters to expect futures not limited to home and hearth.

It is unlikely that most women interviewed closely identified with the women's movement. Nonetheless, they were living testimony to its influence.[12] The fact of their professional positions alone was evidence of social change. Although the routes to career varied, women's engagement in paid work secured their commitment to it. Their upbringings were a mixture of traditional and open-ended messages, and the lives of several reflected both. Some began careers after years of marriage or after a divorce; others were attempting to balance family and profession without sacrificing either. Single women did not necessarily expect to stay that way, nor did they necessarily feel an urgency to marry. In the absence of traditional ideological and economic bases for marital arrangements, women seek more singularly the benefits of relationship in their commitments with men.[13] Social change had revised the reasons for marriage.

A Shifting Basis of Marriage

When women believed that their choices were restricted to a marriage based on a gender division of labor, that choice shaped not only their lives but also their images of themselves. When the range of choice and their self-images were revised, so were their expectations in marriage. This revision was precipitated by social change that operated on psychological, economic, and ideological levels.

Under a gender-based division of labor, women depended upon their husbands to provide for them and their children. Men depended on their wives to care for the needs of home and family. This seemingly mutual dependency turned out to be the basis of inequality between the sexes. Women's economic dependence served to subordinate them to a far greater extent than did men's family needs.

Social change challenged the ideology that relegated women to a financially dependent, caretaker role within marriage. Articulation of different needs and abilities precipitated their revised behavior and self-perception, which, in turn, influenced other's perceptions of women and their place. A changed social belief system coupled with the establishment of an economic base provided women with new choices in and outside of marriage.

When women become economically self-reliant, the traditional marriage contract is undercut. Some women interviewed entered marriage with established professional identities; others began with traditional ideas that changed during the life of the marriage. Shifts in the economic balance of power and in the self-images of both partners can seriously test a marriage.[14] Often, it is not changed consciousness or ideology that initiates a shift but rather financial exigency, as in Heidi's case. In chapter 2 Heidi spoke of the overturning of her expectation to "get married and live happily ever after" when an inability to meet bills precipitated her getting a job.

> It was established as a very traditional marriage. I had no ambitions then. I hoped that he would find a job that made enough money that I would never have to work. I got a teaching degree so that if my husband died or something . . . I would have something that I could fall back on. That was the attitude. So because he didn't make very much money, that's when I started working. It started out as a very traditional marriage, so it's kind of grown. There have been times when it's been a bit of a conflict, and he would complain a little bit about the overwork, yet at the same time he's supportive and has given me guidance himself.

Not all marriages that are initially based on traditional gender roles survive transition. A marriage predicated on female economic need and dependence begins with a weak foundation that may ultimately prove its undoing. When women choose a partner out of their own weakness, the basis of the relationship is shaky. Differences that divide formerly united couples are too numerous and complex to chronicle here, but certainly a marriage that begins under one premise and shifts to another is severely tested.[15] Some relationships can accommodate the changes made by individuals within them, but usually not without a struggle. A woman's professional achievement can threaten male investment in gender imbalance. A conflict arises when Teresa, who does not want to sacrifice her six-year marriage in her late thirties, is unable to accept the limitations that a traditional marriage would impose.

> we were slowly killing whatever we had. . . . I knew that my job was bothering [her husband], but I had to feel that I was not restricted that way [and] he has struggled with dealing with me, with my salary, with my position, what I'm doing. . . . these times are very difficult for men of our generation, because his father and his uncle and his aunts and his mother, they all have a totally different pattern of living. . . . I know it's very difficult for his generation because they're really the first ones to have to deal with this. But I told him it has to start somewhere. And this is where it started.

Men who were socialized to adopt the family's financial support as their primary role are not comfortable with wives whose accomplishment equals or surpasses their own.[16] The more a man's self-worth hinges on his economic capacity in relation to his wife's lack thereof, the more difficult his adaptation to her career. Women with serious career commitments need mates who are secure within themselves and content with their own lives. Such men are sources of strength and support that can enhance a woman's work and home life. A woman's success depends upon her own and her partner's psyche.[17]

Sometimes the conflict between husband and wife who are both employed reduces to an impossible choice between self and other.[18] A husband's demand that a woman relinquish career opportunity in favor of the marriage cannot ultimately be met. To do so, a woman whose profession is central to her identity would be giving up an integral part of herself. In the long run, women are no better at sacrificing themselves for their mates than men are. When Hope cannot suppress herself to meet her husband's needs, he reacts by equating her professional fulfillment with his abandonment. Either she abides by his wishes, or she has betrayed him and the marriage covenant.

> They offered me a job in sales. First, conflict, because my husband felt that . . . women just didn't sell. . . . So I turned the opportunity down and had a lot of anger and rage about missing this opportunity, and what did I really sacrifice it for? I suppose if I pinpointed one place when I began to become aware of what was really happening to women, it was that point. They offered it to me again about three months later, and I took it. That was probably the beginning of the deterioration of my relationship with my husband, because he never really got over that. He saw it as being a threat and an action that proved I really didn't care about him or our relationship . . . but certainly that was a devastating conflict for me, because it started with his feeling that I somehow was abandoning him.

And that quickly became that I thought I was superior to him. And then I became the bad person. And that resulted in a lot of anger and frustration on his part. And for me it meant . . . about three years . . . before I was able to say, "Enough of this, . . . just because I want to work, I don't deserve this."

A marriage based on the subordination of one member's needs to another often has a short life. A woman is surprised to find her husband expecting from her the kind of subservience that his mother might have demonstrated. A man's mother may have sacrificed her own achievement for her family, but his wife is not necessarily prepared to do so. When a man's self-worth depends upon his wife's complicity in her own subordination, the marriage and its members are at risk. Her development in any direction aside from domesticity can constitute a major threat to a husband whose self-esteem is so fragile as to hinge upon another's being less than he.

Hence, women's subordination has its roots in the psyches of both sexes as well as in our economic and sociopolitical arrangements. When women gain substantial earning power and like it, their perceptions of self and other shift. Moreover, their new currency within the marital relationship changes the customary inequality that had been in force. A woman's earnings give her more than financial power; they contribute to her sense of personal power independent of and within the marital relationship. In most instances, however, men still earn more than their wives, and even when they do not, there remains a tendency to believe in "the validity of the male provider role."[19]

Even women who have grown up with messages to the contrary do not altogether escape the entrenched ideology. In developing concepts of identity and capability, people are not rendered immune to the influence of others in their immediate environments and in the larger society. Wanting to work even if her marriage had not dissolved, Ursula lost confidence when her husband denigrated her ability, but self-doubt was overruled as she reestablished her footing outside the marriage and within herself.

Well, my former husband . . . would undermine me. When I decided that I wanted to work he told me that the best I was going to be able to do was sell behind a counter or something. I remember thinking about asking the lady who ran [their apartment] building if I could wash windows or something. I mean it was that stupid, that I was buying into this thing . . . it was that realization that I did not have to plan my life around pleasing this man, and the dishes, and keeping the place dusted, and that kind of thing. So it was anger with him that pushed me out the door. . . . that was a weird period in my life, because I was always the high achiever, in high school especially. That was just a brief period in my life where I allowed whatever fears or doubts I had about myself to really take over. And I lived with it for three years. I don't remember what day or what time or which person I talked to, when it turned around. But I did find people to talk to; I sought out people who would be more positive than I was willing to be, because there was a part of me that really didn't believe that, that I had to settle for less.

Oppression is contrary to a human inclination toward growth and self-actualization. However, the development of self-concept and aspiration does not occur in a vacuum. People's view of themselves and their potential is influenced both positively and negatively by others and by the social context of their lives. It is not by chance that Ursula's period of low confidence coincided with her stay in a traditional marriage, a context that perpetuated female subordination. Reaching down within herself, a woman can find her temporarily obscured self-esteem; reaching out to others, she can find support for her assertion against the inhibiting forces in her life.

What Shapes Choice and Change in Marriage

Men and women are not always explicitly aware of their own or the other's needs and expectations when they enter marriage. Further, they may not realize how much of their socialization they carry with them into the new partnership. The upbringings of many have included a variety of messages about what it means to be a male or female in our society. Even now, two decades into the current women's movement, there exist on both a societal and an individual level vestiges of a traditional ideology about men's and women's places. Our institutions still have not been revamped to accommodate working parents and their children.[20] Discrimination remains in the workplace. The weight of household tasks and child care still falls on women, working or not.[21] Children continue to be taught, if not explicitly, by example, that mothers caretake and fathers earn. Juxtaposed to those messages are those that spell equality of opportunity and shared family responsibility for men and women.

An individual's development cannot be wholly explained by environmental influences or social ideology, however. One who rejected domesticity when it was the agreed-upon definition of women's lives, Esther entered marriage thirty years ago knowing that she needed independent achievement in addition to family. By communicating clearly her needs and expectations to her future husband, she maximized their chances for endurance as a couple but still experienced social sanctions for her life choices. Esther acknowledges her lack of conformity with prevailing reasons for marriage and the unusual forthright approach that her self-awareness allowed.

> I thought that the whole basis for marriage thirty years ago was entirely different than the reasons for marriage today. . . . And I was looked upon as a bit of a maverick, in all truth, because I wanted everything. I wanted a career, and I wanted marriage, and I wanted children. . . . there were women who felt that way, sure there were, because I knew them, but on the whole they didn't feel that way. And you paid a bit of a price sometimes in terms of being accused of neglect of either your children or your marriage or your husband.

To defy prevailing ideology about one's nature and place in society requires a degree of self-understanding and strength that young people may not yet possess. When people married in their late teens and early twenties, their identities were still largely adopted from their socialization.[22] In the process of individuation, separating from family and background to define an individual identity, some aspects of one's socialization are deemed agreeable and others are discarded. A period of time free of social obligation is necessary for this separation and identity resolution to occur.[23] The person must be free to experiment and decide what suits her, some of which will be familiar and some new; the identity that results represents both assimilation of her past and individuation from it. That period without social responsibility was ordinarily thought to be adolescence, but it more often than not extends into the twenties, especially for women. Women seem to have had to struggle more than men in defining their identities and life direction, probably because of the more restrictive ideology prescribing a female path. Males have customarily been expected to have full lives of work and family; a man who chose not to be gainfully employed would be likely to face a struggle more akin to a woman's than to a man's.

An early marriage can preclude the development of an identity that picks and chooses. Commitments made prior to this process later feel like cases of mistaken identity. Unlike Esther, whose self-certainty permitted clear articulation of her needs prior to marriage, women and men commonly discover during the course of a marriage individual purposes and directions that are discrepant from original expectations. Jill's experience after a decade of marriage is not atypical:

perhaps the most significant [decision] was that I realized after quite some time that what I wanted out of my life and what my husband wanted out of my life were very different and were in conflict. And perhaps what I wanted out of him certainly was in conflict with [the way] he saw his role. . . . all these conflicts . . . had displayed themselves. And in an effort to try and work them out, it never worked. So I certainly could have stayed in the marriage, because he wanted to keep it together, but I knew that it was going to be continually destructive for me. I realized that if I was going to really make any changes I had no choice but to get out.

Individual change comes more readily when a person is free of close commitments to others. To facilitate the formation of an adult identity that both assimilates and departs from one's background, a young person often physically moves away from family of origin, thereby making a difficult process easier for all concerned. When personal change occurs, involvement in an intimate relationship can at least complicate if not actually thwart it. The other person and the premises upon which the relationship was built are called upon to change also. If the relationship does not accommodate change, the individual is faced with a conflict between relationship and self. Although that conflict is not easily resolved, individuals in our culture find it far more difficult to ignore the press of personal change. Women who entered marriage before attaining developmental maturity, that is, an adult identity, found themselves changing over time in ways that refuted the bases of the marriage. When their partners cannot make complementary changes, women struggle with a choice between self-suppression and divorce. The choices women make after they have launched them- selves in a career are generally better-informed ones, in that they can take into account the needs of a fully formed adult.[24] Our current high divorce rate can in large part be attributed to the kind of process that Colleen, a mother of grown children who divorced after twenty years of marriage, describes.

he always felt that he made the decisions for the family. Consequently, his decisions were the right ones and the good ones. And if I requested something or I felt something should be done, that was selfish on my part. I think basically I always had the same gut-level feelings, but I did not really have the strength. My ex [husband] is the kind of person that comes out as a very strong, domineering type of individual . . . maybe I was looking for a father image. . . . But I grew in that amount of time, and I didn't need a father. And there really wasn't any change in him. As a matter of fact, that's one thing that he said: "I haven't changed. I've always been the same." And I said,"Yeah, that's right. I agree with you, but I have." . . . I think I finally just got to the point that nothing's going to change, not that my ex [husband] is a bad person or anything. It's just that we grew apart. We had different ideas and beliefs about life. And it was a choice, really: Do I accept life this way, or do I want more for me out of it? Well, the answer was I wanted more for me. . . . And then there was no longer a choice. [*What was important to you at the time?*] I think basic [economic] survival. I thought maybe I could. But I really wasn't sure that I was going to be able to do it . . . setting up a place to live . . . and really, you have nothing. I had no real credit establishment myself or anything. So I had to work through those things. [*How did you feel about yourself at the time of the decision?*] I had a few doubts about my sanity, if I was really going to keep it all together. One thing that I was a little afraid of was being alone. And after I was on my own I realized I had spent a whole lot of years being married being alone. So it took care of the fear real quick.

A woman who has been dependent in a marriage is at considerable risk, pragmatically and psychologically, when she must choose between her own development and the long-standing relationship. A marriage that presumes traditional gender roles keeps women in a dependent, childlike position. When they "grow up," even in the confines of such a relationship, women find their images of self and life direction significantly revised. Either their husbands change in a similar direction or the relationship is jeopardized. Repeatedly, women are unable to deny their independent identities once they begin to emerge.

When Marriage Fails to Accommodate Personal Change

No matter how desolate a relationship becomes, divorce is never easily embraced. The fulfillment that a woman's employment provides can serve to postpone a difficult decision. That employment is connected to a self-image that more readily entertains independence; paradoxically, it also can forestall the shift to single life. Work assumes varying importance in Jill's life as she experiences personal change. Married for ten years, Jill had left a small organization for a larger one, where she moved to a personnel management position within eighteen months.

I really see [work] as a very positive portion of my life, because it didn't start out with the same balance in my life that it has now. Initially, it was down on the scale, whereas my marriage and personal life had a far greater role to play. And as that situation deteriorated over a period of time, and my career developed in a positive way, the two were going in very different directions. As the marriage really started to fall apart, the only thing I really had that was satisfying was my work. So . . . in one sense it had a very, very positive effect; in another sense, what it did was to delay the ultimate decision of getting a divorce. Because it was so offensive to me initially to think of getting a divorce, I would just throw myself into my job and not deal with it, so that a lot of time passed that probably shouldn't have if I had really dealt with my marital problems earlier. But because I was working so hard and I was satisfied with what I was doing and growing and developing, I could just, Monday through Friday, virtually forget about the problems at home. So in one sense it was positive; in another, I think, it probably prolonged the whole thing.

Women with a separate source of income are in a better practical position when a marriage ends. They still contend with considerable psychological struggle about identity and life direction. Their marriage commitments were, after all, a sizable part not just of their daily lives but of who they were.

Gainfully employed married women initially may have viewed their work as secondary to their relationship, but we have seen how their perspectives shifted with further career involvement. A marriage that can accommodate change in roles and self-image is likely to survive the personal transitions of its partners. Others are strained by such shifts. Women's work not only provides them with a way out of the marriage, it also sustains them during the conflict. Their work lives can become especially important in times of marital difficulty. Hope's immersion in the job served as a welcome refuge from domestic stress and also furthered her proficiencies.

When I was going through a lot of real difficult times at home, most of my productive and creative energy went into work, because I just had to cope at home. That's all I could really do. Once I got out of that situation, I found that [in] all those years of working so hard I'd really developed a lot more skill and resource than I realized, so that the work thing got much, much easier. And I had this energy to give at home. I genuinely love my children and my family life, and [now] it's just a real good balance.

When domestic crises are resolved, an employed woman can restore a balance between work and family. The job serves as an outlet for her energy and devotion when channels at home are blocked, and she subsequently reaps the benefits of her hard work through skill mastery. Her family remains vital to her, and she is able to become more active at home when conflicts there are no more. Both family and career are integral to her identity; when one wanes, the other may strengthen until an equilibrium has been regained.[25]

The working woman who divorces still has part of her life intact. Although she struggles with questions of identity around intimate relationships and commitment, there is another part of her life that remains whole and gratifying. Work is a significant source of self-esteem when one's personal relationships are thrown into doubt. Moreover, established economic independence gives her an option on freedom that her unemployed sister does not have.

The plight of a woman who devoted herself to home and is now divorcing is substantially more difficult. When domestic endeavors account for the whole of life, the family's disintegration leaves a woman psychologically and pragmatically bereft. Without work, a woman's self-image is centered in home and family. With that source of identity undermined, she has little recourse. Her psychological foundation shaken, she lacks the preparation to resort to work for a greater share of her self-esteem. She is faced with the task of rebuilding her identity in a more complete and fundamental way than her divorced but employed sister. Economic insecurity further compounds her real and psychological vulnerability. The woman without work must decide not only who she is now but also how she is going to survive.

In contrast, women with established careers have accumulated more apparent resources to carry them through divorce. Though a major part of their lives has been overturned, women's financial wherewithal and identities independent of domesticity are vital mainstays that anchor them psychologically and tangibly.

Marriage as an Unfettered Choice

Economic advantages notwithstanding, women's careers can provide enough fulfillment that marriage is viewed as volitional rather than required. Being on her own may not be Jill's preference, but remarriage is not as necessary for her as others believe it to be.

> There was certainly much more comfort being a married career woman than a single career woman from the standpoint that you're on your own. And I think my family thinks, "Well, she's been through a difficult time and now she's on her own, and the next important thing for her to do is to find a new husband" [*laugh*]. And that's not my objective. Certainly it's to reestablish my life, but the end result of all of that effort is not just to find a new husband. It's to fulfill my life in whatever direction it takes.

Now in her midthirties, Jill's priority is to reestablish herself psychologically and develop a new life that may or may not include another marriage. Her perspectives on the future are open-ended, and her career gives her license for leisurely choice that is not available to women who must perforce be occupied with survival.

Nina, a can-do person who preferred work to school and now successfully manages former peers through collaboration, had been married for a few years in her late twenties. She is even more forthright about the primacy of her career; it would not be subjugated to a marriage.

> I'm not sure that I want to get married again. I want companionship, but [what] scares me is, . . . knowing how important my career is, finding somebody that's willing to let me have my career and my aspirations. I'm just really starting to do the things that I want to do, so I have another twenty years to go, of things that I want to do. And I don't want to have to cut that off at this point.

Once women establish themselves in careers, they are unwilling to relinquish that aspect of themselves for the sake of a relationship. Their first commitment is to themselves; they do not seek their wholeness in another. If they are complete within themselves, women can enter marriage as equal contributors, not relying on a man for economic and psychological sustenance. Women who have been socialized to view marriage as essential to their completion can revise their perspectives, as Leslie, a single woman in her late thirties, did.

> my personal goals have changed. I wanted to get married, and I don't necessarily think that that's a goal anymore. My goal is just to be happy within myself, and I am. I have a fantastically supportive family. So my goal is to be at peace and not to put that pressure and stress on myself about marriage, because I don't really think it's that important at this point in time. So that has definitely changed.

Women who feel complete within themselves are free to choose marriage or not.[26] Ina is in her early thirties and ready to leave a company that has not recognized her outstanding sales prowess. Aware of her desire for family, she knows that her life does not literally or figuratively depend upon it.

> I've come to a decision at this point in my life. I would like marriage and a child. And I used to think there was something wrong in saying that. You know, women's lib; it's not necessary. But at this point in my life, it would be very nice. And if it doesn't come, well, it doesn't come. But I'm not going to kill myself over it.

Ideology can work in either direction: to persuade women that they are incomplete without a man or to argue that they are lacking to want one. With opportunity to develop oneself in any direction, women can become whatever they might, and their choices are more freely made.

Men and women benefit from a marriage that is a true partnership where neither must lean on the other for the meeting of primary survival needs and where both freely give emotional support. Some women do have marriages that nurture them and their careers without conflict. Esther attests:

> As far as my husband is concerned, a liberated woman could not be married to a better person. He has no qualms whatsoever—never has had about career versus marriage or anything like that. And I made sure before we were married that he knew I didn't do buttons and I did not like housework, and he's very supportive—always has been.

Marsha, a thirty-year-old finance executive, also enjoys a relationship based upon mutuality with her husband.

> I think that's another reason we get along so well. We respect each other's individuality, which I think is also important for any type of relationship. I don't push him and he doesn't really push, but he's supportive. I think there's a big difference between pushing and supporting. I'm very supportive of what he does. He likes what he does. And he knows that I like what I do, and he's supportive of that. So it's worked out pretty well.

Marriages that are formed independent of a gender-based division of labor look and feel very different from traditional ones. The mere possibility that husband and wife will be working outside the home creates expectations that are at odds with separate spheres. Social change and economic realities have made it possible for men and women to be more equally responsible for the functions of their partnership where neither sex is solely burdened with domestic caretaking or with financial provision; both can participate in gainful employment and in household activity. This statement continues to express an ideal, as data repeatedly demonstrate that regardless of their employment status, women continue to carry primary responsibility for the home. Even full-time, professionally engaged women report a significantly greater amount of time tending to household chores and children than do their male counterparts, married or single.[27]

Freed of gender convention, women and men can choose partners on different grounds. A man's earning power and a woman's domestic aptitude are no longer pivotal in the marriage contract. The measure of a husband turns less on financial provision and more on active support in promoting an equal relationship. The measure of a wife turns less on homemaking and more on partnership. Ideally, without sole responsibility for one or the other domain and with a true partnership in both, women and men would be freer and more wholly fulfilled. Until boys as well as girls are socialized in a gender-free way and until our institutional structures catch up with revised ideology, we fall short of the ideal. Women nonetheless seek husbands who support their achievements apart from domesticity and who participate in home caretaking. A marriage that seemingly meets these new expectations is put to the test when children are contemplated.

Children

Whether or not they have reached a level of ease with each other in new roles, most wives and husbands today are members of the labor force.[28] When it is just the two of them, the running of the household does not seem so severely undermined by a woman's employment outside the home. In many cases, the wife's job is less demanding and time consuming, perhaps even part-time, and she simply does the bulk of household chores as well. Women who are working to supplement the primary income, which is their husband's, often leave the labor force to have children, returning at varying intervals subsequent to birth.[29] Dual-career couples, where husband and wife are fully involved in professional careers that are both highly compensating and demanding, have the resources to purchase domestic services and meals prepared by someone else. A mutually supportive couple, in the financial and emotional sense, can find this arrangement satisfactory, albeit hectic. Household tasks and meal preparation require more planning than they did when women were reliably at home, but these things can be accomplished through shared domestic responsibility, be it fiscal or corporeal. Such solutions are not so readily available where children are concerned.

Family Arrangements in a Preindustrial Economy

In a preindustrial economy, there was little worry about who would tend the children. The entire family lived and worked together in one location, and children were an integral part of family endeavors. They were tended by other family members, often older siblings, until able to assume some share of the work themselves. Tasks still were delegated to some extent by gender, but the lines seemed less absolutely drawn when everyone labored together in a common purpose and place.[30]

An industrialized economy shifted the provision of goods and services to centralized regions away from the home and thereby divided the family's work and its members.[31] The shift from household manufacture to wage work precipitated a new arrangement such that women were designated as nurturers and men as providers. The social and political imbalance of that arrangement in conjunction with increased economic needs brought women out of the home to join men in the paid labor force.

Women's full-fledged paid labor participation found social acceptance during both world wars when they were needed to compensate for the depletion of the male labor force. Despite women's efforts to retain their jobs, active political forces sent them back to domesticity when men returned from overseas. Women wanted to remain at work, and many did, despite ideology to the contrary. Women's wage labor participation has been more continuous, even in the 1950s, than prevailing ideology would have us believe.[32]

Women's large-scale postwar entrance into the paid labor force challenged long-standing assumptions about "their place" and about the future of the family. Prior to the Industrial Revolution children were needed as labor contributors to the family. Subsequent to it, the assumptions that kept women as domestic caretakers also precluded choice about reproduction. According to a societally shared belief in their intrinsic domesticity, women would naturally want children. Once married, a woman would be caring for the home and the needs of her family; if she worked at all, it was only until the children arrived. Their arrival was not a choice, since women were assumed to be naturally so inclined; a childless married woman was unable rather than unwilling. To be a woman and not to want children was antithetical; indeed, women who professed an antipathy toward children were the subject of pity, scorn, or both.

Women's movement out of the home into the work force raised the question not only of domestic responsibility but also of children. Having choices for life direction and identity, women could more readily contradict prevailing notions about what was natural to them and what was not. Work and career became a choice; so did children.[33] No longer was it assumed that every woman, by dint of being female, wanted or would have children.[34] Social change enabled women to assert their needs for achievement independent of family and even to go so far as to eschew family altogether.

To Mother or Not to Mother

Single or married, women now make conscious decisions about having children.[35] Whereas child rearing was once a given in the life of a woman, it has become the focus of active psychological exploration and soul-searching. At various points in their development, women may answer the question of children differently. Thirty years old and married for the second time to a man who had a family earlier in his life, Carla finds her views have changed with time and circumstances.

> No, I don't want children. And I used to. But I don't; there's no way. I'm not going to take the time out of my career to have children right now. My husband is older than I am . . . so he's not into diapers and midnight feedings either. He's had his . . . he's had plenty of experiences with having children, and I don't think that he would really press it.

Career interruption is a serious consideration for women contemplating children. Women managers who become mothers do not want significant interruptions in their careers. Moreover, control of family size has enabled professional women to work continuously or with very small intermissions.[36]

When a mate has already been a parent in a former marriage, women sometimes feel freer not to bear children. Having a husband with children allowed Teresa to come to an independent decision about her own fecundity.

> once you get married, you should have a little time alone. You don't need a child right away to complicate that whole bit. . . . I did not feel at that time that I was mentally or emotionally prepared to have a child, or materially . . . so I guess that might have been a dilemma, so to speak, but I have not regretted it. My husband was married before; I know that had he not had children I probably would have. But he did, so that made it easier. [*How did you decide?*] Mentally and emotionally, I had established a certain patterned way of living that I knew a child would completely disrupt and change. Ah, and there were certain things that we wanted out of life; . . . financially, we wouldn't have been able to do both. . . . I decided based on those things. And I had [children as relatives]. We have [her husband's] children . . . so that was the decision.

Women do not necessarily have to bear children in order to enjoy them in their lives. Moreover, women are not inherently mothers just because they are female. Some, like Jessica, who has been married and divorced, have had little or no inclination toward maternity for as long as they can remember.

And I won't [have children]. I decided that independent of my husband. . . . you get a bunch of women together, and they talk about kids and blah, blah. I have never wanted children. Never. I can remember being sixteen and seventeen years old and thinking, "I really don't want to do that." And at that young age, saying to people, "I don't care what you call it. If you think I'm selfish, then I'm selfish. I don't want to have them."

In a home economy when children were needed for labor and later when women were relegated to domesticity, a female's unwillingness to have children was tantamount to social sabotage. Refusal to serve society in the way deemed appropriate to her gender labeled her selfish. For a female to want what was a male's birthright, that is, pursuits independent of family and procreation, was unnatural and therefore morally repugnant. We still hear traces of that ideology when women who have rejected childbearing refer to themselves as "selfish."

Women raised between the two eras of traditional gender roles and liberation grappled with questions of what was right for them as opposed to social prescription. For some of these women, both maternity and career become a focus for decision. The combination causes conflict for psychological reasons of traditional expectation and structural reasons of nonaccommodation in the world of work.

Although men still do not face these dilemmas, and our institutions have not been sufficiently revamped to make child rearing compatible with career, we see evidence of social change in the psychological processing of women who now grapple with decisions of children and career. Women who have not been pressed into a mold of traditional ideology can decide about childbearing without the burdens of social sanction and moral implication. Married and divorced more than once before turning forty, Renee's considerations are not riddled with the conflict and psychological suffering that would accompany a choice tinged with social obligation and meanings for personal worth.

[*Do you think about having children?*] Sure, every once in a while. I go back and forth: sometimes . . . wanting them, sometimes . . . being selfish and knowing I'm being selfish and saying I can't have kids if I'm going to be selfish with my time. I don't know at all, because I go on wide swings. Usually I don't think about it. But when I do think about it, it's only for a short period of time, for an hour maybe. . . . But it won't be a great obsession or a depression for me.

Now that maternity is no longer a given, most women want to make an active and conscious choice about it, not one by default. With their value as females and as contributors to society not at stake, women can search within themselves for their suitability as parents. Some claim to have been certain about whether or not they wanted children. Others have given it little thought or have remained content with uncertainty until advancing age presses them to make a choice.[37] Mary, happily married for some time and moving up with yearly promotions in a technical field, represents many for whom age thirty signals the time of decision.

> It's almost natural. For some reason you think of thirty as your do-or-die date, that you've got to decide to have children or not. . . . One of my major concerns is that I wasn't making a decision one way or the other, and I was just sort of letting it pass without making a decision. And I would hate to just have gone by and never really confronted it. So we finally sat down and said, "Yeah, we think we'd like to have at least one child." But then there's the whole issue of timing. You're looking at your career: "Well, where will I be in two years? Let's see, I want to be in this next job for two years so I can get established, and then maybe I'll have the baby." I want to keep working. Then there's the issue: "Well, can we afford someone to come in and stay with a newborn infant all day?" . . . all these things. It's just so difficult. And you get so mad, because I know my colleagues—men at work—do not have this problem. They have these wives at home, and having children is no big deal. You just get so mad that you have to confront and work out all these problems that men don't have to face. I'm also concerned with my image. Through your dress and everything, you're trying to in essence play down the fact that you're a female. You're trying to fit in. So by the way you dress and work, by your demeanor, everything is playing down the fact that you're female so you can make these men more comfortable with you. Then I say, "Well, what are they going to think when I show up eight months pregnant?" That's so obviously female. It's like you're flaunting it; there's nothing you can do about it. How will that affect my career? Will people think of me differently once I come back? Will they unconsciously not give me responsibilities, assignments, ask me to travel—knowing that I have an infant? Will they be making those decisions for me rather than letting me make the decisions, of whether I want that responsibility or whether I want to go on that business trip? So it's all these things.

Mary's comments represent the feelings and thoughts of many women. Considerations that loom large for them would not even appear in the picture of most corporate men's fatherhood. That women must think about ramifications of such a highly personal decision as maternity in these public terms is significant. Certainly, it reflects social change, which has rendered them a choice where there had not been one. But it speaks also to the limits of change. That our institutional structures have yet to accommodate the current realities of people's lives is evident here. Women are trying to figure out ways of fitting family into a structure that still operates upon the assumption that they are full-time, at-home caretakers.[38]

Moreover, the suspicion is strong that these institutions—in this case, corporations—have yet to accept the family functions of its workers. A female has to work harder to cover up those aspects of herself and her life than does a male.[39] That a cover-up is required attests to the fact that our societal structures are functioning under a traditional ideology that stands in contradiction to people's lives. Although women are commonly depicted as suffering the costs of family and intimate relationships, one study found that fully half of the men also showed evidence of such costs.[40]

The fragility of social change is also alluded to here. As long as women are functioning like men within the corporation, they are perceived and treated so. When their uniquely female functions enter the workplace in the form of pregnancy and motherhood, women suspect that they will be treated like the "little woman at home" again, with decisions made for them in the name of their protection.[41] Thus, women are not simply struggling with decisions about parenting; they are in a position of trying to fit themselves and their lives into an antiquated structure whose surface trappings of modernity are easily shaken.[42]

New Families in Old Structures

Although women are now able to choose career and family, social change has not gone so far as to facilitate their doing so. A gender-free socialization of females has not been accompanied sufficiently by corresponding expectations for males. It is unlikely that most boys are brought up to believe their personal fulfillment and life direction may stem equally from active family responsibility and paid work. We probably would not find many working men contending with the problems of procreation and child care that these women face. Even in dual-career families, financial responsibilities may be shared to a far greater extent than familial ones.[43]

Moreover, social change has yet to penetrate our institutions' structures in such a way that they provide mechanisms to ease the dilemma of work and family that is surely societally shared. In order to retain control over their career and family lives, committed businesswomen are leaving corporations in favor of the greater autonomy and family accommodation offered by independent entrepreneurship.[44] It is to our society's detriment that to date the dilemma articulated by Rebecca, married for a few years by age thirty, remains a "woman's issue." How many men would characterize themselves as selfish for wanting career and family? How many men ask themselves the questions she poses?

> . . . the conflict of wanting to remain in the business world continually, and yet wanting to raise a family. To me right now, of anything in my life, that's probably the foremost thing on my mind. Here I'm hitting the big three-oh; you think, "Well, you've got a few years left in there." But . . . if you're going to raise children, maybe you should be at home doing that. Are you going to trust that to somebody else to do . . . every day? Are you being selfish wanting to work and have a family at the same time? Can you do it? Then there's just the practical things; it's going to be an extremely difficult thing to do for a while. It's going to be an extremely tiring experience. The decision to have a family, I think that's pretty much concrete in the sense that I would definitely love to have children. The decision now is, can I fit that in with this work and with all the other things—having a life of my own apart from a marriage relationship? I think I can do it; I mean, other people have. But it's a timing thing. I just got into supervision, and I think, "Oh, how is this going to be perceived by the company?" But I guess the issue just . . . boils down to work and family, working out that picture.

Individual marriages free of gender stereotypes do not suffice as solutions to the dilemma of work and family. Sharon, professionally trained and established in personnel with a toddler at home, raises similar questions despite a compatible partnership with her husband.

> Well, the only thing that really strikes a chord with me was just the whole process of going through the decision of having a baby and a career at the same time. That was a real tough decision to come to, not so much the fact of wanting to do it or not, but the fact of when to do it. Part of it, I think, is just the anxiety of "How am I going to handle this?" "What am I going to look like walking around here in this very professional, conservative environment in the ultimate female state?" I was thirty-two years old. It would be nice to have gotten a little farther along in my career. But on the other hand, there was this other tug of "Well, how much longer can you wait biologically?" In terms of talking about having children, my mother always said, "You have plenty of time to have children when you're after thirty." I'm sure that in my own personal case . . . it was more the anxiety of knowing that I wanted to work; how was I going to handle this situation? What's going to happen? Things [were] really going great. I think a lot of it was also situational at that time. In other words, can I basically play both of these roles simultaneously? Can I be not only a wife and also have a career, but now can I handle being a mother? . . . I'm up in the air sometimes, but

it seems to be working. Part of the reason I [attribute] to two factors. Personally, I am an organized person, and I can see ahead what needs to be done. And secondly, I have a husband who I feel was liberated before I was—in terms of sharing responsibility and really working together on that.

Sharon was less uncertain about her desire for children than about her ability to fit them into her life and career. Females frequently embark upon adulthood with maternity as an eventual expectation. Even early and long-standing determinations may undergo revision with career involvement. Females who assumed that they would have children someday did not necessarily anticipate the complications wrought by professional commitment. That women are now demonstrating career commitment formerly expected of men only is evident in their reluctance to sacrifice, or even interrupt, work for family.[45] Further, women are demonstrating as much and more career commitment than their male counterparts at the middle management level.[46] Beverly, thirty and childless, outlines the new conflicts faced by women, particularly those in a company that clings to the idea of men only in professional positions.

It [the decision to have children] is a big one. I've always thought I wanted them and probably wouldn't have gotten married if I weren't real sure that I did like kids a whole lot. At the same time, I turned thirty and I'm saying, "How long can I wait?" But I'm also meeting a whole lot of other people; since I started looking at this question, wonderful women have come out of the woodwork, . . . saying, "I waited till I was thirty-six or thirty-seven or thirty-eight, and I'm glad I did." And so now I'm saying, "I don't have to decide this week," which is a real help. I think I still want them—no, I'm sure I do—just not this year, maybe not even next year. Trade-off on that is the further I go in the company, the harder it's going to be to get out, ever, even if I decide that is what I want to do. And they [her company] certainly don't make any provisions for families of any kind—I mean for their men or for their women employees. There's no part-time jobs, there's no flex time, there's no subsidized day care, nothing. I'd probably have to do everything I'm doing now, plus take care of a child in there somewhere. We're fortunate enough that financially we could pull it off, and my whole salary would go for child care, household help, and that sort of thing. At this point, I'd probably do that; I think that'd probably be okay. I worry about energy. I've never been a person that went twenty-four hours a day. I think there are people that do. I get tired. I get impatient and cranky. And I'm trying to figure out how to not get tired and add one more thing in.

Questions of parenthood become far more complicated when women must consider not only whether they want to have children but also how to arrange it. Birth control allowed us to move from having no choice to controlling the number and timing of children born. Social change, in the form of the current women's movement, has made parenthood itself optional, but the decision is not simply one of individual desire and suitability. Women now have gratifying careers that they prefer not to relinquish. Should they want children, women must consider the personal and career ramifications that Susan details. Twenty-eight, married, and childless to date, Susan has moved up through seven positions to become a production manager in a creative, forward-looking technology company.

> Nothing . . . has been a real dilemma other than the decision as to whether or not to have a family. We've been back and forth over the past year very intensely on that one, mainly because I'm getting to the point where I want to make the decision; either . . . yes or no. Because as time goes on and my job gets bigger and bigger, it becomes more and more difficult to take the time out to do that. I think in the back of my mind it's always been "Yeah, someday," and now someday is here. I'm getting older, and I really wouldn't want to be thirty-five or thirty-six starting a family, so I think it's been a future thing, but the future is here now, and the decision has to be made. [*What do you consider in making the decision?*] Probably the first thing is the impact on my relationship with my husband. We've had a lot of freedom and been enjoying it, especially relative to time spent at work, play time; we can essentially do what we want. If I want to work overtime, I do, or he does. If we want to take off for a weekend or take off after work at night, we do that. And the constraints involved in having a child are definitely going to put a damper on that. The second thing is probably child care. What happens with that? Does it make sense in the whole bit of myself and my husband having grown up with our mothers there all the time and the whole thing of "that's the way it should be"? "That's what's best" versus "things have changed, and maybe that really isn't the best way anymore." . . . is it right to bring a person into the world and not take complete 100 percent responsibility for them, 100 percent of the time? Trying to weigh that whole thing. The third thing of course is the whole career-interruption thing. For me even to think of taking two months out is a lot, and do I want to do that? The other thing is walking around in a factory, so obviously pregnant. I mean, people put you into roles. They have perceptions, and there aren't a lot of women who are there who are in management positions to begin with. So trying to work through some of the stereotypes can be tough, and that's just another one that can push you back another five years.

A woman's decision about children involves far more than herself. Becoming a mother would curtail some freedoms that she enjoys, but more weighty are considerations of marital relationship, child-care responsibility, and career continuation. Women are thinking about the effects of their maternity upon their lives at home and at work, as well as wrestling with questions of conscience regarding child care. The psychological depth of traditional gender roles can be seen in women's ascription of guilt and selfishness to their desire for career continuity even as they bear children.

Our society contributes to the maintenance of such beliefs by resisting structural change that would enable women to contemplate career and family in the same unconflicted manner as men presumably do.[47] As long as social change does not fully penetrate our institutionalized practices, we remain at the level of individual accommodation of a mass movement. Societal structure has yet to adapt to ideas and behavior that are now almost universal. Even though they grapple with the same dilemmas, individual women and men must find their own solutions in the absence of collective ones. Further, since children are still seen as falling within the female purview, it is primarily women who contend with the resolution of career and family conflicts, and this maintains females' disadvantage in employment.[48] After all, if women were still at home, there would be no conflict; having brought about the problem, they are left to resolve it.

Some predict that women's ultimate resolution is to retreat from career, even after a decade or two of investment.[49] Hardesty and Jacobs go so far as to assert that women are fulfilling unconscious dependency needs when they drop out for the sake of child care.[50] Moreover, they characterize women as more apt to relinquish work than men, who have an "inborn provider instinct" and are more likely to have ongoing responsibility for the survival of dependent others.[51] The premise is that women, unlike men, still have an option not to work.

Economic reality and the changing composition of family contradict the notion that employment for women is not a necessity. Married or not, with and without young children, the majority of women in this country are expected to maintain, if not increase, their participation in the paid labor force.[52] Practical considerations notwithstanding, women of this study also demonstrate psychological needs for work. They seem to conform to findings of similar psychological profiles between male and female managers, with females frequently demonstrating stronger achievement motivation and career commitment.[53] Those who want children are determined to maintain career continuity while forging individual arrangements.

The lack of structural change has perpetuated female dependency.

Women must depend upon others in their immediate lives for support and assistance when they choose to have children and career. A husband who is an equal partner and trustworthy child care are crucial.[54] Karen, planning coordinator in a retail firm and a mother at thirty-two, is fortunate to have both.

> I'd been thinking about having a family for a while, and I have a great deal of confidence in the woman that's sitting with [her child], and if it weren't for that I couldn't feel comfortable about it at all. Plus my husband . . . he really wanted this [child]. My husband and I have a very equal relationship. So in that respect, it's just like that job: He's accepting of it, and he's willing to share it. If I had a job that required travel, I would turn it down, because I just don't think that it will work well. And I don't think my husband would accept one either, because it really takes both of us being around to manage everything, to make it work out.

The consent and cooperation of her employer are also required if a woman is to continue her career subsequent to maternity. Managers can be supportive even when they are not fully certain that a woman's commitment to her job will withstand the charms of a baby.[55] As the mother of a toddler, Sharon attests to the die-hard quality of customary notions about females' inherent nature.

> I told you about my manager and how supportive he was. He never really believed I would come back. And it got to the point where I said, "I'm coming back. I know I'm coming back, and you're not going to believe it until I'm back." So as receptive and liberated as he was, . . . when it got down to this particular situation, he had some doubts himself [during her pregnancy]. The comments [from co-workers] were typically, "How do you feel?" "You look good." "Is everything okay?" In terms of other people that I worked with, when I got back to work they were really interested in how everything was going, and everything about the baby, and certainly very supportive.

Women appreciate managers whose support eases their decision to have children while maintaining career. Aware of the risk that a manager may be taking in her individual case, Karen also feels a sense of responsibility to female employees who might succeed her.

> [My manager was] very supportive of women, but he certainly took a risk. If I said I was going to come back, I would come back. He was still leery up till the end. People kept saying, "Oh, when you see this little baby, you won't possibly want to go back." But I realized I had a great opportunity and that I really felt that I could do both things. I also knew I wouldn't be happy home forty hours a week. I hate cleaning the house. I do not like to cook. I do not like to plan meals. To have that responsibility

day in and day out, I don't enjoy it. . . . I'm the youngest person that's been in [my current job]; I'm the only woman that's ever been in it. So [I had] all these opportunities, and . . . if I had just not come back, the next person that came along that was in the same situation would've had a more difficult time. Plus my own personal career—you're not going to get another. And I think my child will grow up, still be a good person even if I'm not there. So you can see I'm still dealing with this, the whole guilt trip. But I think it'll work out.

These women contradict traditional beliefs about female identity and life path. Their sex does not necessarily imply domestic suitability. Women may need the fulfillment of career as much as men might; they can simultaneously love and care for children without self-sacrifice. Having two powerful commitments, to self and family, inevitably divides their time and contributes to feelings of guilt. Esther, mother of two grown children knows, however, that her mothering would have suffered if it were a full-time occupation.

I think if you have any intelligence whatsoever, you wonder a little bit about whether you're taking enough time with children. I think you wonder whether you're taking enough time with your husband, whether you're giving enough energy to it. There have been many times in my life that I've gone through the guilts. I'm sure men do too. My husband had to travel a lot. He was away a lot all during our marriage, and he had tremendous guilt feelings about it too. But I think that basically I always knew that I would be a much better mother if I were working. I was really miserable at home. And I need some kind of a competitive—not competitive as much as a challenge, probably.

Feelings of guilt notwithstanding, the women interviewed overcome internal and external obstacles to choose the kind of life that meets their needs for independent achievement and family connection. Support from husbands and managers serves to facilitate a woman's decisions, but the critical impetus for her development finally rests with herself.

A Woman's Sole Responsibility

When marriages do not endure and institutions provide no respite for family concerns, women still choose the double life of children and career. Shouldering sole responsibility for a child, single parents face all of the dilemmas described but compounded by the absence of assistance on either the societal or the individual level. Still, women are unwilling to sacrifice the sense of an independent self. Elena, whose mother gave conflicting messages about what it means to be female, will not relinquish her self-reliance and slip into dependency.

> I think one of the most important problems I've had to work through was to find a way to take care of [my child] while I worked. And that has always been something; it's the first thing you have to take care of before you go to your job. And always having . . . in the back of your mind that you have to have a backup system, because he's going to get sick at school, and . . . school holidays—I hate school holidays. I have had to develop a whole . . . organization to take care of him. Now it's easier as he gets older. So that part has always been a big problem in my career. . . . it's having to fight the idea that you ought to want to stay home and take care of [the child]. That has been difficult for me: feeling like a bad mother because you can't be there instantly. And in the end I'm doing it because I want to do it and not because I absolutely have to. . . . had I wanted to, I could have gone home and been taken care of while he grew up, been free to look after him and do whatever I want to do. I chose this because I wanted it, [but] it's almost like I had to. I would have had to give up so much to be taken care of so that I could take care of him. It just wasn't possible for me to do that.

Women who have achieved independence cannot readily give it up; to do so would amount to a significant regression in their development. The mechanics of life might be easier, but the psychological costs are prohibitive. Single mothers may have lost a marital relationship, but they are determined not to lose themselves or their children in the process. Having a child can certainly produce an existential overturning of consciousness. The parent–child connection contributes to Ursula's awareness in intimate relationships, but it does not displace the rest of her life in the way that a husband who temporarily undermined her confidence threatened to do.

> I think being a parent has changed me. Before I had a child, I don't think I knew as much about loving a person as I do now. I've learned a lot about really caring about someone else and really enjoying, for just the enjoyment of it, another person. And it's really enhanced close relationships that I've had with other people.

Women who continue to work do not love their children any less than those who stay at home. It is no longer a choice between self and other; women have changed the equation so that self and other can coexist.[56] The foundations of marriage may be slow to revision, and our divorce rate consequently soars before equal partnerships predominate. Equality between husband and wife is not restricted to one pattern of dual employment but in any case entails a relationship of mutual encouragement and support for individual growth. Women cannot stay in a marriage that forbids them the freedom of their development. A divorce that spells the double difficulty of career and single parenting is preferable to psychological suicide. For such women as Lisa, raising a child alone can fuel their determination to succeed. Having assessed herself as currently underemployed, for example, she gained a perspective on her own abilities and on opportunities elsewhere from exposure to other women managers.[57]

> I enjoy [single parenting]. There was a time when I worried about it, because people say that the right way to do it is to have two parents. When he was younger, I used to worry about it. I used to worry about my ability to do things. I used to worry about whether I would ever be able to financially support us in a reasonable way. I used to really worry about my own energy, if I wasn't cheating him. In many ways, that put more pressure on me . . . I think the desire to give him as much as I could give in terms of supporting him has pushed me to get ahead. If it was just me and if he wasn't there, I might not have been so willing to push or to put up with quite as much, because you wouldn't need as much money. So I think, in a subtle way, that's been a motivator. . . . Now, obviously, I've survived. It was a force. Because I was so determined—I think [that's] the word—that I would proceed, that he was going to make it with my help, that nobody— family, professional, neighbors, or anybody—was going to prevent us. I was driven, because of his existence, because of my desire to give him the best of what I could. That driving force still carries me.

Exacerbated by the fact of her single parenthood, Lisa's struggle continues to represent that of women who choose career and children. The solutions forged by these women remain, for the most part, individual ones. Resistance to changing institutional practice exists on both the personal and the structural level.[58] That organizations are beginning to recognize their changing composition and the family lives of employees is shown by increased provision of parental leave policies. By the mid-1980s more than one-third of the nation's companies offered some type of paternity leave, compared to fewer than 10 percent just five years before.[59] The impetus for this kind of change comes from men, as well as women, and from corporations' growing need to retain their valuable female employees.

It is certainly the case that such change, even in the absence of resistance to it, does not come easily, as massive overhaul of our social belief system and corresponding practice is required. "The most important change we could make in the United States would be a change in the atittude toward parenting. Being a parent is a normal stage in the life cycle of an adult. When business recognizes this, as it recognizes that being young is normal and being old is normal, then the quality of life of working parents will improve."[60] If the trends continue as predicted, with more rather than fewer women working and more men wanting family time, perhaps our structures will be forced to change. Shifts in ideology lag behind behavioral change. Until ideology is really revised in accord with personal change, our social institutions will fail to accommodate us.[61]

□ **III** □

CONNECTIONS
AND CONTEXT

The first two parts of this book focused, respectively, on the professional and personal development of women with careers in corporate organizations. In Part 1 we learned from firsthand testimony how these women's careers began and evolved. The women interviewed gave us access not only to what had transpired in their work lives but to what they had made of it.

In Part 1 we became familiar also with the women themselves through their descriptions of their career development. As they chronicled their work lives, they talked about themselves: what work means to them, how they planned and strategized, how mobility affects them, and what they did and might do as managers.

Explicitly concerned with personal development, Part 2 pursued the women as people apart from profession. Areas of inquiry were not totally separate from career context, but concentration was on the development of personal characteristics and their relation to social change in women's lives. We once again benefited from their thoughtful responses, as they discussed self-images that shifted with time and experience, families that influenced them in various ways, and the joys and dilemmas associated with marriage and children. Events were given meaning by women's perceptions and interpretations, thereby expanding our knowledge of their diverse lives beyond the bare bones of objective data.

Although we have separated the personal from the professional to some extent in our discussions, we have also noted how intertwined they are. When women talk about career, they talk about themselves. When they talk about themselves, it becomes apparent how integral work is to their lives and sense of self.

In Part 3, we address the connections between the personal and the professional along with the larger contexts within which women work. Women interviewed were queried about the relation between work and home: behavioral similarities and differences and perceptions of others in the two environments. Prevailing economic and political conditions within and outside the company that affect women's work are addressed, including the experience of being a female in a male-dominated organization. As in Parts 1 and 2, each topic's elaboration is guided by the women's words. This section, in particular, focuses on the perceptions of males and females in corporate settings, in families, and in the larger society. Connections between psychological processes and context are drawn in both immediate and larger sociopolitical environments.

□ 8 □

Relation between the Personal and the Professional

In a large corporation, the manager's office and desk are readily distinguishable from those of the support staff. There is more privacy; the desk is bigger, perhaps surrounded by other comfortable, decorative furnishings. The manager's appearance is also distinct. There is a businesslike manner, a professional quality that connotes seriousness of purpose and the weight of responsibility. Even when support staff share that professional attitude, appearance can serve to set the manager apart. The manager of your mind's eye is in all likelihood dressed in a suit, white, and male.

Although the number of female managers has substantially increased over the past decade, their presence at corporate helms still startles us.[1] In 1987 women accounted for 37 percent of corporate managers, but only 2 percent of senior executives.[2] Worldwide, "the higher the rank within the organization, the fewer women one finds there."[3] Women continue to be unexpected in positions of authority by individuals who deal with them as well as by the corporations that employ them. It is as though everyone pretends that there is nothing extraordinary about a woman manager, but signs to the contrary exist on both the individual and the structural level. That corporations have yet to change shape to accommodate the fact that both adults in a family are likely to be employed is but one indication.[4] Top managerial ranks are still composed solely of men who have "enabling wives" at home. In this chapter we see how the women themselves project images consonant with business and contradictory to conventional notions of femaleness. In chapter 9, we shall see how difficult the adjustment has been for their male co-workers.

What It Takes to Be a Manager

As we climb the occupational scale, the skills required for white-collar and executive positions become less tangible and more difficult to quantify. Higher-level jobs do not share the predictable and repetitive quality of those on a lower level and are therefore both more stressful and inherently more interesting.[5] Since the nature of the tasks at hand varies from one project and even from one day to the next, job descriptions are formulated less in terms of fixed skills and more with regard to personal aptitude. Abilities that would have application over a broad range of tasks are called for, including oral and written communication skills, decision making, initiative, and willingness to assume responsibility. Even skills that seem relatively objective can be interpreted subjectively. That is, people who would meet the skill standards are frequently assumed to be of a certain nature. Lists of executive skills melt into descriptions of personal qualities that traditionally were assumed to be gender-related.

What does it take to be an effective professional business person? A look at the curriculum of programs yielding a master's degree in business administration (MBA) can readily answer the tangible-skills question. Knowledge and skill in finance, marketing, production, sales, and organizational behavior, for example, may be essential in varying degrees depending upon the particular position and to some extent the type of company. As technology revolutionizes industry and its functions, technical expertise can surely put one in good stead within an organization. A glance at the composition of corporations and MBA programs could lead to the conclusion that these skills are not and perhaps cannot be evenly distributed throughout our population. Even now, the majority of faces found in these environments are white and male.

That the distribution of power in our country has put corporate and academic control in the male domain only partially accounts for gender bias in business. Such bias receives support and sustenance from a psychological belief system, operating on both the individual and the collective level, that attributes characteristics associated with corporate acuity to an exclusive male preserve. Males and not females have been thought to be naturally disposed toward the skills required by business.[6] Further, females have been considered almost universally incapable of those skills by virtue of intellectual and emotional difference.

Notorious for an alleged disinclination for logical thinking, females were assumed to be inherently ill suited to the technical areas of finance, marketing, and production associated with business. Moreover, a presumed female tendency to put the heart before the mind rendered women unfit for the tough personnel management decisions that accompany responsible corporate positions.[7] Even if a select few females could master the technical skills involved, what was assumed to be their personal natures generally disqualified them from a corporate career. The business world, as it has been constructed in this country, had no place for the soft, other-directed nurturance that presumably characterized females. The qualities of independence, ambition, and aggressiveness that became synonymous with men were those deemed appropriate and perhaps essential to the corporate environment.[8] Those characteristics were viewed as antithetical to a focus on relationships and the well-being of others that supposedly defined what it meant to be female.

There has been of late an emphasis upon a supposedly female style of managing that is touted as more effective than the traditionally aggressive, authoritarian male style. It seems that we have once again transferred our male-female stereotypes to the realm of managerial styles. It is likely that individual managers display a mixture of styles representing both traditional authority and new collaborative modes.[9]

Assumptions about gender-based aptitudes and characteristics die hard. The gender division that structurally denied females access to certain places in society has been challenged as a civil rights violation. In response to charges of discrimination, we have begun to restructure our academic entrance and business hiring practices and to overturn our fundamental beliefs about maleness and femaleness.

We now must recognize that neither gender can be characterized exclusively by one or another set of qualities and capabilities.[10] A high degree of crossover has sharpened our awareness of the differences among males and females and the similarities between them in contrast to an unwarranted emphasis on differences between genders.

In Parts 1 and 2 of this book, we have seen ample evidence of women manifesting aptitudes and characteristics that were formerly assumed to be exclusive to men. These women's derived satisfaction from work, their expressed needs for achievement and independent identities, run counter to traditional notions of the female nature. Family and interpersonal attachment, though of primary importance, do not account for the whole of their lives but share center stage with career. These women feel in no way inferior to their domestic sisters or their careerist brothers; indeed, their sense of wholeness stems from the contribution of both sides of their lives.[11]

How are women able to demonstrate the qualities required for corporate success while retaining caring personalities for the sake of their personal lives? We now know that males and females, while certainly different in many ways, are constitutionally neither aggressive nor nurturant, such that the presence of one type of behavior precludes the other in the same individual.[12] Furthermore, people's personal characteristics are not fixed traits that remain stable and consistent across time and circumstance. On the contrary, personality can change with the demands of the situation.[13]

When business and home environments required significantly different behavior, the women interviewed were able to tailor their personalities accordingly without feeling disjointed or unintegrated. Women were asked specifically whether they thought themselves to be the same or a different person at home and at work. Their responses elucidate the question of female personality traits, their place in the corporate world, and their transfer from home to work.

Self at Home and at Work

In these interviews women were about equally divided with regard to similarity or disparity in themselves at work and in private life. Some acknowledged sizable distinctions between who they were at the office and who they were at home; others did not discern much difference. In either case, women evinced a calm contentment with the comparison between their professional and private selves; they did not seem troubled by what we have assumed to be the very different personal requirements of the two domains.

Women might be expected to affirm disjuncture between their behavior at work and outside, since qualities associated with effectiveness in business are not necessarily required on the home front. A need to project a certain image, for example, may be at the forefront of a woman's awareness at work whereas home is presumably a place where such concerns can be safely left at the door. Ina's behavior at work can vary depending upon who sees it. As to whether she is the same or a different person at work and at home, she replies:

> Oh, different. You're never on guard in the home situation. I'm probably much more emotional at home, and more protective sometimes, of [my] own turf. . . . But also I'm [a] much more relaxed person at home. I tend to be a little more formal in the office, depending upon the day, and depending upon who's around—you know, how visible I am that day.

In addition to the delineation of a professional image, Monica details the kinds of knowledge and skill required of her at work.

> I think I work very hard at trying to put on a professional image. I think that's part of the reason why I've been relatively successful—trying to be rational about things in the way that I make decisions. I'm probably a very political person. . . . But when I'm away from work, I'm much more indecisive about things. I'm much more emotional. If I know someone doesn't like me, that would bother me more than it does at work. I'm probably pretty playful both places, but probably more at home. I guess probably the biggest thing is letting down that image a little bit—that's not really totally me—being able to just say I don't know what to do about something, really leaning on someone because I know I need help. At work I probably need to do that and do it, but I don't like to have it appear that I do it.

Characteristics that have traditionally been associated with females— emotionality, indecisiveness, sensitivity to others' opinions, and help seeking—are recognized by Monica as part of her, but a part that is not to appear at work. There she maintains a professional image that includes political astuteness and ability to make rational decisions. Implicit in her remarks is an awareness of the time and place of her behavior, the circumstances in which she can express various parts of her personality with impunity. Bonnie also differentiates her domestic from her professional side, underscoring the popular notion that her professional image could suffer should she be caught typing at work.

> Oh, I'm definitely two different people. Sure, at home I have no problem whatsoever at being very domestic. I enjoy doing that . . . and no job is too lowly for me. And at work I have to be conscious of those things. I have a tendency to do things that I shouldn't from a visibility standpoint. . . . So . . . it's a conscious effort on my part to remember what position I'm in and how to handle that.

For Bonnie, professional behavior does not include socializing, and she explains this taboo again in terms of visibility and image implications.

I avoid them [social topics] like the plague. I neither have time nor interest in that. It's amazing; there are weddings and babies being born all the time, and I'm really not real conscious of it. [*Why do you choose to ignore those?*] A couple of reasons. I think it's bad for my visibility, number one. I don't want to be engaged in nonprofessional conversation where anybody can see me. Every level of management goes through that office. And I choose not to discuss personal things with the employees, especially women. I suppose I shy away from the women most of all. If they come to me for help, and it's business-related, I am very open and very willing to work with them.

These women are watching themselves at work. They have learned what kinds of behaviors and personal characteristics are expected and acceptable within the company. Especially when visible to superiors they are careful to manifest the appropriate demeanor. What would be considered feminine traits can be controlled easily by women who differentiate their behavior according to environmental demands. Further, the nature of the work itself can determine how much personal life can feasibly enter the workplace. The extent of Alison's involvement in work at a new company, for example, precludes her attention to interpersonal and social matters that might be considered typically female.

I'm very different—more and more very different. Don't get me wrong; I'm never curt or abrupt with people. I'm liked on the job, and I'm nice to people, but I'm pushy, very pushy. And I work very hard at being pushy because it's important to me. I don't socialize very much. But right now I'm so totally wrapped up in what I'm doing that I don't even—I mean, I eat lunch in my office. So what I'm saying is that when I'm at home, a very relaxed person, I'm very nice. I'm very human at home, whereas I'm finding more and more that I'm not a human being at work as I used to be.

There is a difference between monitoring one's socializing according to a visible professional image and having one's interactions all but eliminated by task demands. When the amount of work is the primary determinant of behavior, the person may be too preoccupied even to think about, never mind exert conscious control over, image projection and what that entails. In that case, the difference between the work self and the home self hinges more on production exigency and less on personal characteristics that may be gender-related.

Immersion in the work to the exclusion of interpersonal considerations has also been seen as more typical of males than females. The behavior of the women interviewed, however, contradicts conventional ideas of what can be expected of females. Their articulation of the importance of image and their willingness to forgo in the business environment what have been assumed to be central to their beings—interpersonal closeness and connection—contradict the idea that women behave a certain way and no other. Hope can retain her personal style and meet emotional needs at home without sacrificing her integrity at the office.

> And if something is really bothering me, I certainly may get quieter at work, but there isn't anybody there that I would confide my personal problems to. I just don't think it's wise to have to, first of all. You have to create an image. And the more that people think that you're absolutely totally together, [the better]. You know, you do this total thing with yourself. You dress right. You look right. You behave right. I've got everything. I've got the house. I've got the dog. I've got the healthy, normal, happy children. I've got the man. So to all the outside world I am really together, and that creates confidence inside the office for me. People say, "She's really got her life together." If they knew I fall apart every so often, that would create a problem.

To share one's shortcomings and troubles with others at work is contrary to the image of success. Compartmentalizing the public from the private has been men's wont, given their primary needs for achievement and cognitive stimulation outside of home and family. In contrast, women's nature would render them unable to submerge their affective orientation to the requirements of the corporate context.

The women interviewed, however, were not sacrificing themselves when they left their personal lives outside the office; they were doing what was necessary to meet their equally important needs for independent achievement. Recognizing the limitations placed on their behavior by corporate life, these women make the necessary accommodations without feeling any loss of self. Bonnie echoes Hope's sentiments about the pitfalls of mixing close relationships with professional life.

> And do I take personal things back to the office? Normally, only if it's good news. If I have had something very nice happen to me, I share it with people. . . . I will never take a problem into the office. There aren't any of those people that I am close enough to confide in. And even if there were, I don't think I would allow myself to do that, because I think that would be dangerous from a professional standpoint.

Women can readily confine their needs for close interpersonal relationship and friendship to their lives outside of work. Those needs are not so pervasive and pressing that they interfere with professional functioning. Women quickly discern how mixing the personal and the professional can be a detriment to both.[14]

Hope has been able to separate her emotional needs from her need for professional fulfillment. She feels comfortable calling upon two realms for satisfaction of different aspects of herself. Both ways of being are accurate reflections of her, and she experiences no problem with their segregated expression. On the contrary, she finds the separation most comfortable and appropriate.

> I got a lot of personal satisfaction, and I got a lot of my personal needs satisfied from the job. And I know I need the work because this gives me something—first of all, [it] gives me economic security, which is necessary. But it also gives me a sense of who I am and that I'm contributing to something. But on the other hand, there is this other person that I am too, and that is the person who is the mother, and the wife, and the companion, and that sort of thing. . . . So I never attempt to get support, emotional support, at work now, because I don't think that's where you get it, and certainly not in a major corporation at my level. . . . Because they'd say, "Well, if you need that, go see a psychiatrist or something." I get all of my emotional support at home.

Women's needs for professional fulfillment stand aside from and in addition to those for caretaking and emotional connection. The separation of personal from professional can be, as Hope describes, in terms of the different functions that work and home relationships serve.

Separating the Personal and Professional in the Workplace

Another kind of separation divides the personal from the professional within the work environment. Again, contrary to conventional understandings of what is central to female functioning, women are able to work effectively with others, whether or not they find them personally likable.

> I've come to be able to respect people for their talents and tend to overlook personality traits, and I consider that a maturing within myself. I might deal with somebody and extract from them their accomplishments or deal with them on a business level and maintain a relationship without ever liking any one of their own personal qualities.

Developing the functional abilities of others in the absence of individual compatibility is a skill that Tammy evolved in the course of her work experience. Something that is supposedly natural for males but unnatural, and therefore unattainable, for females can be learned even if it was not initially part of a woman's repertoire.

Such learning is demonstrated by Marsha, who now can follow a heated argument with social pleasantries and not suffer conflict, as these behaviors are not contradictory in the context of business.

> But so far I've managed to be able to go in and sit down, and if I have to argue I'll argue, but after I walk out of a room I'm able to smile and say, "Have a nice day," which I think a lot of them can't understand. And to me that is the most important accomplishment that I've made to date . . . to be able to take me as a person and separate me from the profession and go into a room and do what I have to do and then walk out and say, "Well, that was the job, now I have to go back to who I am." [*How did you learn to do that?*] It wasn't easy. As a matter of fact, I think the main reason for doing it, and I had to work on it very hard, was that I got tired of being depressed. I got tired of taking it around with me. I got tired of taking it home. I just got so tired of carrying the weight of the world on my shoulders, so I decided one day, "Look, I'm going to have to do something about this. I can't take it that personal." I've been working ten years; it took me that long to get to the point where I am. It's not easy. It's something you have to work on constantly. It's a daily job. Every day I have to make sure that I remind myself that it's a job, and after the job is over I might like that person very much, and I have to keep that in mind.

Women have long been depicted as merging the cognitive and affective processes so that they were incapable of reasoned judgment independent of emotion. Men have been characterized as inherent compartmentalizers, easily rendering decisions that are not remotely tinged by affective considerations. Though the connection between heart and mind may be stronger in females, they are certainly able to attenuate that link in the interest of effective professional functioning.

Throughout this volume, empirical evidence attests to women's possession of characteristics contrary to conventional expectation and, moreover, to the interaction between developmental change and contextual demands. That is, the women here have repeatedly traced a process of change within themselves, their thoughts, feeling, and behavior, that was affected by and then served to affect the particular context of their lives. Circumstances on the job, for example, might precipitate a change in behavior, which in turn revises those circumstances, further reinforcing the shape and direction of the new behavior.

A kind of feedback loop also occurs within the person among feeling, thought, and behavior just as it does between the individual and the environment. For Marsha, negative feelings prompted a conscious effort to separate personal responses from job requirements. The result was that her changed thinking and behavior served to influence her feelings in a positive way. Moreover, personal change that begins within one context, work or home, soon spreads to the other.

Connections between Personal and Professional Selves

Women's ability to separate the personal from the professional does not preclude their experience of overall integrity. Though her behavior at home and at work may differ, Jill is aware of the general influence that personal development in either domain has on her being.

> Actually, I think, as I've changed in both of those areas [work and home], one part of your life interacts with another. And I think as you grow personally in your life outside of work, it cannot help but spill over into the kinds of things that you do in the office on a day-to-day basis. Simultaneously, as you gain certain skills and experience on the job, I think it gives you confidence in the rest of your life. . . . I used to psychologically segment the [two], and work life was work life and home was home, and they didn't overlap as much as they do now. And obviously, at this point, I think I more fully understand how you as a person can intertwine both of the areas of your life to enhance them rather than just always fragment your activities.

For every woman who portrayed herself as different at home and at work, there is another who perceived herself as the same person in the two places. Some, like Marie, acknowledge discrepant behaviors but emphasize an underlying constant of self.

> I think I'm pretty much the same. . . . I'm probably a little bit tougher at work than I would be at home—just because I have to be. At home there probably wouldn't be too much of a reason for me to jump up and down and scream and yell, whereas at work there might be. I think I'm pretty much the same, though.

Company context and the kind of position one holds can also exert an influence on how much of one's informal self is brought to work. Cathy's relationship with co-workers is on a peer level so that she is comfortable with the consistency in self at work and outside.

> I think I'm the same, pretty much. I may be a little bit more relaxed at home, but I deal very much on a peer basis with the people that work for me. I'm not terribly formal about my interactions with them. I don't feel as though I have to make an effort to project professionalism. I think that . . .

comes with what you're doing, although I do notice that many of the people I deal with have vastly different personalities at work and at home. But I don't believe that I do.

Cathy believes that her professionalism is apparent from the work that she does. Technical expertise or involvement in the job itself can become foremost so that one is not actively contemplating the projection of an image but is just being professional. Tammy realizes that, when she is immersed in the job, others' perceptions of her differ from her own.

> I think I'm the same person, [but] I don't think I'm perceived as that. I know I'm not. I think a lot of people think I'm a little distant at work. But I think it's just because I'm just so busy that I appear to be removed. But I'm the same person, you know.

Thus, women distinguish between their feelings and their behavior. Although they feel themselves to be the same person across environments, they can acknowledge behavioral discrepancies from one context to another. It would be unrealistic to expect people to be precisely the same in significantly diverse situations. In fact, the ability to feel continuity within oneself and yet behave differently is probably a sign of a healthy, functioning individual.

Aware that others' perceptions are determined by apparent behavior, these women do not modify their views of themselves accordingly. A self-image that is not subject to the vagaries of public opinion has been associated with males. Females, who have been characterized as other directed and field dependent, presumably alter their percep tions in line with those of others.[15] The women of this study clearly do not conform to that stereotype.

Whether the differences described are minor or significant, it seems that women's behavior at home and at work is shaped by the context in which it occurs. They can adapt to such an extent that they do not manifest at work characteristics traditionally associated with their gender, and they do not register psychic discomfort or conflict as a result. Their experience of themselves is one of continuity, whether they claim to be the same or different at home and at work. Whatever personal changes they might have made for the sake of career, the requirements of a professional image have not eliminated the fulfillment of their emotional needs in the appropriate context, that is, outside of corporate life.

Image and the Perceptions of Others

In their descriptions of themselves at work, women directly or implicitly refer to a professional image. On the one hand, they are attempting to project an image that is consonant with their particular company's concept of professionalism (and this can vary from one company, and even from one function, to another). On the other hand, they are aware that there are two sides to the image: what they believe they are projecting and how others receive it. Professional effectiveness is influenced not only by an individual's behavior but also by how it is perceived by others. And once an image has been established, it is very difficult to revise without monumental effort or changing jobs.

A professional image is composed of many elements, from those that are obviously job-related to personal behavior and appearance. Being professional means looking the part and being businesslike, making the right decisions, and putting the company's success first. The implication is that the company's success spells success for the individual.

To behave in what one believes to be a professional manner is not enough, however. The meanings that are attached to behavior by its observers and recipients come to define it and thereby influence its effectiveness. Women have frequently been characterized in ways that are contrary to their self-perceptions and to their intended purposes. Camilla is surprised to discover the connotation attached to a slight variation in her wardrobe.

> Once I started to wear a suit to work every single day religiously, there was a change in attitude. And I was told when I was reviewed, "Well, I see you're looking a little more professional." Not that I ever didn't; I always wore skirts and blouses and jackets. [*What does "professional-looking" mean?*] I think sterner. I think they mean sterner and a little more powerful, or maybe more in control of the situation.

Women often discover after the fact an extant discrepancy between self-presentation and its interpretation by others. It is especially disconcerting to find that the value attached to behavior is less than one had assumed. A disparity between self-perception and others' perception can also be weighted positively in a woman's favor. Abigail summarizes a not uncommon experience for females who tend to underestimate their abilities.[16]

> They tend to see me as much more accomplished than I see myself.

Stella's competence had been apparent to co-workers in advance of her full cognizance of it.

> I noticed . . . that people seem to see in me things that I didn't see in myself. But after a certain length of time on each one of the jobs that I've held, people have always wanted to promote me to a higher position or give me other responsibilities, and it always came as a surprise to me, I think, because I didn't see myself in that light.

Marie elaborates on the distinction between what one is feeling and the external impression.

> she said, "I get so upset when something happens, and you just remain so calm all the time." "Calm? Are you kidding?" And I was really surprised she said that to me. And I guess you just always perceive yourself very differently than other people see you. Or, of course, when it's internal, you can really feel the effects of it while it may just not show.

Given the importance of maintaining a certain kind of image at work, women recognize the need to project a calm, controlled, competent approach regardless of feelings to the contrary. In the course of doing the job, however, they may not be consciously projecting the required image. With increased professional skill and experience, the appropriate image may become a more integral part of their work behavior than even they realize.

In order to focus more specifically on the extent of women's awareness of others' perceptions, we asked how people at work would describe them. This question called upon women to project about their projections. That is, a woman who consciously projected a particular image at work must speculate about how co-workers might have interpreted her behavior and what they in turn project to her. In addition to how people at work might describe her, each woman was asked how she wanted others at work to see her. Finally, her response to how she wanted family and close others to see her provided a further glimpse of the similarities and differences between her professional and personal selves.

We find considerably more variation in replies about how people at work see these women as compared to how they would like to be seen. As we have noted, women tailor their behavior to the demands of the business at hand, and they believe themselves to be perceived accordingly. A woman is likely to expect co-workers' views of her to reflect some of her individual characteristics combined with her manner of treating the work demands. The diversity of the individuals and their work environments tie interactions between them to the particular contexts of their occurrence.

There was far more commonality among women's responses to how they wished to be viewed by people at work. Again, this makes sense in light of the existence of some consensus about what constitutes effective professional business behavior, regardless of specific context. Tammy includes several elements that are found separately in other individual responses.

> I would like them to see me as a reference person. I would like them to see me as somebody who is in control. I would like them to see me as a friend. And I would like them best to see me as somebody who is capable of handling a problem of theirs, be it on a professional level or on a personal level. I would like them to have respect for me as a person who demands quality. I have to have that.

Of paramount importance, repeatedly, was professional respect. This necessarily involved a woman's competence and ability to handle both tasks and people. Being in control frequently meant that workers could rely upon her to cope calmly and effectively with difficulties as they arose. Overall, workers would feel that they could depend upon her to know what she was doing, and her strength would foster their own development in positive directions.

As noted above, not all of these aspects were mentioned by everyone; Betty is perhaps most extreme in her distillation of the essential. When asked, "How do you want people at work to see you?" she boils it down to her own sense of professional ethics.

> I don't really care. As long as I feel that I am doing the right thing for them, with them, and as long as I feel that they cannot dispute that, it doesn't matter to me much whether they like me or they don't like me. I think they do, because I like them. But if my employees did not like me but liked their work and wanted to continue, we could work that out.

As we saw in Part 1, these women are less concerned with interpersonal liking and more with professional behavior. Such behavior includes fair treatment of employees as well as competent discharge of one's responsibilities. With increased experience and maturity, a woman learns to subordinate being liked by others at work to being respected as competent. When we examined career development in Part 1, several women described their transition from a personal to a professional orientation. Here women, regardless of whether they characterize themselves as the same or different at home and at work, make distinctions between their behavior and need fulfillment in the two environments.

Thus, women are able to respond differentially to contextual demands and still feel an integration within themselves that transcends situation specifics. Our understanding of how that happens can be enhanced through examination of an individual's responses to all three questions: How would people at work describe you? How do you want people at work to see you? How do you want your family or people close to you to see you?

With regard to how people would describe her, Ina emphasizes first her diligence and second her personal attributes.

> If a job is given to me, they know it will be done before it's even required, even if I have to work overtime. Somebody who will get it done with the least amount of complaining and a certain flair. Easy to get on with. They would want me on their team . . . with a sense of humor, fun to work with.

Describing how she wants others at work to see her, Ina's response implicitly reflects the possibility that others' view of her might be discrepant from her own.

> At work, [I want them to see me] physically as I am: a hard-working, competent person to be trusted. But even more than trust—they'll trust you if you're competent. I don't question my competence. I just want other people to realize that I'm a bright, competent person.

Uncertain that others at work, probably superiors, recognize the extent of her abilities, Ina is confident about her reliably skilled performance as an employee. Similarly, she doubts that her family perceives her as being as strong and dependable as she feels herself to be. Although Ina claimed to be different at home and at work, there is a common theme of trustworthiness and reliability that she wishes to project in both places. She wants her family to see her as

> not as vulnerable as I sometimes think they think I am. Strong and giving, and to be trusted. They can rely upon me. . . . If they needed me, they know they can call me at any time. I would always be available to them.

Most women's responses to the three questions bore more resemblance to each other than not. Even in the case of Ina, who viewed herself as different at home and at work, the variation in her replies is subtle rather than striking. In interpreting such fine differences, one must consider which constituency is implied by the respondent. Some women are using employees as an audience; others are adopting the perspective of superiors. Thus, the others whose descriptions she portrays, and the others whose perceptions she would like to shape, might be peers, subordinates, or superiors. A woman may feel accurately appreciated by peers and subordinates but not by superiors. Of course, the reverse is also possible, where official recognition surpasses the real or imagined perceptions of equals and employees.

For obvious reasons, women are frequently more self-critical in speculating about how others might describe them than in detailing how they wish to be perceived. Not wanting to gloss over any possible sources of criticism, they seem especially thoughtful in second-guessing others. How they want to be viewed is an easier question to answer, since an ideal image can readily be defined. Connie is a good example of someone whose three responses are more alike than different but who can imagine others' criticism of her.

> On the plus side, they would want to work for me for the promotional opportunities and exposure, and also to learn something. . . . the downside of it would be that they have to work hard and sometimes I'm not there. So they might say, "Well, she has a lot of good information, but she's not that accessible." Accessibility would probably be an issue.

Connie would like people at work to see her

> the way that I am, and I think that's as a professional in my area with ability to produce high-quality work and to be an effective leader of the function, to make a difference, to have some influence and power, to be fair, honest, positive about life.

And her family:

> The same way, probably loving and caring, I would add. And I'd probably add that at work . . . I have the capacity to care, which I do, and that I'm not a cold, calculating person. And I would like my family to see those same things.

Leslie is another whose speculation about others' perceptions of her reveals detail connected to the realities of her position and a somewhat critical eye.

> I'm competent, without a doubt. "Things were never as well organized as they were when we began." A mind for organization. They got to feel that I am competent, which gave them, I think, trust in the decisions I made. Sometimes making decisions that they didn't understand and standing by them, almost like forcing my vision onto people. I'm demanding; I don't like mediocrity. At times, not very patient.

In comparison, Leslie's reply to how she wants others to see her is succinct and more generally applicable across professional contexts.

> As competent, professional, honest, and treating them with respect.

Finally, Leslie does not make many distinctions between desirable professional and personal images, except for the most central one of expectations in the affective realm of life. She wishes her family and close others to see her:

> Probably the same way. Except I think I'd like to see a little loving and caring in with my family that I wouldn't associate necessarily with my peers at work. I see my family much more as a support system to me, although you can't survive in the office without support either, because you'll just go under. But I do see my family more as a support to me, and I hope I can be supportive of them.

Karen's replies to the two questions about professional perceptions have similar themes. Others at work would say

> that I was organized, would pass that on to them, so they felt like they knew what their job was; they knew what was expected of them. I was not overly social, so they would probably say I was somewhat detached from them. I gave them direction as to what they should be doing. I would listen to them on advice about how we could change things and so forth, to make it a better environment for people. . . . I was open to suggestion.

Organization, clear communication, measured receptivity, and professional behavior are the elements that Karen wants co-workers to associate with her. Her remarks about physical appearance indicate an awareness of the customary image of power and capability.

> I don't want them to think of me as a little girl. And I know I have to constantly fight that. Sometimes I wish I was six-five and 175 pounds [laugh]. I'd like them to think of me as a professional manager [who] shows good judgment. Someone . . . they can count on. Someone who communicates accurately. More interested in getting the job done than playing the politics.

Karen expresses a desire for straightforward, effective working relationships rather than corporate game playing. She neither contrives nor laments the social distance that is a by-product of her professional behavior. In contrast, her statements about desired family perceptions include nothing of the professional and only personal closeness.

> I'd like them to think that I really cared about them and that they were the most important things in my life, and that we could have a good time together.

Though some women blended their professional images with intimacy in their personal lives, others seemed wholly to separate the two. Virtually no one brought much of her personal life into the office for display or discussion, however. Women were clear and definite in making those distinctions between the personal and the professional. They did not preclude warm working relationships, but these were based not on interpersonal liking but rather on respect, competence, communication, and development of employees' potential. Even where we saw women including criticism in their thoughtful speculations of how others would describe them, there was also thematic connection to how they wished to be seen. That is, the desired perceptions were not substantially different from those presumably attributed. Minor discrepancies did not sway women from their clear-eyed notions of what was desirable professional behavior. Nor did the exercise of such aspirations make them any less emotive in their lives outside of work. Finally, these women portray thematic connections between themselves at home and at work that reflect a strong sense of self-consistency regardless of behavioral differences.

□ 9 □

Females in Male Organizations

Women who hold managerial positions in corporations are, for the most part, working in male organizations. The majority of large corporations in this country have been and still are populated and run primarily by men. Female employees are usually clustered in clerical positions where they wield little formal power.[1] It is only within the past fifteen years that significant numbers of women have entered the corporate world in other than clerical positions. Forms of social change that have combined to account for this increase include shifting beliefs about "a woman's place," concomitant legislative mandates for affirmative action in employment, and the economic realities of women in droves entering and staying in the work force. Despite their increase in middle-managerial positions, however, females are virtually invisible at the higher executive level and remain a minority in terms of accumulated power within corporations as a whole.[2]

Though they are not the only females at their workplaces, the women interviewed might have been the first or sole female occupant of a particular managerial position within their corporations.[3] Their pioneer or minority experience could be expected to vary considerably with the nature of the organization and work required, the skills and personalities of the people involved, and the resources available for support. Here, as in earlier chapters of this volume, we find variation rather than stereotype in women's descriptions of what it is like to be a female in a male organization.

No interview questions specifically addressed gender. Further, most respondents were not especially oriented to "women's issues," nor did they actively operate from that frame of reference. In fact, at the conclusion of the interview some indicated surprise, and perhaps relief, at the absence of questions about "women's issues." If a special orientation guided these women's responses, it was one of measured consideration rather than feminist consciousness.

Even in the absence of direct questioning, women did talk about their experiences of being female in a male organization. Aware of gender and its influence on their own and others' behavior within the corporate context, they were not and did not wish to be seen as thinking primarily in those terms. If anything, their inclination was to minimize, and in some cases to actively ignore, that factor in the human and organizational equations described in the interviews. When gender did come up, therefore, it was usually part of a woman's discussion of another topic. Her own response or anecdote might trigger a related thought about the experience of being female in a male organization. Gender was ordinarily associated with such topics as discrimination or its absence, the need to prove oneself, availability of support, and minority position.

Minority Position

Women's relatively recent entry into corporate professional ranks places them in a minority position. First, they are in the minority in terms of pure numbers. Alison's description of a *Fortune* 500 company gives a striking example:

> There are very few women—I'd say probably ten women in professional positions that I can think of, out of about 800 positions.

Not only are women sparsely represented, their distribution is not equally spread across the various professional levels of corporate functioning. Even when females are seen in these positions, they seem to be held at a certain level and denied access to those higher. One analysis, referred to as the "pipeline" or "critical mass" concept, attributes the ceiling for females to their relatively short history as corporate executives.[4] If it takes twenty-five years of middle management occupation to gain access to top executive positions, men have a solid ten-year head start.[5] This explanation requires us to wait several years for confirming evidence of male–female difference in corporate access. It also begs the question of differential treatment of males and females in similar positions. It is unlikely, however, that male managers have an experience comparable to that of the female minority.

Women who were few in number had to contend with another aspect of minority status that serves to contribute to it, that is, the customary opinion regarding "women's place." When females first infiltrated the managerial ranks, some were met with what had been the prevailing attitude of men regarding women in the work force. Leigh speaks of her manufacturing employer:

> the men within that organization really felt women belonged at home with the kids, and that [it's] fine to have them working, but they're way down there.[6]

Women's acceptance in the work force was still predicated on their being in the lower ranks and not sharing the job titles and influence held by men. Public opinion polls now show a majority in favor of women working, but that does not necessarily constitute endorsement for females assuming positions of power and prestige traditionally occupied by men. Leslie sums up a typical situation for the professional female in a high-technology industry:

> We are finding it difficult for professional women to be absorbed in an all-male organization where most of the women are secretaries. We are not accepted. It's created a them-and-us situation.

The few women who began in positions that had been predominantly male contended with feelings of isolation that stemmed from their minority status.[7] Further, Marsha believed that the organization structured women's segregation in a technical area of financial services.

> The job was very pressure-intensive because it was basically all males. There were a few women. I would say we were about five percent of the incoming staff. They managed to separate the women throughout the whole training course. . . . Then I was promoted again. . . . At this stage of my career I had people working for me, and this included men as well as women—more men than women because very seldom do they put a woman on the same job with another, not two women together. For some reason they found it very difficult to group them. I don't believe it's difficult; I think it was more intentional than anything. . . . So it was a little difficult dealing with them—not on a professional basis but on a social basis. I ended up eating lunch alone most times, because the guys would go off someplace else. There was no socializing.[8]

Women who were few in number were isolated from each other, either as a function of their scarcity or by design. Their segregation seemed to be further enforced along gender lines, as males tended to group together, resulting in female exclusion, be it intentional or not.[9] Thus, pioneering females functioned virtually alone even when there were others in similar positions in the same company.

The Pioneers

Perhaps the ultimate minority experience is being the only representative of a particular group.[10] Some of the women interviewed described what it was like to be the first female in a company position or function.[11] Marsha gives us an idea of some specific ways people attempted to dissuade her from taking a technical position customarily held by a man.

> I was the first female and the only female on the staff of about twenty. The staff was made [up] mainly of middle-aged men, I would say from the age [of] forty through sixty. I had a very difficult time getting the job. I had to go through their equal opportunity office to get the job, because the guy in charge of the area indicated that they could not have a woman on the staff because of the travel, also because of the living accommodations. . . . I later found out that they never had to share rooms. This was one of the excuses that they used. . . . The reaction to my being there ranged from overprotective, sort of fatherly image, . . . and the other extreme probably was they just totally ignored me. I managed to travel most of the time with some very nice guys who were more the fatherly type, where they felt responsible for me. They felt the need to take me everywhere I had to go. They made it a point to be with me [at] every point in time, whatever I had to do. I found that very difficult. I didn't like to hurt anybody's feelings, but sometimes I just like to be alone.[12]

Unaccustomed to female colleagues, men either avoided contact or assumed a role with a woman that was both traditional and safely defined. Marsha met opposition in applying for a job, ostensibly because of the travel arrangements. Perhaps this issue was used as an excuse to block her entrance, as she suggests, but the choice of that particular job component is significant. This underscores the idea that men view their relationships with females primarily around sexuality rather than professional collegiality.[13] Questionable connotations can be attached to a man's traveling with a woman who is not his wife or his mother. At the very least, men's awkwardness with a female colleague, especially in a travel situation that involves considerable socializing, is a sizable obstacle to her landing the job and perhaps to her functioning once in it.

A female pioneer may be hampered in the office, but a substantial part of the job occurs on social ground where her difference is underscored.[14] Where a work task is not structuring the situation, men are at even more of a loss as to how to interact with women. The social context elicits habitual responses. Monica's experience as a pioneering female in the human resource area of a large, diversified conglomerate sounds similar to Marsha's.

> going through an evening of people saying to you, "Oh, we've never had a woman before," "Oh, what a surprise to see you," "Oh"—that reaction. Or some men just kind of avoided you because they either felt like "We really don't want you here," or "I don't know what to say to you now that you are here." Then the recreation the next day, and I had gone out and learned how to play tennis. I thought, I will be damned if I'm going to sit in the hotel and not play, so I went out and played tennis. And it really didn't work out that badly at all, but again, I think fortunately, there were some men in the organization I had a very good relationship with. And [they] said "Hi, you play with us," and there was no problem in doing it. But [I was] constantly entering their domain that had not heretofore had a woman. And some men reacted fine. Others just either resented it or didn't know how to handle it. You know, it was something brand-new.

Interestingly, these women focus on social rather than strictly in-office professional situations that generate awkwardness associated with gender. And it is the lack of easy, informal connections between colleagues that presumably put women at a disadvantage in corporate climbing.[15] Both women also mention the conservative nature of their organizations as a factor contributing to men's inexperience with women in professional circumstances. Both acted, in a quiet but determined manner, as if they belonged there, and as though this too shall pass. According to Monica, indeed it did.

> I think I just didn't even deal with some of the men that really had a problem. And I let them . . . get used to it over time. I didn't go out and try and make a crusade and say, "Hey, you're going to like me being here." It seems [to have] gradually changed, and now I find that's really not an issue anymore.

Pioneering women in this group report similar strategies. They did not call attention to themselves primarily on the basis of gender, nor did they actively demand acceptance from co-workers. Their energies were concentrated on the work itself, and that may have precluded a focus on interpersonal matters related to gender. In any event, they did not attempt to change the attitudes and behavior of others but focused on their own professionalism and skill development. Rather than directly responding to men's stereotypic behavior toward them, these women chose to develop and display work expertise that would eventually gain them the recognition and respect that are blind to gender.

A woman's attitude and behavior can set the tone for others and shape their perceptions of her in an organization. Leslie's experience on entering a high-technology industry from the social service sector lends credence to the idea that an individual's psychological set affects the social context in which it occurs.

> When I went into the organization and I was the only woman, I had been told by other people that I was going to be, quote, "the sex symbol" in this organization. But I went in believing that I was a professional person in all the other positions I held; I was a professional person here. And I have never been treated any way that's different by the group of men that I work with. But I'm dealing with professional people too. Once they got the message, I've never had any problem with that. So I would say that it's true, the two were really linked together: I just assumed that I would be treated the way I had been treated before, and that is the way I was treated.

Leslie sought not social support but rather fair professional treatment from colleagues. She enjoyed the challenge of being the first woman in the organization, and her clearly defined expectations contributed to her ability to cope with the difficulties surrounding women's minority position that continue to characterize her company.

Before they establish themselves as capable and formidable colleagues, women's presence can be ignored or dismissed by men who might otherwise be threatened. By the time she has proved herself, a woman's acceptance has slowly evolved. She has become assimilated in the organization so that gender in her particular case is no longer salient. Roberta describes the long process of gaining respect based on competence as a consultant in a *Fortune* 500 company.

> I was for a long, long time the only woman in meetings. I knew that, whatever I said, no one listened to me. My input wasn't valued. I generally wasn't accepted. It's only been in the last couple of years that that's really turned itself around. I think that's based on my performance and receiving more respect from my colleagues.

Interestingly, Roberta refers to the situation of nonacceptance as "turn[ing] itself around." That implies that no one actually engineered its change; rather, it changed itself. Neither Roberta nor her male colleagues explicitly worked on the manifestations of nonacceptance. But she is deliberate in repeatedly demonstrating and visibly asserting her competence: "the promotions . . . I fought for myself." And she, like others, attributes her acceptance to the establishment of an unquestionable performance record.

In response to being repeatedly tested, women set their own ground rules, which compel male colleagues to respond to their professionalism or not at all. These women's psychological development can shape social change in their offices.

Beyond Newcomer Status to Proving Herself

It is plausible that any newcomer would face the task of proving competence to co-workers and superiors before achieving full acceptance. Some newcomers, however, are given more latitude at the outset than others. The degree of initial acceptance varies with characteristics such as the newcomer's sex.[16]

A newcomer who is also in the minority receives an initiation that goes beyond that extended to a novitiate who is familiar in all other ways.[17] When a man is the newcomer, other men can make certain assumptions about him as a person and as a co-worker. They begin with a trust that underlies tangible assistance, support, and tutelage. That trust can be overturned, certainly, by the newcomer's behavior, but the point is that it is there at the outset for a man but ordinarily not for a woman. A woman in that same position is granted neither benign assumptions nor trust. On the contrary, her presence often stimulates reactions of doubt, distrust, or at best discomfort and neutral watchfulness. Men do not know how to behave in this foreign circumstance, which asks them to deny long-standing customary roles and settle into new ones for which they have had no preparation or experience. Their reactions are predictable: They either retreat to the roles they know best or they retreat altogether.

In this study, we see women as minority newcomers reeducating in a nonconfrontational manner. They do not directly challenge male attitudes and behavior but rather demonstrate through professional performance that they do indeed belong, even if they are female.

For some women, newcomer status overrides gender minority status. Rebecca, who supervises a technical area within the transportation industry, believed that her primary task was to learn the job, and that was independent of being female.

I think probably being a woman was a very small part of what I had to overcome. I don't think it really had that much impact on them [male co-workers]. I might be calling that wrong. Another person might have said, "It has a lot to do with it." But I think, more than that, I was a newcomer in the group and inexperienced, and I think that was the thing I had to get over the most. But they were super, they really were. They really helped a lot, helped me out in meetings and just in general, in sort of filling me in on things, getting me up to speed.

Rebecca claims no need to prove her competence in light of being female. That is, she felt acceptance and support in undertaking the new job. For her, the task was not complicated by co-workers' extraneous reactions. However, she also recognizes the part that her own perceptions may have played in this interpretation. Once again, these women demonstrate how an individual's psychological set can affect that of others. A woman's attitude about herself and her abilities can shape environmental change.[18]

In Elena's case, the dynamics associated with newcomer status were present, but her experience was not automatically negative. She articulately describes those dynamics, how they are compounded by gender, and how she was able to use her novice status to advantage in monitoring a chemical company's compliance with governmental regulations.

I have really used some of my notions about how people interact and what's important to people in order to preserve their own sense of self and their own sense of importance. Important learning experiences have been mostly in terms of the nature of organizations and how men, especially, will form this rigidly stratified . . . social group—and be able to sit in that group and know where everybody else belongs, which you, an outsider coming in, don't know. You just know that there are ways of addressing that, that men address other men as if they belong to the organization, and sort of sense that there is an order to things, and that they know what the order is, and they can work with it. And then you as an outsider have to figure out what the order is. But they kind of like you because you're an outsider. You also can get away with pretending that you don't know what the order is—and be able to circumvent people. Some of the things that have been done forever because they've been done forever—I can get away with it because I'm not part of the structure, part of the order. I haven't heard the instructions before, and I don't know what the unwritten rules are.

Gender was often, albeit not always, a factor in a woman's acceptance by co-workers in the company. Several interviewees spoke as though the difficulties associated with being a female in a male organization were a given; assumed and therefore not surprising, they were also not a subject of direct focus. Again, we see women dealing with such issues by proving themselves as competent employees first and foremost. Aware that gender compounds this process, women act in accordance with an unwritten proscription against its overt acknowledgment. To bring gender into open forum might lend it legitimacy as a criterion for competence in business. By ostensibly ignoring gender, women are transmitting the message that it is not a factor and that they expect to be judged solely on the basis of their performance. If they ignore it, perhaps everyone else will also. Thus, they are engaged in a dual process: establishing their professional acumen independent of gender and overcoming gender as a possible source of bias. Bonnie, selling a product line of a large, diversified conglomerate, speaks of this double and paradoxical duty:

> But the hardest thing was to get the level of management's credibility that you need to succeed in a corporation. Women come into a major corporation, and they really are on a trial basis. Most of the men—maybe I should say, most of the people, if there are women involved—are going to sit back and not make judgment immediately. But that also means they're not being supportive either. You really have to pay your dues, so to speak, and get that credibility established. And the more credibility that you get, the better off you are, and the easier it is . . . You have to have established a business relationship.

Establishing a business relationship apparently involves more than just business in the case of women. Certainly, interpersonal and social characteristics enter into any newcomer's acceptance in an organization. An ordinary process of getting acquainted and establishing a working relationship is exacerbated when males are required to interact with a woman in circumstances where they usually find men. Females functioning as professionals in the workplace overturn a man's expectations regarding who his colleagues are, and he finds himself unprepared to interact with females outside of the conventional roles. A man may believe that a woman does not belong and therefore ignores her, or he may respond according to traditional male–female relationships. Thus, a female professional may be greeted by an absence of support that is at best neutral and at worst hostile. For example, when she moved into a new managerial position within her consumer products company, Jill was not given the benefit of the doubt that a man so appointed might have initially enjoyed, at least until proven undeserving.

> And irrespective of gender, I saw their [co-workers'] role as one of just extending to the new person on the team . . . a degree of welcome and support, that they would do what they could to make the situation work.

They saw it more as a confrontation: "Well, we've got a woman in this position, and we're going to sit back and see what she does." They held back completely and would not even acknowledge, in essence, the fact that I was in the job. And I had to, in those cases, initiate initial contact with them, set up a meeting, open communication in terms of what we had to perform for the company, what my role was. And I did it, and I did get off to really quite a good start because of it. But I think I have some residual resentment from these people because of it.

Not only did men withhold cooperation from their female manager, but they also resented her for successfully overcoming their resistance. Martha, in a traditionally male manufacturing company, describes a kind of hazing process that is unique to women.

Being taken seriously, number one, by men. That is always a barrier that's got to be overcome. . . . Then, once you're taken seriously, how serious are you? So then we get into the sexual games and that kind of thing. And then, number three is, "Okay, you're here and you're not interested in my alternatives, how rough can we make it for you?" That's phase three. Once you get through that, then it's gravy.

In another historically male industry, transportation, Beverly elaborates upon the experiences just outlined. It is likely that a representative of any type of minority would receive similar treatment. When people are unaccustomed to a certain kind of interaction with a minority representative, they respond in ways that are problematic for all concerned. In this case, a woman must find ways of establishing her expertise while simultaneously handling responses related to gender in an unobtrusive way.

And I certainly am getting information around what it means to be a woman in a world that has no experience with women, other than mothers, daughters, and lovers. I didn't expect the amount of energy it takes to do that—how much energy it takes to be visible all the time, and how people choose to believe what they think, whether or not it's true, and don't even choose to check it out. . . . So the real learning here has been that I came in wanting to get all of the people issues taken care of so that I could go do the work. And the learning has been that the work is the people issues. . . . It's a real problem to getting any kind of work accomplished—not being listened to in terms of my saying something or my helping people say something for themselves and then have it thrown away because it doesn't come from a source that they consider credible. Or they don't want to hear it—whatever. But then it can come from somebody else that looks much more traditional, and it's then adopted or worked with, or whatever. It's difficult, in not knowing how to fit into their play patterns, not knowing whether you ought to go ahead and play golf with them, or you ought to go ahead and go drinking with them, or whether it's important for them to see that you can do your work without doing those things. It shows up in joking, in kidding. And they [the men who are co-workers] either [figuratively] beat you up a lot for being there and for doing what you're there to do or they react in a much more seductive way, which is to act like they believe everything you're saying and act like they think you're just wonderful and treat you like their sweet little girl. And that sometimes feels so good after getting beaten up all the time that you just really buy into it. And you think that they're believing you, and you think that you're really being able to work with them, and all they're doing is just kind of patting you on the head and saying, "Isn't she cute?" So for me that's . . . a constant tightrope, to not fall into either one of those.

In contrast to women like Rebecca, whose entry into the technical area of another transportation organization is met with almost Welcome Wagon hospitality and assistance, Beverly shows us the other end of the continuum where the substance of the work becomes "the people issues."[19] Perhaps as a function of the particular organization or her human resource function within it, Beverly's work cannot be wholly separated from the perceptions, interpretations, and responses of others. Thus, her performance is greatly affected by interpersonal dynamics, and her effectiveness becomes contingent upon her ability to walk a narrow line between men's patent rejection and patronizing tolerance. In proving herself, she cannot totally circumvent reactions of men who are unprepared and perhaps unwilling to take a female colleague seriously.

Many women fall somewhere in between Rebecca and Beverly, in that they must prove themselves as corporate professionals who are also female, but they are able to separate their work content from the social and personal difficulties that male colleagues might have with their presence. The strategies these women develop refer more to matters of pure performance independent of gender. A planner working with high-level retail executives, Karen sees proving herself as a one-time-only occasion, but its accomplishment goes a long way.

it's much more political working with senior management, who are all the traditional breadwinner, wife stays at home, four kids, with the white picket fence, etcetera. If you prove yourself in the beginning, right away, then you seem to be accepted. But there aren't too many second chances around. What I feel is my . . . one strategy for success is to do what you say you're going to do in the time frame you say you're going to do it. There are very few people around, I have learned, that do that on a consistent basis. And it's just amazing how it works over and over and over, no matter what you're doing.

It would make sense that top management would not allow much room for error, as it is likely that the demands on them are exacting and unforgiving. However, not only must a female prove herself from the outset whereas a male might experience a grace period, but she is given less room for error than her male counterpart, for whom acceptance and license are foregone conclusions.

Jessica reiterates the observation that some men actively, albeit covertly, oppose the idea of female corporate professionals, whereas others do not. In charge of site development, she has found an effective way of proving herself to the doubting Thomases of her consumer product chain.

> Sometimes the underlying notion [is] that you're a woman, you're not credible. And I imagine we've all faced that with some men. I'm not saying all, but some. . . . But the ones that I've had problems with, I go out of my way to accommodate them. You need information? I'll get it for you, and I'll have it back [in] half an hour—you know, just sort of bend over backward to prove to them. . . . And by the ability to get information and feed it back to them, you build up your credibility. So then, sooner or later, they say, "Well, she knows what she's talking about. I can always go to her because she'll get it done." . . . And that's basically how I overcame that.

The learning process is multifaceted for women who are proving themselves in the corporate world. Beyond content skills, they must develop a facility with interpersonal styles and modes of communication that have been set by the dominant culture of the organization. Further, women contend with varying degrees of having to prove themselves in the corporation. As we have seen, some are welcomed with a responsive assistance that is blind to gender. Others face what seem to be insurmountable barriers based primarily on gender. Many fall in between; they are met with a modicum of resistance, which probably exceeds that associated solely with newcomer status. The degree of obstacle is likely to vary with the nature of the organization, the type of function within it, and the preparedness of male workers for female colleagues.[20]

Despite variation in their strength, duration, and number, obstacles confronted by a female newcomer in a male-dominated organization commonly involve gender to some degree. Moreover, the gender component of her newcomer status is denied by all concerned. Gender is not acknowledged as an element in the competence equation by either the men or the women in the corporation.[21] In order to prove themselves, then, women focus exclusively on competent performance. To admit gender as a variable could lend it a legitimacy that women reject. Thus, they are in the paradoxical position of having to prove themselves despite being female and as though they are not. Often they are alone in this struggle, but there are instances where others are available for support.

Available Support

The first woman in an organization has to prove herself in light of her minority status, and she is by definition alone. Although they were among the first, most women interviewed did not view themselves as affirmative action hires. Their perception is substantiated by a dedication to achievement that is contrary to findings of lowered commitment and job satisfaction among women who do perceive themselves as tokens.[22] Even in the absence of the burdens of tokenism, a woman's minority status implies that she may have no mentor or female role model immediately present to show her the ropes, counsel her, tip her off to the unadvertised aspects of the job and the organization. She goes it alone.

Regardless of the route taken to the job and the availability of support once on it, without exception women are aware of the need to establish their competence as firmly and quickly as possible. However, the establishment of competence and the projection of a consonant image may involve considerably more than simply job substance. In Part 1 women frequently talked about managers who did not teach the job directly but supplied a more general challenge by leaving them to their own devices. This sink-or-swim mode may be a common corporate way of ascertaining whether a newcomer really belongs in the organization. Or it may be differentially applied to females, whose aptitudes are especially tested whereas a male newcomer would receive the benefit of more formal and informal tuition.

In the absence of coaching, a woman learns as much about herself and her own capabilities as she does about the job. At the time of this kind of hazing process she is too preoccupied with all that is required of her to reflect upon the process itself. It is not until after successful navigation of both the manifest and the latent content of the job that she may become aware of the scope and nature of that learning.[23] As with so many others, Jill's realizations came in retrospect.

the individual I first worked for taught me a lot from the perspective that he didn't do any sort of training—you can say hand-holding, you can say

anything you want—but he really let me sink or swim. And I was amazed
[at] the things he threw me into. But somehow I always survived. And we
never really spoke about it. It was just something that was understood.
And in retrospect I think it was extremely beneficial. But at the time I
couldn't see what was really happening.

Much of what transpires among co-workers is unspoken. While
learning the job, a woman also learns about the existence and character
of different levels of communication. She learns the language of business and of her particular company. She learns the company politics
and symbol systems, how meaning is transmitted and interpreted. She
learns when and when not to question, challenge, confront. She develops strategies that allow her assimilation within the corporation
without sacrificing herself as an individual.[24]

Women have evolved a personal style at work that includes use of an
"androgynous strategy." This involves a deemphasis on gender as an
issue in the workplace and the use of professionalism to deal with
gender-related problems. An androgynous management style for both
men and women has been receiving support in the literature. The
notion that females bring special traits to management, however, harks
back to the sex stereotyping of separate male and female management
styles and their combination under the guise of androgyny. Ideally, a
reciprocal process of acceptance occurs wherein women are not mask-
ing their own identities, and the organization is treating them as individuals rather than as women.

When not actively taught, women must infer the lessons of the
corporation. Thus, these women are doing double duty: They are
learning both the written and the unwritten rules on their own. It often
has been said that a woman must be twice as good as her male counterpart.[25] These women's accomplishments in the absence of support
attest to that.

Much learning can occur on an almost unconscious level unless and
until a woman has the opportunity to articulate and thereby bring it
forth. Sometimes a superior in the company will foster such articulation. Like the women themselves, those who act as mentors and role
models are frequently outstanding individuals.[26] Ina expresses open
gratitude and admiration for a successful female superior.

the director . . . who has taken me and showed me the ropes and pointed
out the rules of the game. It's a woman . . . I appreciate, admire, emulate.
She's gone damn far, and she's shared it with me, which I think a lot of
people wouldn't have. What did she show me? Well, just in the everyday

matters, the big pictures of markets. She showed me how she gets—maybe not even in words—who she spoke with and who she tried to get power with. Even in style of dress. It sounds so strange, but yes, I suppose I've imitated her along the way. She's my model. And I'm not unaware of it.

An accomplished member of the organization can shed considerable light on latent job elements necessary for the depth of understanding pivotal to subsequent success.

I worked for a very highly motivated, aggressive woman . . . she and I really hit it off from the beginning. She did a lot of career counseling with me, and really educated me in terms of aspects of the business that I didn't understand or hadn't understood up until that point.

Further, as Susan points out, a mentor can assist in placing a woman and her position within a larger perspective so that she is thinking ahead even when ostensibly consumed by the task at hand. Like Susan, Roberta's thinking was stimulated in new directions by a superior with a wider perspective on career and its possibilities.

But there was a lot that I was exposed to with this woman. . . . she was a real trailblazer, and it was very valuable just to be exposed to her. She's helped me project more, definitely has helped me to take my career seriously, myself seriously. The whole risk-taking area, which I never dabbled with at all, very much was impacted by her. I have some discussions with her all the time about where I want to go with my career. She gives me a whole menu of things that I would never think of on my own.

Support can come in many forms. A manager who delegates difficult projects and weighty decision making without providing much guidance may be testing an employee as well as covertly communicating confidence in her abilities. A superior who functions as a role model and provides critical information not manifestly available about the immediate task and the organization is teaching invaluable lessons. One who tutors beyond the current circumstance and its many layers can continue to influence a woman's perspectives in the larger sense of career path.

Women interviewed indicated that these various forms of support came to them from both males and females at their workplaces, but they themselves felt an obligation to provide similar support for other women.[27] Camilla explains that even with the support of other women the corporate road can be fraught with difficulty.

I feel like I've had to battle it through at every step of the way. I'd like to make it easier; I do everything I can to bring . . . more women into the department. I've worked with other women who've done the same for me, and it's something that I really believe in strongly.

Whether actively or covertly tutored by other women, several echoed Camilla's conviction about supporting others in their companies. This belief is not necessarily predicated on number and degree of obstacles experienced. Marie, for example, equipped with technical skill suitable to the financial industry, did not find her corporate acclimation unduly trying, but she has her own theories about why females may need extra help.

It's very important, I think, for women to be supportive of other women who are in business. Not that you meet so many obstacles along the way, but it's so important to just know that there's somebody else who's going through the same problems that you go through and meeting the same types of insecurities, . . . and I don't think men have the same experience with that. . . . They're [men] brought up differently, and I think they've learned to do that [delegate authority, for example] from when they were little boys. They just know how to take authority and demand it, whereas I don't think women have that same experience [upbringing]. They're just brought up to believe that someday that's what they're going to have to do, so they just know how to do it.

Marie refers to gender differences in early socialization that presumably prepare males, and not females, for corporate success. For example, participation in competitive team undertakings, such as the military and athletics, is thought to be indigenous to a male's upbringing and thereby prepares him for corporations as they are currently structured. The fact that females are taking advantage of the opportunities for sports only recently made available to them could overturn these notions.[28] Also, whether these assumptions correspond with the reality of male socialization remains to be seen, but cultural belief in them alone can support and perpetuate male dominance in the business world.

In Part 2 women described individual differences in childhood messages about who they were and what their futures held. However, we also witnessed descriptions of changes made in their personal characteristics and behavior to suit business requirements.[29] Women can adopt behavior appropriate to business, usually with some active effort and learning. Perhaps this applies equally to men, and Marie's remarks underscore the benefits of empathetic support by others who have shared similar feelings and experiences.[30]

Lisa, an underemployed planner in a *Fortune* 500 company, reiterates the idea that the insecurities of men and women may differ and that it is helpful to have the understanding and active assistance of another like oneself. Even though she has not been the beneficiary of much support, Lisa's determination to be its provider reflects an inspired optimism.

> When I see somebody, another woman, who's trying to . . . get ahead, if I have an opportunity I go out of my way to encourage them; or if I see them doing something that I know is going to hurt them I'll also go out of my way. It may not always be appreciated, but I feel . . . that I should. I wish I had another woman up there someplace that could guide me, but I don't. But it's okay, I'll make it somehow. Because I feel there are a lot of men out there that accept women. They accept the fact that we're here to stay. We are going to get ahead. We are going to make progress. They are also a lot of men out there who have a hard time. They don't do it on purpose, it's unconscious, but they have insecurities of their own, just like I have insecurities. Whenever I feel I leave something or somebody with a good impression, I feel like I've not only helped myself but maybe I've helped some other woman to get a chance. And I'd like to see that happen. I would like to see our daughters have more opportunities and an easier path. I just think it will get better, and better days are ahead for everybody.

Whether or not women have been the recipients of support from others in the corporation, they are aware of how useful it can be. What constitutes support can range from active mentoring of a particular individual, including explicit tutelage and advocacy in the organization, to a more general lobbying for affirmative action. Even in the absence of support for them individually or as a group, they retain the determination to help other women in whatever ways possible. The learning required for success traverses the manifest job substance to less apparent modes of communication and political strategies. Such learning can be accomplished, and errors avoided, more rapidly and efficiently under the tutelage of one already experienced. Beyond job performance, a minority newcomer can gain emotionally from the psychological knowledge of even passive support. Helpful anywhere, support can be critical in certain situations where discrimination still exists.

Discrimination

The women interviewed were not asked about discrimination. As with gender, there were no questions directly or even implicitly aimed at the subject per se. And as with gender, interviewees were not intent on discussing discrimination. It could be said that the interviews were a microcosmic reflection of attitudes and philosophies adopted by these women in the corporate setting. The interviews took place in a professional context and as such represented an extension of their business, rather than personal, demeanors. Personal matters were certainly raised, and women revealed their personal sides to varying degrees, but the predominant mind-set in the interviews was professional. Therefore, since these women attempted to minimize gender's bearing on the job, it follows that their interviews likewise did not reveal a focus on sex discrimination.

In several interviews the topic of discrimination was never mentioned. When raised by the interviewee, it was, again like gender, in the context of a response to a question about something else. In most cases it was less a discussion and more a parenthetical nod to the possibility of discrimination simultaneous with a denial of personal involvement. That is, by mentioning in the context of something else that they had never been the object of discrimination, women implicitly acknowledged its existence, albeit elsewhere.[31]

It is not surprising that the women spoke little of discrimination. Admittedly, these were a select group who might be termed successful in the corporate world. They had not been barred from opportunity; a few may have even benefited from affirmative action mandates. The majority saw themselves as trading on their talent and accomplishment, not on their sex. They did not seek special allowances, nor did they look for evidence of discrimination. About half of the women had at some time experienced discrimination in matters of hiring, promotion, or compensation, but their tendency was to make short shrift of it and move on.[32] These women were more interested in meeting their achievement needs through substantive job performance than they were in battling sexism in the business world.

Faced with undeniable evidence of discrimination that does not yield to professional efficacy, these women would rather change jobs than change co-workers' attitudes. To divert their energies from the job to a fight against discrimination is contrary to their instrumental goals, which are grounded in the work itself. Hope characterizes a learning process fraught with frustration, which culminated in a decision to change companies.

> Certainly, at that time, even though it was only five or six years ago [late seventies], the . . . men were certainly not accustomed to dealing with women. They didn't have any trouble hearing me at cocktail parties. And

they didn't have any trouble hearing me in private conversation, but they couldn't hear me in the work-related environment. It was as if they didn't know how to operate with me, so they just didn't operate. They just . . . walked away . . . but when a problem came up, they wanted a hard answer. And I could give it to them, because I had been there. But they couldn't take it from me, because they couldn't hear me. So I started going through this whole thing of, "Well, what's wrong with me? I can't talk; I'm not articulating this well; I'm not being clear." Until a real good friend (and colleague) said to me, "It really isn't you," and was kind enough to do an experiment with me. Next time we had a meeting, they'd present a problem. I'd present the answer. They'd smile and move on. Ten minutes later, he'd present the same answer but in a different form, and they'd say, "Goddammit, you're going to go far. You know, we can always trust you. You've got all the answers," and all this stuff. And I said, "I'm going to quit. My shoulders are all tense and hard. I've got headaches. I'm frustrated. I don't like the job, and I especially don't like the mentality of the men,"—there weren't any other women. "And I just don't want to get into this . . . bitter female kind of thing. It's an issue, but I don't want to become real militant about this whole thing." And I could certainly see where it was going. So I quit.

Thus, an idea's acceptability was a function of its spokesman rather than its content.[33] When its proponent was a recognizable member of the club, with whom others could identify if only on the basis of gender, it was heard and moreover applauded. The same idea voiced by an alien in the environment suffers a fate akin to whistling in the wind. Learning the established native language and mode of communication may not suffice.[34] A degree of receptivity and acknowledgment may be necessary for a woman to believe that efforts to prove herself will bear fruit. In the absence of even a whit of positive potential, Hope decided to go elsewhere.

These women see themselves as business professionals, not political activists. They have not adopted as their mission proof that women can make it in the business world. Whether through happenstance or a career exploration process, they discovered their propensities for work in the corporate world. Even women who harbored dissatisfactions with the company of their current employ did not show leanings away from business. These women are concentrating on proficiency at work in whatever company proves suitable. They are willing to foster and encourage other women's similar strivings but not to represent and overtly push feminism at the office. For some, like Teresa, their presence is statement enough.

I know that there have been obstacles and barriers and roadblocks and all kinds of things . . . at least people have attempted to put them in my path.

But I have tried to rise above them or go around them. I tell you the truth . . . if there's anything I can say that I resent sometimes [it's] being expected to be a model. If I'm better, they always say a black has to be twice as good—or a woman. If I am, I just am. I'm not twice as good because I'm black or because I'm a woman. I'm twice as good because I have an inherent ability to be twice as good. I think I resent people expecting me to obviously and constantly be on that damn bandwagon, even as far as a woman is concerned. I recognize that we have problems. If no one recognizes it, I do. . . . But I think just my being is a model. I'm there. I'm doing it, you know. I'm successful. What more do you want out of me? I just get a little tired of dealing with them sometimes. But I'm not going to give up. I'm not going to let anybody run me out because of my color or because of my sex. I'll fight it, I'll do a good job, and I'll ignore it. I will not really confront it unless I actually have to.

Women are not unaware of discrimination's presence despite their frequent reports of no actual or observed experience with it. Even when unmistakably confronted, women choose circumvention whenever possible.[35] In those instances where a woman successfully executes her responsibilities in spite of manifest or latent prejudice, her triumph is a double one. Teresa recounts the details of just such a circumstance.

There were a lot of old-line employees who resented me for one reason or the other. And when I recognize a problem of that nature, I ignore it. I rise above it. As long as I'm being supported and rewarded [by supervisors], I don't deal with it. And I think it bothers people more than anything else, because it . . . tells them, that's not important, and I can't deal with that. I don't have the time to deal with it. But I also did not shrink from letting them know the position I enjoy. I didn't soft-pedal them. If it came time to give them direction or whatever, I treated them just like it didn't exist, like that feeling they had—and I know they had it, and they know I knew that they had it—it didn't exist. And I think that disturbed them more than anything else. And that's probably another reason why I did it, because I knew I was disturbing them even more.

Teresa's experience differed from Hope's in important ways. Prejudice against Teresa emanated from her subordinates whereas Hope's peers were tuning her out. As Teresa points out, managerial support was critical in enabling her strategic performance despite workers' attitudinal barriers. Moreover, recognition and validation, always vital and especially so in an adversarial situation, were available to Teresa but painfully absent for Hope. Teresa's superordinate position in relation to those prejudiced allowed her some affective satisfaction through the exercise of authority as though detrimental attitudes did not exist.

By refusing to deal with workers on their terms and insisting on business as usual, she denied them power and defused the impact of their beliefs. Facing collegial rather than subordinate prejudice, Hope did not have such avenues available; structural elements of her position in comparison to Teresa's left Hope without recognition or recourse for effective performance. In both cases, however, the women chose to focus on their work in preference to direct acknowledgment of the prejudice. In neither situation were the biased attitudes a subject of open discussion.

The absence of its acknowledgment can make discrimination difficult to discern. Long-standing practices having a discriminatory effect may be recognized as such only after studied observation. When discrimination takes subtle and inconsistent forms, it is difficult to detect, and a woman may be reluctant to affix that label to an organization's behavior. Discrimination is supposed to be a thing of the past, and a woman shouting its name may be an object of scorn. Hence, women tend to suspect quietly and try to deal with it singlehandedly. For example, Lisa has seen differential treatment of males and females in her group, but preferences for the work foster her patience and forbearance.

> It's just that it seems as if there are different rules for different people. I think that's what I'm trying to say: There are different rules for different people. If I want to move up, I just have to do more before I get the money that other people do. It's definitely different. But I do know there are parts of the company that are not that way. It just happens in this particular area. And because I like the area, and I like the job, I think I'm willing to plod along rather slowly. . . . It seems like I get the job, and then finally I get the money, if I'm lucky. I . . . accept that as the way it happens, because I haven't seen anybody, any women, do it any other way. [*Why special rules for different people?*] I think it's because I'm female. That seems to be the only difference. I think they're insecure in the sense that, if I took the job and blew it, the person who suggested or recommended me would have stuck his neck out; he could be held responsible. They're trying to protect themselves.

The tentative tone of Lisa's description reflects women's reluctance to admit discrimination. To acknowledge it actively would put them in a state of dissonance, and they might be forced to act contrary to their own interest. This is particularly the case when a woman likes the job and does not want to leave it.[36] Here, as elsewhere, the organizational context plays a crucial role. In large organizations like Lisa's, some areas may be discriminatory whereas others are not. To assist in her avoidance of the issue, Lisa resorts to looking at levels of discrimination. Since she has not seen discrimination within discrimination—that is, other women in her area are treated as she is—she can maintain her patience. Lisa appears to ignore discrimination while she is in fact both circumventing it and watching it closely.

Lisa's interpretation of why females must prove themselves prior to securing a commensurate salary that a male would receive from the start underscores females' alien status in the corporate world. We are reminded of Hope's anecdote, which held the implied message that certain assumptions can be safely made about a male colleague but not about a female. People more readily identify with and attribute a trustworthiness to others evidently like themselves. When males are in the majority, they assume another male will perform competently and contribute significantly. A female represents the unknown, even an enigma, and therefore she is a risk. She may be tested more stringently not only in reference to the work itself but also with regard to affective tolerance of prejudice. Some men are quite explicit in their message that a woman does not belong, as Bonnie's story illustrates.

> This guy one time took me to lunch. [He] took me to the men's health club for lunch—women were not allowed in. And he proceeded to make a big spectacle of it, and he said, "Oh, geez, why do we have women in this organization? You can't even go into where all the businessmen go. You expect business to be conducted, and you can't even get in there. You're really going to be an asset to the company." And I'm thinking to myself, "This guy really deserves a punch in the nose," but I just kept myself very composed and said, "I think we can go someplace where business is conducted; what do you say we find another place?"

To act on her impulse might have had detrimental consequences for Bonnie's future with the company. Instead of responding to her co-worker's baiting actions and words, she stepped over them to the business at hand. In the face of covert and explicit discrimination, women decide what degree of response to make. They seek to maintain a balance psychologically and behaviorally whereby they can continue functioning in their jobs.[37]

Some testing, though not ordinarily as blatant, is not uncommon. The nature and amount of testing applied to a woman are likely to vary with the company and the men with whom she has direct contact. For Tammy, testing was a onetime event that was not burdensome. Although she easily gained the respect of her male superiors, she still witnesses their generally biased attitude toward women on the job.

My bosses are all men. And although I have never been a victim of really being discriminated against because I'm a woman, I did feel this: that they did test me in that I had to do something that impressed them or I had to gain their confidence by having sort of expert knowledge. But once that was accomplished, then there was no problem. But I have heard them sitting and talking and saying all the discriminatory things that everybody accuses their male managers of saying. A week's worth of argument was whether they should hire a male or a female. The argument went, "Well, if we hire a woman, she won't be able to take the pace." "We want her to do everything, and I just don't think a woman could do it."

Tammy represents an exception to her employers. She has been assimilated within the organization, but their acceptance of her has not been transferred to a gender-blind consideration of other female employees. Their stereotypes remain intact even though they enjoy a mutually respectful relationship with at least one female professional employee.

Perhaps, contrary to the belief of many, affirmative action continues to serve a vital purpose.[38] If a woman can get hired, then she presumably has an opportunity to prove herself, but discriminatory stereotyping might still function to block her entrance. Once on the job, a female may be put through a more difficult and complex hazing process than her male counterpart. Furthermore, it is not necessarily the case that a woman who has proven herself is free of discrimination's effects in daily working relationships. However, many people, women included, seem to believe that such obstacles have been eliminated; others assert that women face the same constraints as they did twenty years ago.[39] Hope remarks on the lack of concern about male-female difficulties in the workplace on the part of young professionals.[40]

They don't consider that the male–female issue exists anymore, and I can't believe that, because it seems to me as if that's the thing I'm constantly concerned with. I don't have to deal with the issue of how to solve a problem, or how to get a decision made, or how to implement a solution, or how to motivate people. I know how to do all that. I don't know how to get around these men. All the men that are above me are surprisingly supportive. That's because they're not threatened. I mean, they're secure in who they are, and I'm no threat. I'm not going to take their position away from them or anything. But all these men down here are . . . saying, I think, "How come she's there? You know, I'm a man. I'm supposed to get promoted. I'm the breadwinner, and I've been with the company for a long time, and they brought her in from the outside, and she's a girl."

Although support from above is crucial for any worker, especially one who faces opposition from other factions, it does not remove the stress of regularly dealing with resentment among subordinates. Be it explicit or veiled, hostility generated by discrimination can be a relentless undercurrent that affects working conditions, relationships, and the execution of the work itself. It can make every task more difficult. Moreover, it is not amenable to straightforward problem solving as it is not a straightforward problem. Layers of psychological dynamics, on both individual and collective levels, make it extraordinarily complex and inaccessible to ordinary problem-solving routes and strategies.

A task of enormous proportion in itself, discrimination's abolition is not seen as the job of the corporation, even by the women who suffer its effects. Those women do not feel that they should have to deal with it either, but the reality is that they do, and largely without guidance or support, as Hope points out.

> There have always been problems of relating well to the men, usually below you rather than above . . . but there's a certain kind of man who can work for a woman. I mean, that's the social element. Men just aren't real comfortable working for women. So people are—men are—afraid. Maybe "afraid" is too strong a word. Maybe they just don't know how to deal, so they . . . simply don't attempt it. [*What kind of man can work with a woman manager?*] One who has a strong sense of who he is and isn't hung up in any way on who women are. Some men see women in one role, and they simply can't see beyond that. You know, "You're the wife. You have the babies, and that's what you do." They simply don't yet know how to see them as working equals. So for that kind of man to have to report to a woman is very, very hard. And one of the big failures of corporations is [in providing] any kind of integrating programs. There's nothing that tells you how to get along, or even how to identify the resentment.

Aside from legislative mandates that govern hiring practices, discrimination is largely a matter of individual reckoning. Our institutions, corporations included, offer few large-scale lessons on how to handle discrimination. Since, for the most part, discrimination is no longer applied in a systematic and blanket fashion, institutions and individuals are better able to deny its existence altogether. But pockets of discrimination can be as disabling, albeit in a different way. Resembling a "now you see it, now you don't" phenomenon, sporadic instances of discrimination are more difficult to detect, easier to deny, and less amenable to prediction and control. Societal investment in a belief that discrimination has been eliminated removes it as a focus of attention and strategies. Individuals are left to their own devices in both its detection and its dissolution. Consequently, those who are its object spend considerable time analyzing and strategizing on their own, with mixed results. Understanding the sources of discrimination does not always imply its solution. Other than trying to ignore or rise above it, women remain in a quandary about its detection and treatment. Moreover, they are primarily alone in that quandary.

Far from agreement, we find in this group of women several singular experiences regarding discrimination. Some report a total absence of the faintest trace; Cathy, for example, has held six positions with the same financial service employer since her graduation with a degree in business:

> I've never been in an environment that wasn't supportive, that was in any way hostile or working against what I was trying to do.

Others are convinced that discrimination presents a daily challenge. Camilla, whose seriousness about her career increased with a move to the profit sector coincident with a divorce in her late twenties, currently applies her technical skills in the construction industry. She is puzzled by colleagues from other organizations who deny discrimination's existence.

> I think the issue is just women getting ahead in general . . . being told [a week or two ago], this time by my boss who considers himself egalitarian, that he still felt that women who have children should stay home with their children. And so I think the biggest thing is trying to decide whether it's really worth fighting every single day. Even though times have changed and they've gotten better, I still feel that the discrimination exists, very, very much so. And that I found in every single job. Even with the technical expertise, it's still there. I've spoken to [female peers], and they don't discuss that at all. They're all talking about it as if it doesn't exist. So I guess it's maybe true that the younger ones are not seeing it. But I still see it.

Whether or not a woman perceives discrimination might be, in part, a function of her age and experience, as well as the company culture of her employ. As Camilla and Hope have suggested, recently employed females behave as though discrimination is nonexistent. Young women may reflect current popular belief that those battles are old and have all been fought and won. They have learned that civil rights and equal opportunity issues are history in our country, and their relatively easy access to the corporate ladder serves as corroboration.

In contrast, women who have been in the work force more than a decade are likely to have witnessed the kind of discrimination that has been outlawed but may be on its way back with recent Supreme Court decisions.[41] The establishment of those laws was a struggle; proof of the most glaringly obvious discrimination was met with massive societal denial and resistance.[42] Legislation can begin and enforce a process of change on an administrative level, but discrimination is insidious and can take many forms. Blatant discrimination is easily identified but subtle discriminatory practices may prove highly recalcitrant. A cultural proscription against the discovery of discrimination could confound its detection and therefore its thorough elimination.

Regardless of diversity of views on discrimination or its absence, women are aware of the difficulties that surround being a female in a male organization. The obstacles vary with the nature of the organization and a woman's particular job within it. Organizations that are new, or less conservative, or involved with creative or technological endeavors may be more egalitarian.[43] Technical expertise often serves to mitigate gender bias. Administrative support is crucial, and unprejudiced co-workers are ideal. Short of maximal conditions, women learn to step over bias, find and offer support wherever they can, focus on performance, and prove their competence as often as necessary.

□ **10** □

The Context of Opportunity

Throughout this volume customary assumptions about women have been challenged. By looking at women's lives in a holistic fashion, we have corroborated data from other studies and elaborated new directions. The bringing together of evidence from achievement and affiliative realms has served the purpose of overturning stereotypic notions about women's identities and lives. Through examination of both the personal and the professional development of the same women, we have gathered a fuller picture of where women have come from and where they are headed.

This book has placed women's psychological development within the context of social change. Connections between female development to date and future directions can be clarified by reviewing the premises of this study and placing them within the current sociopolitical context of opportunity in this country.

The Process of Change

This book has been about the interaction between individual psychological development and social change. We know that people have been shaped by their environment, both immediate and larger. Over the past three decades human rights movements have significantly altered

217

attitudes and behavior toward minorities and women. Although this idea seems indisputable, we have little evidence of the process of change as it occurs on the individual psychological level. This volume begins to provide that.

We have seen firsthand accounts not only of the fact of change but of its process. The women of this study are ideally situated to demonstrate this, as most of them have spanned traditional and new ideologies about who and what women were supposed to be. They graphically describe how they moved from traditional ideas to new conceptions about themselves derived from experiences in a heretofore "man's world." Their individual changes, paralleling social change, are traced in both their personal and professional lives.

The premise upon which this volume has been built is that individual development affects and is affected by social change. People's changed consciousness influences social restructuring. Similarly, social restructuring shapes people's attitudes and behavior. These ideas have face validity, but there has been little documentation of their occurrence.

The disciplinary nature of academic research has separated the study of individuals from that of society. For the most part, individual change has been delegated to psychologists, social change to sociologists. A study of their interaction has usually been deemed too unwieldy for the kind of controlled variable research that these disciplines ordinarily pursue.

Thus, a phenomenological approach was appropriate here. A close-up look at people's lives from the point of view of their own perceptions, interpretations, and understandings could yield information unattainable through the experimental methods typical of psychology or the survey methods of sociology. Listening to women chronicle their own personal and professional histories has enabled us to witness the process of psychological development in relation to social change.

The Different Levels of Change
within the Individual and Society

The idiographic study of individuals at home and work allows us insights into the connections among attitudes, behavior, and psychological development. As noted in the introduction, psychological views of development have gone back and forth between personality trait and behavioral theories. Since Freud, we had believed that individual personalities were composed of traits that developed early and permanently. A countervailing theory of behavior change revised our thinking so that people were seen as changing in response to environmental circumstances. We even went so far as the notion that behavior change could precipitate attitude change; thus, the nature of the change was not merely a surface phenomenon.[1] People's "personalities" were not necessarily fixed early but rather responded to situational context.

Like gender stereotypes, views of personality traits die hard. The most popular recent theory of female development describes differences between the sexes that parallel traditional notions of male and female traits.[2] Male identities are said to be formed through interpersonal separateness and independent achievement whereas females' are shaped by interpersonal connectedness and care. When this idea is extrapolated to management women, we find them depicted as behaving one way but feeling another; their adaptation to the corporate world supposedly is surface behavior which ultimately betrays their true and primary unconscious needs for interpersonal connection.[3]

The question that arises, then, is what constitutes psychological development and change. When are revised behavior and professed attitudes believed to represent true psychological change? Have we reified personality so that it is neither visible nor changeable? In that case, even behavior and attitude change are not thoroughgoing enough to constitute genuine psychological development. The testimony of these women contradicts that kind of dualistic thinking. Their descriptions of behavioral and internalized affective change illustrate the dynamic interaction and ultimate consonance between the two.

Because this study looks at human development from the inside out, from the point of view of women's internal processing of change, it begins to examine the meanings of change on various levels. That is, women describe revised thoughts and feelings as well as behavior and the synergism among them. These aspects of self are ultimately reconciled with each other, although not necessarily all at once.

Thus, these women have demonstrated the process of psychological development on the individual level, whereby changes in thought, feeling, and behavior occur at different rates but are ultimately attuned in the interest of personal integration. Similarly, social change proceeds at varying rates and on different levels. And the interworking of individual change and social change, each with its different levels and rates within those levels, is far from a uniform process. Rather, it is one of ebb and flow, with variable degrees of effect at different points of intersection among the agencies of change.

Individual Change and Structural Change

What is the most viable approach to understanding change? Two positions have been clearly articulated: the individual and the structural.[4] To date, considerable emphasis has been placed on the individual approach to change for women who desire professional corporate careers. The basis of this approach is the idea that women have to overcome shortcomings, whether stemming from their socialization or from their inherent natures, such as lack of assertiveness, independent achievement motivation, and managerial know-how. A structural approach focuses on how social structures, including political apparatus and practice and the setup of the organizations themselves, hinder the progress of individuals.

When women began to enter managerial ranks in the early seventies, both individual and structural approaches to change were employed. Women were steered toward self-improvement programs that would better equip them for business.[5] Meanwhile, affirmative action legislation required organizations actively to recruit women for positions that had been for men only.[6] Now, as we move into the nineties, there is increasing awareness that change on the individual level will not suffice to bring about equal opportunity. Although some structural change has occurred, its circumscribed nature to date is also apparent. Legislation is necessary but insufficient and too dependent upon aggressive enforcement. Structural change that stops at legislative mandate, even with active enforcement, is not enough. Moreover, some speculate that there are structural limits even to the internal reforms that organizations in a profit-based economy can make, and that we must examine connections between capitalism and corporate structures, the stratification among firms in the economy.[7]

Despite an unprecedented increase in the number of female managers in the last decade, the trend may be turning around with corporations cutting back and women leaving for other pursuits, including their own private enterprises.[8] Hardesty and Jacobs explain this retreat as serving the release of suppressed affiliative needs inherent to females. The emphasis had been on how women can adapt to the corporation, and now that they have achieved apparent adaptation their reluctance to stay with it is again mistakenly attributed to female traits. Apparently, women have realized that they do not need to adapt further, as their career commitment and established strengths can be transferred to other business endeavors. Having their ambitions and independence limited by the corporate environment, women have turned to entrepreneurship in an unprecedented way. Owners of one-third of the nation's businesses, female entrepreneurs have the same skills and motives—strong needs for achievement, independence, and control—as their male counterparts.[9] A point of this volume is that, if corporate women are dropping out, it is not because of unmet, subconscious needs for connection but rather because of structural obstacles and persistent, albeit subtle, discrimination.

The Precipitants of Current Opportunity

The women whose voices we heard in this volume had opportunities that had scarcely been available to their predecessors. Within the past fifteen or twenty years sizable numbers of females have secured positions in other than clerical ranks of corporations. Several factors conspired to produce professional opportunity for women in business, with perhaps the most far-reaching being our changing economic realities and the psychological and political ramifications of the current women's movement in this country.

In the past two decades we have witnessed the obsolescence of the single-income, middle-class nuclear family. Ideologically, we had been committed to a notion of the middle-class family that is associated culturally with the 1950s but perhaps was never much of a reality. Presumably, husband/father worked full time outside of the home, and wife/mother was full-time caretaker of home and family. The adequacy of his sole support of family marked the measure of a man. If a woman "had to work" beyond homemaking, her husband was either physically incapacitated or otherwise deficient. A wife could seek gainful employment without her family's suffering social censure if it were for a circumscribed time period or purpose, for example, the children's college education. Men did not want their wives to work, and presumably neither did the women themselves.

Patently stereotypic and frequently at odds with reality, this picture nonetheless represents an ideology about the respective places of men and women that has proved extraordinarily tenacious. When a single family income became inadequate on purely economic grounds, women's work still was seen solely as a financial supplement, not as a primary source of satisfaction.

Betty Friedan's *Feminine Mystique* is often credited with kicking off our country's current women's movement. This book described a nameless dissatisfaction that women whose sole occupation was homemaker had been feeling. Psychological needs for socially recognized, compensated, meaningful work were not confined to males; females shared similar yearnings. Women entering the paid labor force in the sixties were doing so not simply out of financial necessity but rather for myriad psychological reasons related to self-esteem, life satisfaction and meaning, independence, and need for extrafamilial achievement.

As a society we have been reluctant to overturn cultural ideology, even in the face of abundant evidence to the contrary. The persistence of entrenched ideology is seen when women, and not men, still must contend with the conflict between family and career.[10] Women interviewed for this volume present firsthand testimony that females can want a career as much as home and family.

Wanting is not getting, however. Resistance to a new understanding of female identity, needs, and abilities was not simply psychological. The unidimensional caretaker view had extended beyond individual and collective psychic representation to the structures of our institutions and politics of our legislation. Consonant with a belief in female unsuitability for a career, our laws and practices enforced women's inability to do what they should not.[11] Efforts to disinter evidence of discrimination on the basis of sex were met with massive societal denial and its concomitant obstacles. Repeated long and hard court battles resulted in unimpeachable confirmation of the charge, and legislation was enacted to allow women access to the opportunities that men had monopolized. The fragility of these enactments has been demonstrated by the major blows dealt to affirmative action legislation in recent Supreme Court decisions.[12] The sociopolitical culture of the time surely shapes opportunity and prospects for individual economic and psychic fulfillment.

The Limits of Legislation

Legislation is a beginning. It renders discrimination illegal, but it does not automatically overturn long-standing assumptions, attitudes, and practices.[13] People can become so inured to custom that they are unaware of its meaning. It is likely, for example, that Monica's employer did not think of his company's conventions as constituting discrimination.

> it was an entry-level trainee job in personnel. And I went in and talked to the boss. I said I would like to be considered for that job, at which time he

fell off the chair, because at that time there wasn't one woman in a professional capacity in that division. And he just said to me, "You know, we've never had women in personnel jobs, professional personnel jobs." And I talked to him about it. It wasn't that confrontive or anything; it was just he really had not thought about it, even with laws on the books about discrimination. It was just like nothing had really sunk in. I happened not to get that job, but it at least made him very aware of what I wanted.

Women who have gained entry to professional corporate ranks learned not to rely on laws to pave the way. Theoretically, doors can no longer be shut to them, but those on the other side are not always aware that a door exists. Further, some who are aware may be extremely slow in granting access. Legislative help notwithstanding, women learned that they must actively forge awareness and willingness where there had been none.[14] Betty reiterates Monica's lesson regarding the importance of proclaiming goals.

I found out that, if they ask you what you want to do, it's wise to tell them, because they don't really know. It's a woman's tendency to say, "Well, you know what I can do, you know all the jobs that are available, . . . you place me." And [a] man just doesn't know; he isn't thinking about you in that way. It's up to you.

Women's inexperience in business can foster assumptions that hinder advancement. Betty also points out differences between females and males that stem from women's having been largely untutored in business interactions.

[Men are] very competitive with one another, and when they were very competitive with me, at first I didn't understand it, and I decided to blame it all on the fact that I was a woman and they were just trying to push me around. After I got a little perspective on it, I realized that it didn't have much to do with that—a very small percentage—they were just treating me the way they treat one another. They're competitive with one another; they're competitive with me. If I showed any weakness, any vulnerability, boy, there was someone right in there with the knife. No wound was left unopened. And that was very hard for me to deal with as a woman. . . . there are many, many women in the same position who are ill prepared, who think they're prepared but are not. Telling women that they deserve this or they deserve that, that they're smart enough to do this or that, is just not enough, because they believe it, and then they get into these positions in competition with men and they can't hack it. They're not prepared properly.

Granting women rights to opportunity is not tantamount to preparing them for it. Females may represent more heterogeneity in their preparation than males do. Nonetheless, women can be as assertive and appropriately competitive as their male counterparts in the corporate context.

The women whose development was chronicled here demonstrated an impressive variety and depth of learning that served their ambitions and achievements well. In retrospect, they can see how their paths might have been more efficiently forged, but a lack of formal preparation or male socialization was quickly overcome, and they used what they had learned to advantage. Esther provides an example.

> I've learned to be a little smarter than I used to be in terms of who you talk to, what you don't say, what you do say, where you show up, where you don't show up. I was terribly naive twelve years ago, in terms of a corporate structure. . . . I think if I had [it] to do over again I would have found out much more about the structure of the corporation itself. I went in at too low a salary. I didn't ask for the right position. I didn't realize how much titles meant. I didn't realize how much official status meant. But when I think back, I acted as though I [had the title], and everybody that I had to work with probably thought I [did]. And I didn't know I wasn't that important. And then, when I found out, I made sure that I became [that important].

In the absence of formal preparation or training for a career in business, women are able to learn essential strategies on the job. They can benefit from the opportunities that do exist for access and for learning and consequent advancement. Those opportunities materialized as a function of the larger political and economic context of our country and are currently being dismantled by the conservative shifts of the past decade. Changing economic conditions, with concomitant corporate streamlining, can mitigate against women's management opportunities.[15] Particular corporations, however, can vary considerably in their responsiveness to women as competent corporate executives equal to men. Women might experience more equitable treatment from one corporation than from another. Further, the people within any one company may be less susceptible to bias. Legal mandates and companies' policies, however, cannot totally eradicate diehard discriminatory attitudes.

Overcoming Obstacles on the Job

Having gained entry and technical expertise, women continue to face gender-based obstacles in their daily interactions. According to Teresa, who described dealing with subordinates' prejudice in chapter 9, her greatest difficulty is

> getting the respect, in terms of getting people to overlook the fact that I'm a woman, that I look younger than . . . I am, whatever their hang-ups are . . . but that's so [much a] part of their nature you just learn to work around that. . . . But I think that's the biggest thing, getting over those first damn impressions. Having to expend the energy to establish yourself, whereas if I was a blond, blue-eyed six-footer male, hey, half of my damn job would be accomplished. But first I've got to let them know that I know what I'm talking about. I know what to do and not to do. I have to show them that. They won't accept that at face value.

By virtue of their sex, females may be subjected to an informal testing that is perpetuated by deeply ingrained beliefs about their nature. Traditional sex role stereotypes and their respective characteristics are not as pervasive as they once were, nor is it as socially acceptable to proffer such notions.[16] Even twenty years of a countervailing ideology, associated legislation, and revised public practices have not completely eradicated those notions. The reasons for their tenacity undoubtedly span political and psychological arenas.

Women still represent the unfamiliar and less predictable colleague to many in business. Where females are concerned, the need for proof may be greater and more persistent, and such proof may not readily generalize to other situations for the same woman, or from a trusted woman to others unknown. Here we have witnessed women, when faced with this circumstance, adopting an attitude of belonging, ignoring or working around barriers of bias, and concentrating their energies on performance. This has been effective only up to a point. Women who have been required to be exceptional are being held at a certain level considerably below top management.[17]

The barriers are more subtle now, however, and increasingly resistant at the higher rungs.[18] Men, who remain the gatekeepers, are less likely to select a female for the most precious corporate positions. At the top, subjective criteria, such as comfort, trust, and fit, work to place men and not women in those positions of power.[19]

The dearth of women at the top formerly was seen as a function of their scant numbers throughout corporations.[20] However, their increased numbers, rather than making women more commonplace and therefore acceptable, have been met with increased resistance.[21] Moreover, we can no longer attribute women's absence at the top to their lack of aspiration. More likely it is, as Rosabeth Kanter has suggested, that powerless positions are the cause, not the effect, of lowered career aspiration.[22]

Again, women's current corporate circumstance provides clear illustration of the limits of individual approaches to change. The proof of their abilities has been firmly established in the field and in research findings. They have taken advantage of the provisions of equal employment opportunity and have stepped over and around bias when confronted with it on the job. Yet current literature depicts women's professional advancement at a standstill. Reasons offered have less to do with female managerial acumen and more to do with male prejudice, often unconscious, and the lack of structural change throughout the organization. As with our study of women managers, a holistic approach to change is needed that encompasses both psychological and structural realms.[23]

The Future of Opportunity

Our society's institutions are legally enjoined against discriminatory practices, but prejudice remains interpersonally extant. Parallel to obstacles on the individual level is a sociopolitical threat to opportunity, as affirmative action is dismantled by the courts and by inertia. Since it is neither legal nor socially acceptable, the remnants of discrimination take subtle forms on both the individual and the societal level. Here women discuss how current governmental leanings are reflected politically in corporate practice. Opportunities provided by social change that moved us away from discrimination and toward affirmative action slacken with diminishing political support. Hope observes:

> There are subtle things going on. I have a real sense that . . . women are losing ground. . . . I sense inside [her company], since Reagan has been elected, a slackening of all of our affirmative action energy. I mean, we just . . . aren't pushing and doing things that we were doing in the past. . . . I don't see as many women being given opportunities for good jobs. I don't see the push to bring talented women in from the outside. It used to be that if you were sitting in a room, and you were talking about a particular project, and you needed to bring in some good people, always someone would say, "Well, don't forget we've got to . . . balance this out." And they weren't talking about a black. They were generally talking about a woman. That doesn't happen so much anymore. I definitely think men have stopped thinking in those terms. And unfortunately they're still the ones that have all the power.

Again, the shift is subtle, but a laissez-faire tone has displaced active efforts to insure opportunities for women. The government's view and priorities are translated into a less stringent monitoring of affirmative action procedures, and underlying discrimination is allowed rein, albeit in the subtle form of passivity.[24] It is not that corporations are purposefully discriminatory but that their legally raised consciousnesses have slid into inertia. The larger political context shapes the strength of action taken by institutions within it. Teresa echoes Hope's assertions:

> the recognition of the unfairness that has been perpetrated on women and minorities in the past . . . is not as important on a federal, on a national, level. And that federal administration sets the tone for the country. And as a result, a lot of the people who were trying to understand and be more fair, although they were struggling with it, but because that was the social norm, they were doing it—well, they aren't doing it anymore, and they feel very comfortable doing just the opposite. I'm sure my company has breathed a sigh of relief at times and cooled out on that if they thought they could, just like everyone else has. I mean, I can tell the difference. I think corporate culture is very adaptable . . . can be what it has to be when it has to be.

Just as the political climate of the country shifts with administrative and economic realities, so does that of the corporation. Our country's institutions and populace reflect the larger context's prevailing ideology and practices. The forces of social change, however, are ordinarily mobilized by groups who feel the press of inequity. Organized protest and judicial action lift change to the legislative level where it can become institutionalized. The degree to which legislated change permeates society's functions hinges at first largely on enforcement and later on actual assimilation. Assimilation in the case of equal opportunity for women involves far more than affirmative action. It calls for change within the deepest recesses of our individual and collective psyches. And it calls for substantive support and active promulgation from top management.[25]

Thus, women have had access to more opportunity within the corporate world than perhaps ever before. They have proven themselves in terms of competence and personal suitability. They are ostensibly accepted, but full assimilation has yet to occur. In the absence of active monitoring, corporate power can too easily slip back into traditional hiring and advancement practices that passively exclude women from consideration. People, notably men, are still not convinced. Women's full participation does not yet come naturally; it requires active vigilance and continuous striving. The blatant barriers are temporarily gone, but passive resistance is still encountered on both the individual and the institutional level. Karen aptly characterizes the current woman's dilemma:

> I'm among the women in a number of different industries that are having opportunities, maybe for the first time, to advance. [But] society as a whole accepting them and, although it's somewhat difficult, providing alternative child care so you can get out of the house—it's not easy to set all that up. Somebody twenty years from now is going to have a [much] easier time. I don't know how much society's really contributed. They probably don't put as many roadblocks, but they're certainly not paving the way.

In the absence of systemic change and active structural support, the women interviewed seem to be working individually to maintain a context of opportunity for themselves and their successors. They certainly give us ample evidence of women's capacity for both the professional and the personal requirements of corporate careers. Unquestionably remarkable, their professional achievements and personal adaptations might not be enough to guarantee future opportunity for women who seek self-fulfillment in business. Active, large-scale change must continue so that passivity and other complex, subtle forms of discrimination give way to truly gender-blind employment access and opportunity.

Appendix

First Interview

Introduction

Open-ended, semistructured interviews with a career-path format were used to trace the manager's background, career choices, work history, and future plans. The interview was introduced by explaining who the interviewers are and the goals of the project. The interviewers emphasized the primacy of the women's own perceptions and ideas, their reflections on experiences in their professional and personal lives. We were looking for responses that represented not prepackaged notions found in the literature but rather the diversity and individual meanings that the women brought to their experiences.

Interview Questions

A. Looking back on your work history, which of your assignments or jobs have proven to be particularly important learning experiences for you?
    What have been the significant problems, or difficulties, that you have had to work through in your job situations?
    [In the case of frequent job moves] What has the experience of frequent changes in position/frequent moves been like for you?

B.   Have there been any particularly important persons in your career development so far?

What role do you think your family has played in your career development?

C.   Looking back at your work and life in general, have there been situations that represented real dilemmas to you, where there was a conflict between what you believed in/what you wanted to do and what you thought you should do? Was there a moral dimension to that or a question of conscience?

Do you feel that you have had to make moral decisions, at work or in your life in general, that other women might not have had to face?

D.   How would you describe the styles of managers that you've worked with so far?

How is your own style of dealing with others evolving? Can you give an example?

How do you think your present staff would describe you?

E.   How do you see your participation in this program with regard to your career?

How has this group of women (in the management program) been for you?

F.   In conclusion, what did you think of this interview?

Do you have any suggestions for how we might change the interview?

Was there anything that you wanted to say that we didn't ask? If something does occur to you, we will be happy to meet and talk with you again.

Finally, much gratitude was expressed by the interviewers.

Second Interview

Introduction

The second year we continued with questions about work history, the dilemmas faced at work and outside, and the development of the women's managerial style; we also caught up with their work and personal lives during the past year. As always, we were interested in their own ideas, experiences, and perceptions; we viewed them as the experts. The interviewers explained that all identifying information was changed on the transcripts and assured confidentiality. Copies of final studies were offered, and we indicated our interest in their reactions to them.

Interview Questions

A. Since last year, what's happened in your work, or in your life in general, that stands out to you?
   Have your perspectives on the future changed?

B. Are there significant changes that you've seen in yourself in the past year?
   Have those changes posed any dilemmas for you? What impact have those changes had on you?
   To what do you attribute those changes? Are there any circumstances in your life or in the larger society that have contributed to those changes?

C. What are your managerial responsibilities, direct and indirect, in your present position?

D. In the last five years or so, has your company undergone any reorganizations? How have those changes affected you? How have they affected others in similar positions?

E. In your mind's eye, we want you to take us into your office as it's been this past year. What have been some of the major (non-technical) topics of discussion, debate, or controversy? Are there major themes that dominate office discussion? How did you feel about these topics at the office?

F. Whom do you go to when you need help or a different perspective on a decision or problem at work? Whom do you go to when you want something done?
   What's the biggest difficulty that someone in your position is faced with in a company like yours? What have others done about it? What do you do?

G. Do you think that you are the same person or a different person at home and at work? Do you take your problems at work home or your problems at home to work? One more than the other?
   How would people at work describe you? How do you want

people at work to see you? How do you want your family or people close to you to see you?

H. How did you feel about coming back to the program this year? How has being in this group of women in the program been for you?

Combined Interview

In some very few cases, a woman who had agreed to the interview but could not be interviewed twice was given the following combined interview in the second year.

Interview Questions

A. Looking back at your work history, can you pick out some examples of jobs or work situations that have proven particularly important learning experiences for you?
   What have been the significant problems or difficulties that you have had to work through in your job situations?

B. Have there been any particularly important persons in your career development so far?
   What role do you think your family has played in your career development?

C. Are there significant changes you've seen in yourself in the past year? To what do you attribute those changes? Are there any circumstances in your life or in the larger society that may have contributed to those changes?
   Have these changes posed any dilemmas for you? Have you faced difficult dilemmas, tough choices, situations where you weren't sure what was the right thing to do, at work or in your broader life? Did any of those dilemmas involve a question of conscience?

D. In the past five years or so, has your company undergone any reorganizational changes? How have these changes affected you? How have they affected others in similar positions?

E. How would you describe the styles of managers that you've worked with so far? How is your own style of dealing with others evolving? How do you think your present staff would describe you?

F. Do you think that you are the same person or a different person at home and at work? How do you want people at work to see you? How do you want your family or people close to you to see you?

G. How do you see your participation in this program with regard to your career? How has this group of women in the program been for you?

At the conclusion of every interview, the interviewers thanked the manager and offered the option of talking again should something come to mind. As it turned out, follow-up conversations were not found necessary by the interviewers or the managers.

Notes

Introduction

1. Carol Gilligan, *In a Different Voice: Psychological Theory and Women's Development* (Cambridge, Mass.: Harvard University Press, 1982).

2. Sarah Hardesty and Nehamah Jacobs, *Success and Betrayal: The Crisis of Women in Corporate America* (New York: Franklin Watts, 1986).

3. Felice N. Schwartz, "Management Women and the New Facts of Life," *Harvard Business Review,* Jan.-Feb. 1989, pp. 65–76.

4. Walter Mischel, *Introduction to Personality* (New York: Holt, Rinehart and Winston, 1971).

5. Albert Bandura, *Principles of Behavior Modification* (New York: Holt, Rinehart and Winston, 1969).

6. Such studies can be found in many psychological sources; the abundance of findings necessitated the formation of a separate publication, *The Journal of Applied Behavioral Analysis.* Classic early texts include Leonard P. Ullmann and Leonard Krasner, eds., *Case Studies in Behavior Modification* (New York: Holt, Rinehart and Winston, 1965); Leonard Krasner and Leonard P. Ullmann, *Behavior Influence and Personality: The Social Matrix of Human Action* (New York: Holt, Rinehart and Winston, 1973).

7. Rosabeth Moss Kanter, *Men and Women of the Corporation* (New York: Basic, 1977).

8. Dale Feuer, "How Women Manage," *Training* 25 (1988): 27.

9. S. M. Donnell and J. Hall, "Men and Women as Managers: A Significant Case of No Significant Difference," *Organizational Dynamics* 8 (Spring 1980): 60–77.

10. Nancy Chodorow, *The Reproduction of Mothering: Psychoanalysis and the Sociology of Gender* (Berkeley: University of California Press, 1978).

11. Susan K. Boardman, Charles C. Harrington, and Sandra V. Horowitz, "Successful Women: A Psychological Investigation of Family Class and Education Origins," in *Women's Career Development,* ed. Barbara A. Gutek and Laurie Larwood (Newbury Park, Calif.: Sage, 1987), chap. 5; Robert L. Dipboye, "Problems and Progress of Women in Management," in *Working Women: Past, Present, Future,* ed. Karen S. Koziara, Michael H.

Moskow, and Lucretia Dewey Tanner (Washington, D.C.: Bureau of National Affairs, 1987), chap. 5.

non-mgr 12. Dana E. Friedman, "Why the Glass Ceiling?" *Across the Board* 25 (1988): 34.

13. Diana Zuckerman, "Career and Life Goals of Freshmen and Seniors," *Radcliffe Quarterly*, September 1982, pp. 17–20.

14. Glenn Collins, "Future MBA's Learn Value of a Home Life," *New York Times*, October 16, 1985, C-1, C-12.

15. Jill K. Conway, Address at Smith College, July 28, 1989.

16. Throughout this book, the term "work" will be used to refer to paid labor force participation. This is not to deny that women's traditional domestic occupations are work.

17. Michael E. Lamb, ed., *The Role of the Father in Child Development* (New York: Wiley, 1981).

18. For a thorough scholarly description of American women's paid labor force participation, see Alice Kessler-Harris, *Out to Work* (New York: Oxford University Press, 1982).

19. That women worked outside of the home only because they had to was always more ideology than reality (ibid.). See also Cynthia Fuchs Epstein, *Woman's Place* (Berkeley: University of California Press, 1970).

20. Mirra Komarovsky, *Blue-Collar Marriage* (New York: Vintage Books, 1967).

21. Mary Lindenstein Walshok, "Occupational Values and Family Roles: A Descriptive Study of Women Working in Blue-Collar and Service Occupations," *Urban and Social Change Review* 11 (1978): 12–20.

22. Thirty-seven percent of corporate management positions currently are held by women.

1. Work

1. Mary Frank Fox and Sharlene Hesse-Biber, *Women at Work* (Palo Alto, Calif.: Mayfield, 1984), p. 2. Work serves various social and emotional needs, including those of personal identity and social status, and both of these contribute to the evaluation of an individual by self and others. In a postindustrial society, the work one does is an integral part of who one is. Further, a person's occupation is an important determinant of social standing, particularly as it is tied to opportunity in a circular fashion.

2. Ibid., p. 3.

3. Ibid., p. 5. What has been called work and traditionally studied by social scientists is paid labor, that which "is assessed in wages, output, and employment, and in which productivity is defined in terms of capital (money and wealth) created. . . . it never encompasses child care, meal preparation, food processing, or other work that is done exclusively by women."

4. Veronica F. Nieva and Barbara A. Gutek, *Women and Work: A Psychological Perspective* (New York: Praeger, 1982), p. 2. "At the turn of the century women workers were either young unmarried women or mothers whose husbands had deserted them." This century has seen increased labor force participation by women whose marriages and families are intact.

5. This assumption has been successfully challenged and overturned by recent research (see, for example, Susan Hesselbart, 1978, 1980, as cited in Fox and Hesse-Biber, *Women at Work*), which finds men declaring family rather than work as "the greatest source of satisfaction."

6. On the contrary, there is now considerable documentation that "men and women have similar motivations for working" (ibid., p. 4).

7. A very thorough scholarly description of American women's paid labor force participation can be found in Alice Kessler-Harris, *Out to Work* (New York: Oxford University Press, 1982).

8. Ibid., p. 301.

9. Ibid., p. 49.

10. Ray Marshall and Beth Paulin, "Employment and Earnings of Women: Historical Perspective," in *Working Women: Past, Present, and Future*, ed. Karen S. Koziara, Michael H. Moskow, Lucretia Dewey Tanner (Washington, D.C.: Bureau of National Affairs, 1987), chap. 1.

11. For a full discussion, see Barbara Welter, "The Cult of True Womanhood, 1820–1860," *American Quarterly 18* (Summer 1964): 151–74.

12. Marcia Lynn Whicker and Jennie Jacobs Kronenfeld, *Sex Role Changes: Technology, Politics, and Policy* (New York: Praeger, 1986), chap. 6.

13. The classic source for this theory of family and men's and women's places in it is Talcott Parsons and Robert Bales, *Family Socialization and Interaction Process* (New York: Free Press, 1956). See also Jean B. Elshtain, "Moral Woman and Immoral Man: A Consideration of the Public-Private Split and Its Political Ramifications," *Politics and Society 4* (1974): 453–73. Feminist scholars of the past two decades have argued that societal and scholarly biases reflect each other.

14. Summary indicators on women in the labor force for the third quarter of 1986 showed white women's civilian labor force participation rate to be 55.3%, black women's 56.4%. "Employment in Perspective: Women in the Labor Force," Third quarter 1986, U.S. Department of Labor, Bureau of Labor Statistics, Report 733.

15. Jean Piaget, *The Moral Judgment of the Child* (New York: The Free Press, 1965), p. 117.

16. Nieva and Gutek, *Women and Work*, p. 2. "The history of women's participation in the labor force shows a great deal of resistance and reservation expressed by segments of society including many women. At various times women who worked were viewed as immoral, unfeminine, negligent mothers, or objects of pity. They were often not taken seriously by their employers, colleagues, significant others, or society in general."

17. Betty Friedan, *The Feminine Mystique* (New York: Norton, 1963).

18. Whicker and Kronenfeld, *Sex Role Changes*, p. 112.

19. Wartime working women fell prey to the concept of "last hired, first fired" because they had less seniority than the men whose places they had taken. Further, veterans took priority over wartime workers in civilian jobs. Finally, companies in the postwar period suspended nepotism practices and eliminated women through restrictions on age and marital status. Women who had helped during the war were now supposed to move over and yield their jobs to their rightful owners, the returning men. See ibid., pp. 114–15.

20. Women interviewed by the author for an earlier study described the difficulty of leaving their family responsibilities to enter the paid labor force as a dilemma with moral overtones. Women who wanted but were not compelled to work outside of the home were especially troubled by abdicating what they had learned to be their "place," but in every case pursuit of an identity independent of home and family constituted a dilemma of moral proportions. See Sue J. M. Freeman, "Women's Moral Dilemmas: In Pursuit of Integrity," in *Women Living Change*, ed. Susan C. Bourque and Donna R. Divine (Philadelphia: Temple University Press, 1985), pp. 217–54.

21. In the report of an April 1982 conference on problems of women managers at Cornell University, Juanita Kreps declared: "We now know that women are in paying jobs to stay; that women's work lives are approaching men's; that the drive for comparable pay will continue until the earnings gap is substantially reduced; and that, in contrast to the World War II era and the postwar era, when women returned to hearth and home as quickly as possible, most young women today take for granted that they will have both

jobs and marriages." Juanita M. Kreps, "Changing Economy," in *The Woman in Management,* ed. Jennie Farley (Ithaca, N.Y.: ILR Press, 1983), p. 5.

22. Cynthia Fuchs Epstein, *Woman's Place* (Berkeley: University of California Press, 1970), p. 43.

23. Women and other groups of minority status have been characterized according to psychological attribution theory as having an external locus of control. That is, they are likely to attribute their successes to external factors such as luck or chance rather than crediting their own abilities or efforts, and they are apt to blame themselves for mistakes or failures. Self-esteem is lowered since one is not instrumental in positive outcomes and is blameworthy for negative ones. Feelings of helplessness and powerlessness result. Hence, recent literature has focused on a characteristic called "learned helplessness" as peculiar to women (C. S. Dweck, "The Role of Expectations and Attributions in the Alleviation of Learned Helplessness," *Journal of Personality and Social Psychology 31* [1975]: 674–85). In contrast, men of the dominant group are likely to credit themselves with positive outcomes and externalize blame for negative ones (Nancy E. Betz and Louise F. Fitzgerald, *The Career Psychology of Women* [Orlando: Academic Press, 1987], p. 118).

24. Kathleen Gerson, *Hard Choices: How Women Decide about Work, Career, and Motherhood* (Berkeley: University of California Press, 1985), chap. 4.

25. High-achieving women have been plagued by a feeling of unworthiness and lack of genuine competence. With each successive accomplishment, they fear "being found out this time." This view of themselves is obviously detrimental to confidence and self-esteem. By rendering each achievement a function of accident or fate rather than honest ability, this notion works in a circular fashion to keep self-doubt high and confidence low.

26. Sarah Hardesty and Nehamah Jacobs, *Success and Betrayal: The Crisis of Women in Corporate America* (New York: Franklin Watts, 1986), chap. 4.

2. Career Planning

1. For extensive recent documentation of this idea, see Grace Baruch, Rosalind Barnett, and Caryl Rivers, *Lifeprints: New Patterns of Love and Work for Today's Women* (New York: New American Library, 1983). The authors make the point that women need both pleasure and mastery to lead healthy, fulfilling lives.

2. Women who "fell into" corporate careers, as opposed to formally preparing for them, have been called "accidental careerists." See Sarah Hardesty and Nehamah Jacobs, *Success and Betrayal: The Crisis of Women in Corporate America* (New York: Franklin Watts, 1986), chap. 3.

3. The configuration described here would typify "accidental careerists" rather than a more recent generation of young women who actively prepare for professional careers.

4. This, of course, refers to the customary debate in psychological literature about the relative weight of innate characteristics and socialization practices in contributing to behavior. While the pendulum has swung between emphasis on nature and on nurture as the more influential at various times in psychohistory, for most topics resolution has centered on a melding of the two. Recent work in sociobiology and cerebral orientation has again focused attention on possible physiological origins of sex differences. In general, however, the evidence still seems to add up to the conclusion that difference within the sexes outweighs that between. See Anne Fausto Sterling, *Myths of Gender: Biological Theories about Women and Men* (New York: Basic, 1986); Julia A. Sherman, *Sex-Related Cognitive Differences—An Essay on Theory and Evidence* (Springfield, Ill.: Charles C. Thomas, 1978).

5. Hardesty and Jacobs, *Success and Betrayal,* make the point that women are still seen by themselves and others as having the option to work.

6. Currently available are "workbooks" for teenage girls which include chapters about

work that pose the question, "Could you support a family on your income alone?" See, for example, Mindy Bingham, Judy Edmondson, and Sandy Stryker, *Choices: A Teen Women's Journal for Self-Awareness and Personal Planning* (Santa Barbara, Calif.: Advocacy Press, 1984), chap. 3.

7. Hardesty and Jacobs (*Success and Betrayal*) describe women as developing nebulous but grandiose career ambition before they enter the work force. While growing up, females were given messages that they could do anything and everything, that all would be available to them. As a result, Hardesty and Jacobs maintain, females grew up with great expectations but without the preparation necessary for their actualization. In contrast to those findings, the women interviewed here, who also were given open-ended messages about their potential, seemed to develop ambition once on the job, and that ambition was therefore concrete and specific to the work and organization at hand.

8. Barbara A. Gutek and Laurie Larwood, "Introduction: Women's Careers Are Important and Different," in *Women's Career Development,* ed. Barbara A. Gutek and Laurie Larwood (Newbury Park, Calif.: Sage, 1987), p. 8.

9. Hardesty and Jacobs, *Success and Betrayal,* chap. 4, have characterized this stage of a woman's career as the "proving-up" phase. Proving up to oneself, to the corporation, and to other women and men is an exciting, rewarding phase, a positive and energized experience for women.

10. Ibid., p. 102. Hardesty and Jacobs concur that women at this stage are too busy proving themselves to map out strategy.

11. F. D. McMahon, "Relationships between Causal Attributions and Expectancy of Success," *Journal of Personality and Social Psychology* 28 (1973): 108–14.

12. Piaget maintained that changed consciousness follows revised behavior in the course of psychological development.

13. This example stands in contrast to Hardesty and Jacob's thesis that women operate according to the Myth of Individual Recognition and the Myth of Meritocracy.

14. Hardesty and Jacobs (*Success and Betrayal*) contend that women see the corporation as father or lover and are therefore unable to leave a particular company, even in the absence of reward or recognition.

15. Hardesty and Jacobs (ibid., pp. 183, 186) identify boredom as common in corporate work. They maintain that women want the growth and expansion that comes with new learning, not the repetition indigenous to the corporation. Women had been lured by the style rather than the substance of corporate work, and they face its meaninglessness after the exhilaration of the proving-up phase. A woman's desire to learn more is ultimately self-defeating in the corporate setting (p. 98).

16. Ibid., p. 109.

17. Ibid., p. 287.

18. Hardesty and Jacobs describe these characteristics as the Myth of Meritocracy and the Myth of Reward; ibid., pp. 31–34.

19. Ibid., p. 97.

3. Mobility

1. This is assumed to be in contrast to men, who actively plot direction prior to or at least simultaneous with corporate employment.

2. Sarah Hardesty and Nehamah Jacobs, *Success and Betrayal: The Crisis of Women in Corporate America* (New York: Franklin Watts, 1986), pp. 262–63; Ellyn Mirides and Andre Cote, "Women in Management: Strategies for Removing the Barriers," *Personnel Administrator* 25 (April 1980): 26.

3. Hardesty and Jacobs (*Success and Betrayal,* pp. 36–42) describe women as forming a familial attachment to the corporation in the Myth of the Corporation as Family. Some

women expect a kind of marital commitment from their employer, hence the Myth of the Corporation as Lover. Finally, these two female modes of relating to the corporate entity culminate in the Myth of the Loyal Retainer, which keeps women in positions that have become unsatisfying. According to this thesis, women have transferred their relationship needs onto the corporation and therefore resist mobility. "Women's nurturance of the ideal of connection forces them to order their experience in continuous terms" (p. 41).

4. In a 1978 study of 124 women managers, "sixty percent of the women managers cited financial incentives as their major reason for employment and many commented on the pleasure they received from their earning power." Corine T. Norgaard, "Problems and Perspectives of Female Managers," *MSU Business Topics 28* (Winter 1980): 26.

5. Thomas J. Peters and Robert H. Waterman, Jr., *In Search of Excellence* (New York: Harper and Row, 1982); Robert B. Reich, *The Next American Frontier* (New York: Times Books, 1983); Alice G. Sargent, *The Androgynous Manager* (New York: AMACOM, 1983).

6. Apparently, daily corporate work is rather boring and repetitive, for the most part (Hardesty and Jacobs, *Success and Betrayal*, p. 36). Little challenge exists once a job is learned within the first year or two.

7. There is some difference of opinion about what staying with one company does or does not do for career progress. Hardesty and Jacobs attribute women's longevity with a company to a typically female ambivalence about advancement (ibid., p. 262). Unrealistic expectations about rewards combined with a passive waiting for those rewards fixate women on one company. The assumption is that greater gains can be made by making company shifts than by moving within a single company. However, women who have been targeted as on the path to top executive positions "have been with their present employers for an average of five years." Basia Hellwig, "The Breakthrough Generation: 73 Women Ready to Run Corporate America," *Working Woman*, April 1985, p. 100.

8. As seen in chapter 2, Cathy's career-planning strategies involved considerable mobility, first within the company of her current employ and then projecting out to other organizations.

9. Hardesty and Jacobs, *Success and Betrayal*, chap. 4.

10. Philip L. Quaglieri and Joseph O. Pecenka, "Making It to the Top," *Leadership and Organization Development Journal 6* (1985): 26; Lawrence R. Quinn, "After 20 Years Women Face the Same Barriers," *Executive Financial Woman 2* (1987): 25.

11. In a 1978 study of 124 women managers, women who had changed jobs by going to another company were at higher salary levels than those who had not. Norgaard, "Problems and Perspectives," p. 27.

12. See, for example, Hardesty and Jacobs, *Success and Betrayal*, p. 183.

13. An individual's abilities are still vital commodities for corporate employment. "With all the emphasis career strategists put on political skills and gamemanship, intellectual abilities often seem to take second place. Yet high intelligence was mentioned more than any other single factor by the [executive] recruiters, who characterized particular women as 'strong, strategic thinkers,' 'cerebral with a great grasp of concepts,' 'analytical.'" Hellwig, "Breakthrough Generation," p. 99.

14. There are many articles and books about how to manage people for the most productivity. The classic psychological finding is known as "the Hawthorne effect," whereby factory workers' productivity significantly increased as a function of their feeling included in decision making about aspects of their work environment (Anne Anastasi, *Fields of Applied Psychology* [New York: McGraw-Hill, 1964], pp. 133–35). See also, Mirides and Cote, "Women in Management," p. 28; Hellwig, "Breakthrough Generation," p. 100.

15. Hellwig, "Breakthrough Generation," p. 101.

16. The power of ideology is such, however, as to make female assertiveness and male passivity less acceptable than the stereotype. Men and women often are perceived less

favorably when they behave in a manner contrary to stereotype. See Mary Frank Fox and Sharlene Hesse-Biber, *Women at Work* (Palo Alto, Calif.: Mayfield, 1984), p. 138.

17. Hardesty and Jacobs, *Success and Betrayal*, pp. 231–232, point out how one woman's failure, caused by artificial promotions, becomes institutionalized as gender failure such that another female is not similarly placed. That is, a woman's shortcoming is generalized as the inability of all women to do the job, whereas a man's failure is confined to that particular person, and he is readily replaced with another male.

18. Quinn, "After 20 Years Women Face the Same Barriers," p. 25.

19. We met Nina in the first chapter's discussion of the evolution of interest in work. One of the few interviewees without a college degree, Nina professed a preference for work over school from her high school days.

20. This advice is echoed by others. "[Women] must learn to tell others—specifically those who count—exactly what they can do well. This is not bragging; it's simply being confident enough about yourself to let it show." Donna N. Douglass, "For Women: How to Get Where You Want to Go," *Supervisory Management*, May 1984, p. 34.

4. Managing

1. A secretary's advancement also can have the opposite effect on her clerical peers. See Joanne Martin, Raymond L. Price, Robert J. Bies, and Melanie E. Powers, "Now That I Can Have It, I'm Not So Sure I Want It: The Effects of Opportunity on Aspirations and Discontent," in *Women's Career Development*, ed. Barbara A. Gutek and Laurie Larwood (Newbury Park, Calif.: Sage, 1987), chap. 4. The dearth of female role models is frequently mentioned in management literature. The beginnings of the affirmative action philosophy that Gwen describes would have been a time of few women in managerial positions serving as role models. Even as recently as 1986, Hardesty and Jacobs decry a lack of role models for women managers. Sarah Hardesty and Nehamah Jacobs, *Success and Betrayal: The Crisis of Women in Corporate America* (New York: Franklin Watts, 1986), pp. 96–97, 179. Of course, the classic work documenting the many ramifications of women's scarcity in management ranks is Rosabeth Moss Kanter, *Men and Women of the Corporation* (New York: Basic, 1977). This book provides an important structural analysis of corporate gender bias.

2. Gwen's experience is corroborated by research findings of a positive correlation between age of male managers and their acceptance of female managers; that is, the older the male manager, the more accepting he is of women as managers. Several explanations are offered for this finding. The older the manager, the presumably more established and therefore less threatened he would be by women managers. Female managers, who are relative newcomers, would not be competing with older male managers for positions. See Linda K. Brown, "Women in Business Management," *Signs* 5 (Winter 1979): 278. More exposure to women managers would also confirm the experience of no operational difference between male and female managerial behavior. See Virginia E. Schein, "The Relationship between Sex Role Stereotypes and Requisite Management Characteristics," *Journal of Applied Psychology* 57 (April 1973): 99. Given the social change of recent decades, older men may have had more interaction with women at work and at home who have a worker rather than a caretaker identity.

3. Brad Chapman, "Comparison of Male and Female Leadership Styles," *Academy of Management Journal*, Sept. 1975, p. 648, cited by Ellyn Mirides and Andre Cote, "Women in Management: Strategies for Removing the Barriers," *Personnel Administrator* 25 (April 1980): 28.

4. Common advice for female managers is: "Remember, first of all, that your aim should be to gain respect, not love, in your role as manager. Don't mother your subordinates; manage them with confidence, compassion, and care. . . . This takes self-

confidence—a trait not easily acquired by males or females but a trait successful managers have in abundance." Donna N. Douglass, "For Women: How to Get Where You Want to Go," *Supervisory Management,* May 1984, p. 36.

5. Freud maintained that the resolution of the Oedipal conflict in boys' psychosexual development equipped males to perform higher mental functions, such as executive and moral decision making, free of affective considerations. The lack of an Oedipal conflict in female development left women unable to make the clear distinctions between reason and emotion necessary for society's management. See Sigmund Freud, *Some Psychical Consequences of the Anatomical Distinction between the Sexes* (1925). In *The Complete Psychological Works,* vol. 19, trans. and ed. James Strachey (New York: Norton, 1976).

6. See Michael D. Ames and Dorothy Heide, "Training and Developing Women Managers: Are They Really a Special Case?" *Personnel Administrator* 27 (Nov. 1982): 22.

7. The findings of several studies have established that managerial skills cannot be differentiated by gender. See S. M. Donnell and J. Hall, "Men and Women as Managers: A Significant Case of No Significant Difference," *Organizational Dynamics 8* (Spring 1980): 60–77. The conclusion that "differences in management potential are far more attributable to individual rather than sex differences" was made by Richard J. Ritchie and Joseph L. Moses, "Assessment Center Correlates of Women's Advancement into Middle Management: A 7-Year Longitudinal Analysis," *Journal of Applied Psychology 68* (1983): 231.

8. Some writers have asserted that women are particularly suited for a new direction in management that emphasizes teamwork and the "people skills" of facilitation and support needed for a participatory operation. Jane Kay, "A Positive Approach to Promoting Women," *Personnel Administrator,* June 1975, p. 38, quoted by Mirides and Cote, "Women in Management," p. 28. Other writers have advocated females as managers on the basis of their domestic skills of human relations, persuasion and participation, household organization, and care of subordinates. For discussions on both sides of this idea, see W. Goode, "Family Life of the Successful Woman," in *Corporate Lib: Women's Challenge to Management,* ed. E. Ginzburg and A. Yohalem (Baltimore: Johns Hopkins University Press, 1973), p. 99; E. Janeway, "Family Life in Transition," ibid., p. 119; J. Lannon, "Male vs. Female Values in Management," *Management International Review 17* (1977): 12, cited in Brown, "Women in Business," pp. 276–77.

9. Hardesty and Jacobs, *Success and Betrayal,* p. 121.

10. Ibid., p. 112.

11. A case study of employee resistance to a female manager can be found in Marjorie Bayes and Peter M. Newton, "Women in Authority: A Sociopsychological Analysis," *Journal of Applied Behavioral Science 14* (1978): 9, 15. "A woman given primary authority for a work group or for an organization faces a basic incongruity between role requirements of the position and the sex-linked role conception she and her staff have learned. Subordinates will respond to her partly as an individual, and partly according to the cultural stereotype of woman." A psychosocial history of a gender-stereotyped division of labor has left workers with "no important previous social experience which enables them to perceive a woman as having legitimate power to control and protect the external boundary of an adult group (a mother's function is internal to the family group whose external boundaries the father protects), to stand alone as a figure of authority (mother is second to father's authority in the traditional family), to delegate authority, and to evaluate output of other adults."

12. Much has been written about the exclusion of women from informal information networks and sources of power such that their ability to function successfully as managers is severely curtailed. Virginia E. Shein, "Sex Role Stereotyping, Ability, and Performance: Prior Research and New Directions," *Personnel Psychology 31* (1978): 266.

13. Dale Feuer, "How Women Manage," *Training 25* (1988): 25.

14. "If the woman leader consistently directs her attention to the work task instead of to the dependency needs which have been evoked in part by her gender, she may enable the group to learn after a time that she will not play a primarily nurturant role." Bayes and Newton, "Women in Authority," p. 18.

15. The risks involved in delegating are numerous, particularly given the fact that it is the manager who is held accountable for the performance of subordinates. Some find women less inclined to risk taking and to delegating than men. Edith L. Highman, *The Organization Woman* (New York: Human Sciences Press, 1985), pp. 45–47.

16. That women still might have to demonstrate more ability than male counterparts is at least partly due to the tenacity of traditional gender stereotypes. Laurie Larwood and Marion M. Wood, *Women in Management* (Lexington, Mass.: D. C. Heath, 1977), p. 113; Dale Feuer, "How Women Manage," p. 26.

17. Women may assume more responsibility and work harder than men of equal rank in an organization. "The productivity of the average woman per dollar in salary is higher than of men in many high-ranked jobs." Larwood and Wood, *Women in Management*, p. 101. This finding could also be a function of a salary differential by gender wherein women have not received pay equal to men holding the same position.

18. Women who had been identified as contenders for top executive positions favor the cultivation of subordinates' abilities and teamwork for task accomplishment. The manager leads and develops her staff to prepare them for responsible participation in the group's outcome. Basia Hellwig, "The Breakthrough Generation: 73 Women Ready to Run Corporate America," *Working Woman*, April 1985, p. 99. Workers' productivity and morale are enhanced by the adept delegation of responsibility. Highman, *Organization Woman*, p. 80.

19. Executive recruiters and female contenders for top corporate spots refer to communication and "people skills" as fundamental for managerial success. Hellwig, "Breakthrough Generation," p. 99.

20. Larwood and Wood, *Women in Management*, p. 112; Ritchie and Moses, "Correlates of Women's Advancement," p. 230; Robert L. Dipboye, "Problems and Progress of Women in Management," in *Working Women: Past, Present, Future*, ed. Karen S. Koziara, Michael H. Moskow, Lucretia Dewey Tanner (Washington, D.C.: Bureau of National Affairs, 1987), pp. 123–24.

21. Management literature has designated two styles of management, Theory X and Theory Y. Theory X refers to an authoritarian style where the manager essentially dictates to subordinates what is to be done and how to do it. A Theory Y manager retains authority but allows subordinates more participation in the work's planning and implementation. Theory Y is said to be the more productive style. Highman, *Organization Woman*, p. 73.

22. A participatory management style is widely recognized as being most effective for both workers and management. Hardesty and Jacobs, *Success and Betrayal*, p. 398; Hellwig, *Breakthrough Generation*," p. 99; Highman, *Organization Woman*, p. 74.

23. Highman, *Organization Woman*, p. 78; Douglass, "For Women," p. 34.

24. Feuer, "How Women Manage," p. 31.

5. Self

1. Calvin S. Hall and Gardner Lindzey, *Theories of Personality* (New York: Wiley, 1957).

2. Traits have taken on considerably more meaning than their original formulation as psychological dispositions. Stereotyping gave rise to a cultural ideology that associated certain attributes with gender to such an extent that those characteristics were presumed to be inherent, perhaps even innate, and immutable. Gender-based traits took on a connotation of biological imperative so that individuals of either sex who behaved to the

contrary were denounced as unnatural, or misfits. Feminine traits were deemed antithetical to a professional life, especially a business career, which was sex-typed as a male role. The past two decades of social change and related psychological research now support the idea that "There are no inborn sex differences that affect managerial behavior or ability." Laurie Larwood and Marion M. Wood, *Women in Management* (Lexington, Mass.: D. C. Heath, 1977), p. 84.

3. Walter Mischel, *Introduction to Personality* (New York: Holt, Rinehart and Winston, 1971).

4. Surely, many have written of personal metamorphosis in connection with social change. Ruth Halcomb, *Women Making It* (New York: Atheneum, 1979), pp. 12–14, attests to women's choosing who they are and what they might do and be well into adulthood. She cites Cynthia Epstein's criticisms of early socialization theories: "after the women's movement had been sufficiently developed to make career opportunities available to many women, I could see distinct changes in the personalities of women. Those who had severe self-doubts regarding their own competence found that, when they were given additional responsibility, they could handle it well, although they were frightened to begin with. Women who were afraid of taking on new jobs normally reserved for men found they could not only learn things they thought they couldn't, but they found they liked the new activity. They also liked the power and they liked the success. Nothing, it seems, succeeds like success." Cynthia Fuchs Epstein, "Mind, Matter, and Mentors," in *The Frontiers of Knowledge,* ed. Judith Stiehm (Los Angeles: University of Southern California Press, 1976), p. 29.

5. The classic work in the study of women managers' personal and professional paths was Margaret Hennig and Anne Jardim, *The Managerial Woman* (Garden City, N.Y.: Anchor Press/Doubleday, 1977). Restricted by the small population of women in management at the time, the authors' portrayal of twenty-five women who reached top executive positions by the late fifties is a fascinating study in itself. Its findings, however, cannot be generalized to the much larger and more diverse population of current women managers.

6. Sarah Hardesty and Nehamah Jacobs, *Success and Betrayal: The Crisis of Women in Corporate America* (New York: Franklin Watts, 1986), pp. 32–34, discuss and document what seems to be a corporate female as opposed to male tendency to seek individual excellence through learning and contribution. Instead of playing the corporate political game, women live according to the Myth of Growth, seeking self-improvement through achievement and job satisfaction. Men's goals of recognition through money and power more readily coincide with the structure of corporations. According to this view, women emphasize performance over politics (the Myth of Meritocracy, p. 31). In so doing, they risk disappointment because individual performance does not always bring commensurate recognition in large corporations, which are structured to reward luck and gamesmanship inordinately.

7. Hardesty and Jacobs call the dawning of this realization in women the "seeds of disenchantment" (ibid., chap. 6), which follows the "proving-up" stage (chap. 4).

8. Thomas J. Peters and Robert H. Waterman, Jr., *In Search of Excellence* (New York: Harper and Row, 1982); Robert B. Reich, *The Next American Frontier* (New York: Times Books, 1983). These books describe the most desirable managerial style as one that seems to draw upon what have been characterized as female strengths: interpersonal sensitivity and communication skills as well as high internal standards for achievement performance.

9. Christine D. Hay, "Women in Management: The Obstacles and Opportunities They Face," *The Personnel Administrator* 25 (April 1980): 32.

10. S. M. Donnell and J. Hall, "Men and Women as Managers: A Significant Case of No Significant Difference," *Organizational Dynamics* 8 (Spring 1980): 60–77.

11. Alma S. Baron, "The Achieving Woman Manager: So Where Are the Rewards?" *Business Quarterly,* Summer 1984, pp. 70–71.

12. David C. McClelland, *The Achieving Society* (New York: Van Nostrand, 1961); J. W. Atkinson and N. T. Feather, eds., *A Theory of Achievement Motivation* (New York: Wiley, 1966).

13. Larwood and Wood recognized that women in these positions are "violating a still-potent cultural norm. These women are not attempting to be average, but they are concerned with what seems most suitable for them. . . . the woman who enters management is a specially selected individual; there is no reason to suspect that she will behave in an average or 'feminine' way unless that way seems justified. If it turns out that particular behaviors are more useful than others in successful management, she will use them because she desires success" (*Women in Management,* p. 85).

14. See Hay, "Women in Management," p. 32.

15. Dale Feuer, "How Women Manage," *Training 25* (1988): 27.

16. For the pioneer work on females' alleged fear of success, see Matina Horner, "Toward an Understanding of Achievement-Related Conflicts in Women," *Journal of Social Issues 28* (1972): 157–75.

17. Feuer, "How Women Manage," p. 31.

18. Baron, "Achieving Woman Manager," p. 72.

19. James R. Terborg, "Women in Management: A Research Review," *Journal of Applied Psychology 62* (Dec. 1977): 659; Laurie Larwood and Barbara A. Gutek, "Working Toward a Theory of Women's Career Development," in *Women's Career Development,* ed. Barbara A. Gutek and Laurie Larwood (Newbury Park, Calif.: Sage, 1987), p. 172.

20. This difference between women and men in what they choose to talk about has been documented elsewhere, for example, in literature on interpersonal relationships and clinical psychology. It is a common finding that women will talk about connection and caring as well as feelings about the self in a way that is both quantitatively and qualitatively different than most men. However, it may be a mistake to assume that what is underemphasized by either sex is merely ignored by them.

21. Achievement motivation can be divided into different, albeit related, dimensions: aspiration, mastery, and career. The latter two are particularly applicable to the women of this study. Mastery motivation comes closest in meaning to Atkinson's and McClelland's definition of achievement motivation: "Mastery represents the motivation to achieve on challenging tasks, including the motivation to persist until mastery is achieved." J. Atkinson, "The Mainsprings of Achievement-oriented Activity," in *Personality, Motivation, and Achievement,* ed. J. Atkinson and J. Raynor (New York: Halsted, 1978); D. McClelland, *Human Motivation* (Glenview, Ill.: Scott Foresman, 1985.) Career motivation represents long-range commitment to a career and, as such, can be thought of as cumulative achievement motivation. Helen S. Farmer, "A Multivariate Model for Explaining Gender Differences in Career and Achievement Motivation," *Educational Researcher 16* (March 1987): 6. The work lives of several women interviewed may have been characterized initially by mastery motivation, but career motivation soon accompanied it.

22. According to Hardesty and Jacobs, "most women define the satisfactions of career success [as] flexibility, creativity, the yearning for individualized, meaningful contribution, the desire to grow" (*Success and Betrayal,* p. 403).

23. It is important to note that Connie was already holding a relatively high position when considering this move to another even higher. Her weighing the consequences to others was uncharacteristic of the kind of thinking that had gotten her to this point. The high level of the new position may have prompted some questioning within her along the lines of the "Who, me?" phenomenon. Or the move may have represented risks that she could avoid while still being assured a good deal of success following the path she had originally forged for herself.

24. Hardesty and Jacobs, *Success and Betrayal,* chap. 8.

25. Ibid., chaps. 6 and 7.

26. Terborg, "Women in Management," p. 648; Nancy E. Betz and Louise F. Fitzgerald, *The Career Psychology of Women* (Orlando, Fla.: Academic Press, 1987): p. 115.

27. Sharon Nelton and Karen Berney, "Women: The Second Wave," *Nation's Business* 75 (1987): 18.

28. Dana E. Friedman, "Why the Glass Ceiling?" *Across the Board* 25 (1988): 32–37; Linda Currey Post, "Where Do We Go from Here?" *Communication World* 5 (1988): 30–32; Julia Kagan, "Cracks in the Glass Ceiling," *Review of Business* 8 (1987): 10–12; J. Benjamin Forbes, James E. Piercy, and Thomas L. Hayes, "Women Executives: Breaking Down Barriers?" *Business Horizons* 31 (1988): 6–9; A. M. Morrison, R. P. White, and E. Van Velsor, *Breaking the Glass Ceiling* (Reading, Mass.: Addison-Wesley, 1987); Carol Hymowitz and Timothy D. Schellhardt, "The Glass Ceiling," *Wall Street Journal,* March 24, 1986, sec. 4, p. 1.

29. Peter F. Drucker, *Managing in Turbulent Times* (New York: Harper and Row, 1980), p. 121.

30. Ruth Halcomb, *Women Making It* (New York: Atheneum, 1979), p. 172. In *The Organization Woman,* Edith Highman concurs and adds self-confidence, professional attitude, and organization (chap. 2). She maintains that a woman has to be better than a man to get commensurate recognition (p. 21).

31. A lack of confidence has been consistently associated with females, as opposed to males. In a thorough review of sex differences, Eleanor Maccoby and Carol Jacklin found self-confidence to be the one achievement-related characteristic that consistently differentiated the sexes (*The Psychology of Sex Differences* [Stanford, Calif.: Stanford University Press, 1974]). Moreover, females' lack of self-confidence is not tempered by reality. That is, they will consistently underestimate their ability, past and predicted performance, in achievement-type tasks despite clear evidence of skill and aptitude (Jacquelynne E. Parsons, Diane N. Ruble, Karen L. Hodges, Ava W. Small, "Cognitive-Developmental Factors in Emerging Sex Differences in Achievement-Related Expectancies," *Journal of Social Issues* 32 [1976]: 47–61). In contrast, males tend to overestimate their abilities, aptitudes, and performance expectancies in relation to known evidence.

32. Larwood and Wood, in *Women in Management,* point out the interconnectedness of confidence and independence in risk taking with supportive circumstances. "Women can be self-reliant, then, when circumstances support their independence. Continued independence probably lowers perceived risks and could allow many women to accept additional challenges more boldly. . . . having the confidence to handle a variety of situations independently undoubtedly leads to a willingness to become involved in a wider range of activities and to a more flexible repertoire of responses in existing activities" (p. 76).

33. Women's attitudes toward themselves have been recognized as having a self-limiting effect. Obstacles caused by deficits in female self-confidence and self-image can be overcome through personal development within an improved social climate, according to Ellyn Mirides and Andre Cote, "Women in Management: Strategies for Removing the Barriers," *Personnel Administrator* 25 (April 1980): 27.

34. Terborg, "Women in Management," p. 659.

35. It is interesting to note that this is also the formula for good teaching in any setting: home, school, work. Herbert Ginsburg and Sylvia Opper, *Piaget's Theory of Intellectual Development—An Introduction* (Englewood Cliffs, N.J.: Prentice-Hall, 1969): p. 223.

36. Hardesty and Jacobs recommend that women develop "their own inner core of values" as the real benchmark of adjustment to the corporate world (*Success and Betrayal,* pp. 380–81).

37. Hardesty and Jacobs, *Success and Betrayal,* p. 390.

6. Family

1. This is undoubtedly as true for men as for women.

2. The tendency to integrate and treat experience globally has been attributed to females and contrasted with a male proclivity for compartmentalization. Traditionally, women's integrative approach has been negatively valued. Freud believed that females' inability to separate the emotional from the intellectual rendered them unsuitable for higher executive and moral functioning. More recently, cognitive psychologists have characterized females' cognitive styles as more field-dependent and other-directed than males' (Bernice Lott, *Women's Lives* [Monterey, Calif.: Brooks/Cole, 1987], p. 74). Again, a contextual approach indicates a perceptual and interpersonal dependence that is seen as less desirable for society's executive functions and more suitable to its domestic ones. It is only in recent years that psychologists such as Carol Gilligan have offered a more positive interpretation of an integrated approach to experience.

3. Linda K. Brown, "Women in Business Management," *Signs 5* (Winter 1979): 287.

4. Margaret Hennig and Anne Jardim, *The Managerial Woman* (Garden City, N.Y.: Anchor Press/Doubleday, 1977).

5. Lott, *Women's Lives*, p. 6.

6. Such macro factors as societal attitudes and economic conditions accounted for differences in educational and vocational ambitions among three generations of women. Sue C. Whisler and Susan J. Eklund, "Women's Ambitions: A Three-Generational Study," *Psychology of Women Quarterly 10* (1986): 361.

7. Ibid., p. 361; Grace Baruch, Rosalind Barnett, and Caryl Rivers, *Lifeprints: New Patterns of Love and Work for Today's Women* (New York: New American Library, 1983), p. 289.

8. "Sex roles are expectations for behavior and attitudes that a particular culture defines as appropriate for men and women." Such roles are learned through socialization, which is administered by various societal agents and institutions, including the family. Marcia Lynn Whicker and Jennie Jacobs Kronenfeld, *Sex Role Changes: Technology, Politics, and Policy* (New York: Praeger, 1986), p. 8.

9. Marjorie Bayes and Peter M. Newton, "Women in Authority: A Sociopsychological Analysis," *Journal of Applied Behavioral Science 14* (1978): 9.

10. Brown, "Women in Business," p. 287.

11. Hennig and Jardim, *Managerial Woman*, chaps. 6 and 7.

12. Ibid., p. 99.

13. In contrast to earlier findings on family background exemplified by the work of Hennig and Jardim, more recent evidence indicates less uniformity in antecedent influences among female managers. The fact of their vastly increased numbers alone would point to variability. Instead of seeing these women as father-identified firstborn or only daughters, we admit to not knowing what the definitive familial factors might be. Brown, "Women in Business," p. 287; Cynthia F. Epstein, *Women's Place* (Berkeley: University of California Press, 1970): p. 80.

14. Brown, "Women in Business," p. 288.

15. Betty Jane Jarman, "The Effect of Parental Messages on the Career Patterns of Professional Women," *Dissertation Abstracts* (Fresno: California School of Professional Psychology, 1977), Jan Vol 37 (7-B), 3580-B.

16. In the early 1970s psychologists embraced a new concept called androgyny to account for the crossover between stereotypic male and female "traits" found in many individuals. The term "androgynous" has been used to refer to people who exhibited both typical male and typical female traits. Diane F. Halpern, *Sex Differences in Cognitive Abilities* (Hillsdale, N.J.: Erlbaum, 1986), p. 114; Sandra L. Bem, "The Measurement of Psychological Androgyny," *Journal of Consulting and Clinical Psychology 42* (1974): 155–62.

17. James R. Terborg, "Women in Management: A Research Review," *Journal of*

Applied Psychology 62 (1977): 659; Helen S. Farmer, "A Multivariate Model for Explaining Gender Differences in Career and Achievement Motivation," *Educational Researcher 16* (1987): 8; Whisler and Eklund, "Women's Ambitions," p. 361.

18. Baruch, Barnett, and Rivers, *Lifeprints*, p. 84.

19. Sarah Hardesty and Nehamah Jacobs, *Success and Betrayal: The Crisis of Women in Corporate America* (New York: Franklin Watts, 1986), p. 101.

20. One study found no significant differences in the early socialization of matched groups of employed executive and nonexecutive women, but the executive group was significantly higher in mental ability, the need for power, and the need for achievement. Brown, "Women in Business," p. 288.

21. Sex roles define self and appropriate behavior according to cultural conceptions of gender. "Dominance and independence are linked with the masculine role, while submissiveness, passivity, and nurturance are linked with the feminine. These sex-linked role conceptions are learned through socialization, primarily within the nuclear family." Bayes and Newton, "Women in Authority," p. 8.

7. Marriage and Children

1. Historically, marriage has been an institution of the civilized world that sanctioned sex, especially for procreation, and formalized economic and social commitments, not just between individuals but between families. Marcia Lynn Whicker and Jennie Jacobs Kronenfeld, *Sex Role Changes: Technology, Politics, and Policy* (New York: Praeger, 1986), p. 61.

2. The traditional American nuclear family is not now nor has it historically been a universally applied arrangement. It may have been more of an ideological myth than a lived reality for most Americans, even those of the white middle class. Other kinds of family arrangements have characterized different classes and ethnic groups. An ethnographic study of black family patterns, for example, is seen in Carol Stack's *All Our Kin* (New York: Harper and Row, 1974). There is growing recognition, and perhaps acceptance, of the fact that our society is dominated by diverse family patterns and that the traditional nuclear family currently represents a statistical minority.

3. The traditional marriage contract and corresponding expectations of its participants did not include the more modern ideas of love and intimacy as fundamental. Whicker and Kronenfeld, *Sex Role Changes*, p. 61.

4. Cynthia Fuchs Epstein, in *Woman's Place* (Berkeley: University of California Press, 1970), p. 47, writes: "American society in many ways is more pragmatic than ideological, in the sense that economic gain is accepted as a better rationale for behavior than any other ideological value."

5. This is an oversimplified summary of very complex economic and social-political phenomena in our country's history. Many have written in sophisticated detail about various aspects of the history of the American family and wage labor. For an emphasis on women's participation in paid labor and corresponding ideology, see, for example, Alice Kessler-Harris, *Out to Work* (New York: Oxford University Press, 1982); Karen S. Koziara, Michael H. Moskow, Lucretia Dewey Tanner, eds., *Working Women: Past, Present, Future* (Washington, D.C.: Bureau of National Affairs, 1987).

6. An entire constellation of traits and functions was attributed to the nineteenth-century woman. These became the basis of a belief system regarding her inherent nature and what she was suited for. The evolution of her position as a moral guardian confined to home and hearth is described by Barbara Welter, "The Cult of True Womanhood, 1820–1860," *American Quarterly 18* (Summer 1964): 151–74.

7. Evelyn Nakano Glenn, "Gender and the Family," in *Analyzing Gender*, ed. Beth B. Hess and Myra Marx Ferree (Newbury Park, Calif.: Sage, 1987), p. 360.

8. Sarah Hardesty and Nehamah Jacobs, *Success and Betrayal: The Crisis of Women in Corporate America* (New York: Franklin Watts, 1986), pp. 305, 306.

9. Ibid., p. 304.

10. Sharon Nelton and Karen Berney, "Women: The Second Wave," *Nation's Business* 75 (1987): 18–22.

11. Esther E. Diamond, "Theories of Career Development and the Reality of Women at Work," in *Women's Career Development,* ed. Barbara A. Gutek and Laurie Larwood (Newbury Park, Calif.: Sage, 1987), p. 23.

12. In their book, *Lifeprints* (New York: New American Library, 1983), Grace Baruch, Rosalind Barnett, and Caryl Rivers maintain that women's lives can heavily reflect the influence of social change even in the absence of its verbal acknowledgment (p. 289).

13. Modern marriages fall short of the ideals of love and intimacy for women. When women have established their financial independence, there is less reason for them to remain in marriages that do not meet their emotional needs. Marcia Lynn Whicker and Jennie Jacobs Kronenfeld, *Sex Role Changes: Technology, Politics, and Policy* (New York: Praeger, 1986), p. 64.

14. When a marriage contract changes from its initial premises, both partners feel the effects. What happens to the marriage depends upon a number of factors, both psychological and structural. See Harold H. Frank, "The Two-Career Family," in *Women in the Organization,* ed. Harold H. Frank (Philadelphia: University of Pennsylvania Press, 1977), p. 305.

15. Case studies of dual professional couples illustrate the process of change in a woman's perception of herself and her husband as she acquires professional status. Her view of herself as more capable, masterful, and desirable can significantly influence the marital relationship. In addition to these psychological changes attached to the reality of her growing economic self-sufficiency, a woman now receives more social acceptance for leaving a marriage that lacks emotional support or satisfaction. Ellen Berman, Sylvia Sacks, and Harold Lief, "The Two Professional Marriage: A New Conflict Syndrome," in Frank, *Women in the Organization,* pp. 297, 302.

16. It seems to be the case that men still are threatened by a woman whose accomplishments surpass their own. The competition between spouses is kept at a tolerable level when she makes less than he and works in a different field. Hardesty and Jacobs, *Success and Betrayal,* p. 130. It also seems that women continue to believe in the notion that their men must be better than they. Ruth Halcomb, *Women Making It* (New York: Atheneum, 1979), pp. 199–200.

17. Halcomb, *Women Making It,* pp. 195–98, 202; Linda K. Brown, "Women in Business Management," *Signs* 5 (Winter 1979): 286.

18. For a description of this conflict in nonmanagerial women who demonstrate psychological change in line with social change, see Sue J. M. Freeman, "Women's Moral Dilemmas: In Pursuit of Integrity," in *Women Living Change,* ed. Susan C. Bourque and Donna R. Divine (Philadelphia: Temple University Press, 1985).

19. Whicker and Kronenfeld, *Sex Role Changes,* p. 67.

20. There are countless articles on this topic. For a succinct review of the dilemmas of both women and corporations, see Hardesty and Jacobs, *Success and Betrayal,* pp. 406–15.

21. Bernice Lott, *Women's Lives* (Monterey, Calif.: Brooks/Cole, 1987), pp. 136, 230; Roberta L. Valdez and Barbara A. Gutek, "Family Roles: A Help or a Hindrance for Working Women," in Gutek and Larwood, *Women's Career Development,* p. 158.

22. The idea that most people have not met the developmental tasks of full adulthood by the early twenties is now commonly recognized. Daniel Levinson, who writes about male development, describes the period of the twenties as one of provisional adulthood when one has begun a life independent of parents but is still following a "programmed" path. In the late twenties or early thirties, significant questioning begins the process of

establishing a more autonomous, self-selected path. Daniel Levinson et al., "The Psychosocial Development of Men in Early Adulthood and the Mid-Life Transition," in *Life History Research in Psychopathology,* ed. D. F. Ricks, A. Thomas, and M. Roff (Minneapolis: University of Minnesota Press, 1975). Gail Sheehy, in *Passages* (New York: Bantam, 1977), p. 340, agrees that in their twenties most women have yet to achieve the personal integration necessary to make a successful combination of marriage, career, and motherhood.

23. Erik Erikson has called this period a psychosocial moratorium (*Identity and the Life Cycle* [New York: Norton, 1980]).

24. Early studies of women managers—Margaret Hennig and Anne Jardim, *The Managerial Woman* (Garden City, N.Y.: Anchor Press/Doubleday, 1977), for example—found them remaining single or marrying later in life, often subsequent to their childbearing years. Career and marriage were seen as an either/or choice until perhaps the past decade or so. Current research finds women who know that they want both marrying later; further, those later first marriages are less likely to end in divorce. Alice M. Yohalem, *The Careers of Professional Women* (New York: Universe Books, 1979), pp. 30–31; Halcomb, *Women Making It,* pp. 181–82.

25. "Women's definitions of success emphasize not only achievement in their jobs but also relationships. . . . Success to us is the total picture of our lives." Halcomb, *Women Making It,* p. 180.

26. Several studies find that women managers are less likely than male managers to be married. "Compared with the general population, a substantially larger percentage of women in middle management are not married, and those who are married tend to marry late." Brown, "Women in Business," p. 286.

27. Yohalem, *Careers,* pp. 45, 47.

28. In 1987, two-thirds of all school-age children had working mothers, and 80% of the mothers with babies under one year are expected to be employed by 1990. Tamar Lewin, "Day Care Becomes a Growing Burden," *New York Times,* June 5, 1988, p. 22.

29. Despite women's advances in the labor market, men still significantly outearn them, even in the professional realms. About 10% of married women earn more than their spouses. Francine D. Blau and Marianne A. Ferber, "Occupations and Earnings of Women Workers," in *Working Women: Past, Present, Future,* ed. Karen S. Koziara, Michael H. Moskow, and Lucretia Dewey Tanner (Washington, D.C.: Bureau of National Affairs, 1987), chap. 2.

30. Ray Marshall and Beth Paulin, "Employment and Earnings of Women: Historical Perspective," in Koziara, Moskow, and Tanner, *Working Women,* p. 3.

31. Kessler-Harris, *Out to Work,* chaps. 2 and 3.

32. Veronica F. Nieva and Barbara A. Gutek, *Women and Work: A Psychological Perspective* (New York: Praeger, 1982), p. 2.

33. Whicker and Kronenfeld argue in their book, *Sex Role Changes,* that birth control technology is a primary impetus for social change in sex role relationships.

34. The reality of reproductive choice is illustrated by fluctuations in birth rates concomitant with birth control technology and the current women's movement. Until recently, the birth rate in this country has steadily declined since the post–World War II baby boom. Currently, people are explicit in their exercise of more choice in deciding whether and when to have children, and if so, how many. See, for example, Stephanie Dowrick and Sibyl Grundberg, eds., *Why Children?* (London: Women's Press, 1980).

35. The latest era of birth control technology enables women to reproduce without sexual intercourse. Whicker and Kronenfeld, *Sex Role Changes,* p. 29.

36. Brown, "Women in Business," p. 274; Yohalem, *Careers,* pp. 33, 41.

37. Halcomb, *Women Making It,* p. 191.

38. Hardesty and Jacobs, *Success and Betrayal,* pp. 406–15; Jane Meredith Adams,

"When Working Women Become Pregnant," *New England Business,* Feb. 20, 1984, p. 19.

39. Adams, "Working Women," p. 20.

40. Susan K. Boardman, Charles C. Harrington, and Sandra V. Horowitz, "Successful Women: A Psychological Investigation of Family Class and Education Origins," in Gutek and Larwood, *Women's Career Development,* p. 76.

41. Ibid., pp. 20, 21.

42. For a proposal about how corporations might accommodate managers who would also be mothers, see Felice N. Schwartz, "Management Women and the New Facts of Life," *Harvard Business Review,* Jan.–Feb. 1989, pp. 65–76. For some of the debate that ensued, see *Harvard Business Review,* May–June 1989.

43. Earlier surveys of married female middle managers indicated that they shouldered primary responsibility for children and spent more time with them than did their male counterparts. Brown, "Women in Business," p. 286. There is some evidence that young men now express more appreciation for family priorities. Helen S. Farmer, "A Multivariate Model for Explaining Gender Differences in Career and Achievement Motivation," *Educational Researcher 16* (March 1987): 8.

44. Richard Scase and Robert Goffee, "Women Managers: Room at the Top," *Management Today* (March 1987): 64–67; Dana E. Friedman, "Why the Glass Ceiling?" *Across the Board 25* (1988): 32–37; Nelton and Berney, "The Second Wave," pp. 22–24, 26–27.

45. Farmer, "Multivariate Model," p. 7; James R. Terborg, "Women in Management: A Research Review," *Journal of Applied Psychology 62* (1977): 657.

46. Scase and Goffee, "Women Managers," p. 65.

47. "Although there have been isolated appeals to consider ways to maintain the continuity of the female manager's work experience, most American analysts still focus on getting women into the managerial pool rather than redesigning jobs to retain them." Brown, "Women in Business," p. 273.

48. Patricia Voydanoff, "Women's Work, Family, and Health," in Koziara, Moskow, and Tanner, *Working Women,* p. 91; Friedman, "Why the Glass Ceiling?" p. 37.

49. Caryl Rivers, "Reaching for the Top," *Working Woman,* Sept. 1983, p. 138.

50. Hardesty and Jacobs, *Success and Betrayal,* pp. 301–10.

51. Ibid., p. 101.

52. "Women Face Job Bias, Experts Say," *New York Times,* March 25, 1984, p. 1.

53. Robert L. Dipboye, "Problems and Progress of Women in Management," in Koziara, Moskow, and Tanner, *Working Women,* p. 123; Dale Feuer, "How Women Manage," *Training 25* (1988): 27; Carol Hymowitz and Timothy Schellhardt, "The Glass Ceiling," *Wall Street Journal,* March 24, 1986, sec. 4, p. 1.

54. Increasing numbers of women entering the work force diminish the availability of child care to working mothers. Lewin, "Day Care," p. 22; Yohalem, *Careers,* p. 44.

55. Adams, "Working Women," p. 19.

56. This corresponds to the final stage of Gilligan's theory of women's psychological development, where the needs of self and other are given balanced attention.

57. See chapter 5.

58. Hardesty and Jacobs, *Success and Betrayal,* pp. 336, 409–14; Adams, "Working Woman," p. 21.

59. Lisa Collins, "More Firms Giving New Fathers Time Off to Share Chores and Joys of Infant Care," *Wall Street Journal,* July 5, 1985, p. 9.

60. Gail Bryant Osterman, "Does Becoming a Parent Mean Falling off the Fast Track?" in *The Woman in Management,* ed. Jennie Farley (Ithaca, N.Y.: ILR Press, 1983), p. 60.

61. "As Komarovsky has noted, 'The ideological support for the belief in sharp sex role differentiation in marriage has weakened but the belief itself has not been relinquished.'" Yohalem, *Careers,* p. 47.

8. Relation between the Personal and the Professional

1. In the ten-year period from the early 1970s to 1982, the number of female managers increased 96%; during the same time, the number of male managers grew 14%. Jane Meredith Adams, "When Working Women Become Pregnant," *New England Business*, Feb. 20, 1984, p. 19.

2. Dana E. Friedman, "Why the Glass Ceiling?" *Across the Board* 25 (1988): 33.

3. Nancy J. Adler, "Women in Management Worldwide," *International Studies of Management and Organization 16* (1987): 18.

4. Eleanor Byrnes, "Dual Career Couples: How the Company Can Help," in *The Woman in Management*, ed. Jennie Farley (Ithaca, N.Y.: ILR Press, 1983), p. 52.

5. There is considerable evidence that managerial work is stressful insofar as the work demands too much and is too difficult. Debra L. Nelson and James C. Quick, "Professional Women: Are Distress and Disease Inevitable?" *Academy of Management Review 10* (1985): 208. An imbalance between degree of responsibility and amount of authority in a job, however, is associated with the most stress. Such jobs are frequently pink-collar or clerical, those heavily populated by female employees. Grace Baruch, Rosalind Barnett, and Caryl Rivers, *Lifeprints: New Patterns of Love and Work for Today's Women* (New York: New American Library, 1983), p. 179.

6. Virginia E. Schein, "The Relationship between Sex Role Stereotypes and Requisite Management Characteristics," *Journal of Applied Psychology 57* (1973): 95–100.

7. Nelson and Quick, "Professional Women," p. 209.

8. I. K. Broverman, S. R. Vogel, D. M. Broverman, F. E. Clarkson, and P. S. Rosenkranz, "Sex-Role Stereotypes: A Current Appraisal," *Journal of Social Issues 28* (1972): 59–78.

9. Robert B. Reich, *The Next American Frontier* (New York: Times Books, 1983); Thomas J. Peters and Robert H. Waterman, Jr., *In Search of Excellence* (New York: Harper and Row, 1982); Caryl Rivers, "Reaching for the Top," *Working Woman*, Sept. 1983, p. 138; Alice G. Sargent, *The Androgynous Manager* (New York: Amacom, 1983).

10. S. L. Bem, "The Measurement of Psychological Androgyny," *Journal of Consulting and Clinical Psychology 42* (1974): 155–62.

11. Baruch, Barnett, and Rivers, *Lifeprints*, chap. 3.

12. Anne Fausto-Sterling, *Myths of Gender: Biological Theories about Women and Men* (New York: Basic, 1985).

13. Thomas S. Szasz, *The Myth of Mental Illness: Foundations of a Theory of Personal Conduct* (New York: Harper and Row, 1974).

14. John A. Byrne, "No Time to Waste on Nonsense," *Forbes*, May 6, 1985, p. 110.

15. Bernice Lott, *Women's Lives* (Monterey, Calif.: Brooks/Cole, 1987): p. 74.

16. That females typically underestimate whereas males overestimate their performance and abilities is a repeated finding across experimental and field studies in psychology. Ibid., p. 47.

9. Females in Male Organizations

1. That women have been channeled and kept in low-paid, low-power, and low-prestige positions has been documented as occupational segregation. Mary Frank Fox and Sharlene Hesse-Biber, *Women at Work* (Palo Alto, Calif.: Mayfield, 1984), pp. 34–36; Francine D. Blau and Marianne A. Ferber, "Occupations and Earnings of Women Workers," in *Working Women: Past, Present, Future*, ed. Karen S. Koziara, Michael H. Moskow, Lucretia Dewey Tanner (Washington, D.C.: Bureau of National Affairs, 1987), chap. 2.

2. Anthony F. Buono and Judith B. Kamm, "Marginality and the Organizational

Socialization of Female Managers," *Human Relations 36* (1983): 1126. A brief summary of studies of attitudes toward women as managers can be found in Cynthia Berryman-Fink, "Male and Female Managers' Views of the Communication Skills and Training Needs of Women in Management," *Public Personnel Management 14* (Fall 1985): 307; Ann Morison, R. P. White, and E. Van Velsor, *Breaking the Glass Ceiling* (Reading, Mass.: Addison-Wesley, 1987).

3. The classic work on this subject is Rosabeth Moss Kanter, *Men and Women of the Corporation* (New York: Basic, 1977).

4. J. Benjamin Forbes, James E. Piercy, and Thomas L. Hayes, "Women Executives: Breaking Down Barriers?" *Business Horizons 31* (1988): 6.

5. Julia Kagan, "Cracks in the Glass Ceiling," *Review of Business 8* (1987): 10.

6. Sarah Hardesty and Nehamah Jacobs, *Success and Betrayal: The Crisis of Women in Corporate America* (New York: Franklin Watts, 1986), p. 145.

7. Glynis Jane Bean, "Professional Women: Role Adaptation Strategies and Their Correlates," *Dissertation Abstracts International 44* (Nov. 1983): 1635-B.

8. Debra L. Nelson and James C. Quick, "Professional Women: Are Distress and Disease Inevitable?" *Academy of Management Review 10* (1985): 210.

9. Helen Rogan, "Top Women Executives Find Path to Power Is Strewn with Hurdles," *Wall Street Journal*, Oct. 25, 1984, p. 35.

10. This can be tokenism, whose meaning and experience was aptly described in Rosabeth Moss Kanter, *The Tale of "O": On Being Different in an Organization* (New York: Harper and Row, 1980).

11. Buono and Kamm, "Marginality and Socialization," p. 1132.

12. Though there has been an emphasis on age as salient in male acceptance of female colleagues, there is evidence that other aspects of a man's life can be more influential. For example, the attitudes and occupations of the females in his own personal life have a significant impact; wives and daughters can educate and serve as models. Julia Kagan, "How Management Myths Hurt Women," *Working Woman*, Dec. 1980, p. 76.

13. James R. Terborg, "Women in Management: A Research Review," *Journal of Applied Psychology 62* (Dec. 1977): 660.

14. Buono and Kamm, "Marginality and Socialization," p. 1136.

15. Rogan, "Top Women Executives," p. 35; Dale Feuer, "How Women Manage," *Training 25* (1988): 28; Alicia Johnson, "Women Managers: Old Stereotypes Die Hard," *Management Review 76* (1987): 37.

16. Terborg, "Women in Management," p. 652.

17. Buono and Kamm, "Marginality and Socialization," p. 1134.

18. Alma Baron, "Women in Business: Are They Still Fighting Shadows?" *Training and Development Journal*, May 1976, p. 12.

19. Alice G. Sargent, "Women and Men Working Together: Toward Androgyny," *Training and Development Journal 37* (April 1983): 72.

20. Rosabeth Moss Kanter, *The Change Masters: Innovation for Productivity in the American Corporation* (New York: Simon and Schuster, 1983).

21. Faye J. Crosby, *Relative Deprivation and Working Women* (New York: Oxford, 1982).

22. Thomas I. Chacko, "Women and Equal Employment Opportunity: Some Unintended Effects," *Journal of Applied Psychology 67* (Feb. 1982): 119–23.

23. Her retrospective reflections might be assumed to be quite different, given unsuccessful navigation of those same hurdles.

24. Bean, "Professional Women," p. 1136-B; Alice G. Sargent, *The Androgynous Manager* (New York: Amacom, 1983); Kagan, "Management Myths," p. 75.

25. Hardesty and Jacobs, *Success and Betrayal*, pp. 125, 227; Nancy Austin, "Goodbye to All That: The Mythology of the Professional Woman," *Healthcare Forum 29* (Jan./Feb. 1986): 14.

26. Eleanor Mimi Schrader, "Personality Characteristics of the Woman-to-Woman Mentor in the Career Arena," *Dissertation Abstracts International 42* (July 1981): 404-B.

27. Hardesty and Jacobs, *Success and Betrayal,* 375; Nelson and Quick, "Professional Women," p. 213.

28. The idea that males' early socialization prepares them for executive leadership and females' does not harks back to the pioneer study by Margaret Hennig and Anne Jardim, *The Managerial Woman* (Garden City, N.Y.: Anchor Press/Doubleday, 1977); see also Berryman-Fink, "Male and Female Views," p. 308.

29. In an interview, the late Linda K. Brown underscored Rosabeth Kanter's message that "people rise to the jobs they're given, not the other way around." Kagen, "Management Myths," p. 76.

30. Nelson and Quick, "Professional Women," p. 214.

31. Crosby, *Relative Deprivation.*

32. Based on results of a questionnaire completed subsequent to this study.

33. Candace West, "Why Can't a Woman Be More Like a Man?" *Work and Occupations 9* (1982): 5–29.

34. The stereotype that women are less effective communicators than men was not supported in tests of written modes of expression. Biased, inaccurate, folk-linguistic beliefs and the sex of the recipient are some of the variables influencing effectiveness of communication. Larry R. Smeltzer and James D. Werbel, "Gender Differences in Managerial Communication: Fact or Folk-Linguistics?" *Journal of Business Communication 23* (Spring 1986): 41–50.

35. John A. Byrne, "No Time to Waste on Nonsense," *Forbes,* May 6, 1985, p. 110.

36. Leon Festinger, *A Theory of Cognitive Dissonance* (Stanford, Calif.: Stanford University Press, 1957).

37. Women recognize that whistle blowing may not be in their own best interests. Finding other ways to deal with discrimination and knowing when to blow the whistle require careful balancing. Linda Bartlett, "Coping with Illegal Sex Discrimination," in *The Woman in Management,* ed. Jennie Farley (Ithaca, N.Y.: ILR Press, 1983), pp. 40–44. For an excellent, thorough study of whistle blowing and its complexity, see Myron Peretz Glazer and Penina Migdal Glazer, *The Whistleblowers: Exposing Corruption in Government and Industry* (New York: Basic, 1989).

38. Fletcher A. Blanchard and Faye J. Crosby, eds., *Affirmative Action in Perspective* (New York: Springer-Verlag, 1989).

39. Lawrence R. Quinn, "After 20 Years Women Face the Same Barriers," *Executive Financial Woman 2* (1987): 21.

40. Amanda Bennett, "A Road Already Traveled," *Wall Street Journal,* Nov. 24, 1986; Rogan, "Top Women Executives," p. 45.

41. John W. Martin et al. petitioners v. Robert K. Wilks et al. #87-1614.

42. The Equal Pay Act of 1963 and Title VII of the 1964 Civil Rights Act rendered discrimination on the basis of race or sex illegal. 1972 court cases were the first to uphold legislation prohibiting discriminatory hiring practices.

43. Kanter, *The Change Masters.*

10. The Context of Opportunity

1. A well-worn debate in psychology focused on whether behavior change preceded attitude change or vice versa. A change in attitude could be presumed to imply revised behavior. The real question arises when attitude change is desired but not spontaneously forthcoming, as in the case of prejudice, for example. If action precedes consciousness, the implication is to work on behavior change first, and attitude change will follow. This is the premise underlying civil rights legislation whereby people were forced to act in ways that were contrary to their inclinations. In their resistance, people still claimed that

forcibly changed behavior would not affect attitudes. It has been found, however, that revised behavior does precipitate shifts in attitudes in a consonant direction. Cynthia Fuchs Epstein, *Woman's Place* (Berkeley: University of California Press, 1970), p. 203; Charlotte Decker Sutton and Kris K. Moore, "Executive Women—20 Years Later," *Harvard Business Review,* Sept.–Oct. 1985, p. 52.

2. Carol Gilligan, *In a Different Voice: Psychological Theory and Women's Development* (Cambridge, Mass.: Harvard University Press, 1982).

3. Sarah Hardesty and Nehamah Jacobs, *Success and Betrayal: The Crisis of Women in Corporate America* (New York: Franklin Watts, 1986).

4. Mary Frank Fox and Sharlene Hesse-Biber, *Women at Work* (Palo Alto, Calif.: Mayfield, 1984), introduction, pp. 70–85.

5. Scores of books, manuals, and articles as well as workshops and training seminars have been aimed at women's self-improvement and preparedness for business. See, for example, Alma S. Baron, "Communication Skills for the Woman Manager: A Practice Seminar," *Personnel Journal,* Jan. 1980, pp. 55–63; L. Larwood and M. Wood, *Women in Management* (Lexington, Mass.: D. C. Heath, 1977), p. 162.

6. For a succinct overview of the history and current status of such legislative mandates, see Marcia Lynn Whicker and Jennie Jacobs Kronenfeld, *Sex Role Changes: Technology, Politics, and Policy* (New York: Praeger, 1986), pp. 130–39.

7. Linda Blum and Vicki Smith, "Women's Mobility in the Corporation: A Critique of the Politics of Optimism," *Signs: Journal of Women in Culture and Society 13* (1988): 528–45.

8. Hardesty and Jacobs, *Success and Betrayal,* p. 278.

9. Sharon Nelton and Karen Berney, "Women: The Second Wave," *Nation's Business 75* (1987): 23; Richard Scase and Robert Goffee, "Women Managers: Room at the Top," *Management Today* (March 1987): 65; Julia Kagan, "Cracks in the Glass Ceiling," *Review of Business 8* (1987): 10.

10. Female executives are more likely to be single, divorced, or separated than their male counterparts and nonexecutive women. Fraker, "Why Women Aren't Getting to the Top," p. 44; Helen Rogan, "Top Women Executives Find Path to Power Is Strewn with Hurdles," *Wall Street Journal,* Oct. 25, 1984, p. 44; Caryl Rivers, "Reaching for the Top," *Working Woman,* Sept. 1983, p. 138.

11. Fox and Hesse-Biber, *Women at Work,* pp. 13–29, 84–94.

12. John W. Martin et al. petitioners v. Robert K. Wilks et al. #87-1614.

13. David D. Van Fleet and Julie G. Saurage, "Recent Research on Women in Management," *Akron Business and Economic Review 15* (Summer 1984): 21.

14. Larwood and Wood, *Women in Management,* p. 150.

15. Sharon Caudle, "The Bedrock Capping 'Uppity' Women," *Bureaucrat 14* (Summer 1985): 27.

16. "You've Come a Long Way, Baby—but Not as Far as You Thought," *Business Week,* Oct. 1, 1984, p. 126.

17. Carol Hymowitz and Timothy D. Schellhardt, "The Glass Ceiling: Why Women Can't Seem to Break the Invisible Barrier That Blocks Them from the Top Jobs," *Wall Street Journal,* March 24, 1986, sec. 4.

18. Rivers, "Reaching for the Top," p. 137.

19. Ibid.; Marilyn Gardner, "Women's Next Frontier: Top Management," *Christian Science Monitor,* April 3, 1986, p. 31; "You've Come a Long Way, Baby," p. 130.

20. Karen Blumenthal, "Room at the Top," *Wall Street Journal,* March 24, 1986, p. 9.

21. Anne Harlan and Carol L. Weiss, "Sex Differences in Factors Affecting Managerial Career Advancement," Working Paper no. 56, Wellesley College Center for Research on Women, 1980.

22. Rosabeth Moss Kanter, "The Impact of Hierarchical Structures on the Work Behavior of Men and Women," *Social Problems 23* (1976): 415–430.

23. Hardesty and Jacobs, *Success and Betrayal,* pp. 399, 428.

24. Judith M. Von Seldeneck, "A Time to Recharge," *Management World*, Nov. 1982, p. 1; Fraker, "Why Women Aren't Getting to the Top," p. 42; Whicker and Kronenfeld, *Sex Role Changes*, p. 136; Hardesty and Jacobs, *Success and Betrayal*, p. 389; Caudle, "'Uppity' Women," p. 28; Joanna S. Lublin, "White Collar Cutbacks Are Falling More Heavily on Women Than Men," *Wall Street Journal*, Nov. 9, 1982.

25. Fraker, "Why Women Aren't Getting to the Top," p. 45; Van Fleet and Saurage, "Recent Research," p. 22; Barbara Carlson, "A Long Way," *New England Business 3* (Oct. 5, 1981): 18, 19; Hardesty and Jacobs, *Success and Betrayal*, p. 421; Lenora Cole Alexander, "Director's Journal: Steadying the Corporate Ladder to Help Women Move Up," *Women and Work: News from the U.S. Dept. of Labor,* Office of Information, Publications and Reports (Oct. 1984), p. 2.

Index